ENNIS AND NANCY HAM LIBRARY
ROCHESTER COLLEGE
800 WEST AVON ROAD
ROCHESTER HILLS, MI 48307

Herring Gull.
Gull Island, June 20, 1938. R. T. Hatt.

Island Life: A STUDY

of the Land Vertebrates of the
Islands of Eastern Lake Michigan

by Robert T. Hatt &
Josselyn Van Tyne
Laurence C. Stuart
Clifford H. Pope
Arnold B. Grobman

CRANBROOK INSTITUTE OF SCIENCE
Bulletin No. 27

Copyright 1948
Cranbrook Institute of Science
Bloomfield Hills, Michigan

Printed by the CRANBROOK PRESS, *Bloomfield Hills, Michigan*

Preface

THIS VOLUME IS the outcome of many studies of the land vertebrates of islands lying off the western shore of the Lower Peninsula of Michigan. It is more particularly, however, the product of a series of investigations by field parties from the Cranbrook Institute of Science and the University of Michigan, extending from 1937 to 1944. These had the object of determining the distribution, both geographic and ecologic, of the amphibians, reptiles, birds, and mammals on these islands and of learning, if possible, the means by which the various species reached the islands, the factors restricting species which were unrepresented or limited in their distribution, and of making such other discoveries about the island faunas as were practicable in the time available. Toward the clarification of the zoological history of the region, geologic studies were made of the Fox Islands. However, since most of the geological data seemed, in the end, largely irrelevant to the zoological studies, the manuscript on the glacial geology of the Fox Islands, originally intended for inclusion in this volume, was released for publication elsewhere, though it is extensively quoted and abstracted in the pages which follow.

The collections resulting from these island investigations are mostly incorporated in the holdings of the University of Michigan Museum of Zoology, though a few items remain in the Cranbrook Institute of Science, and some are in the collection of Dr. Max Minor Peet. Specimens secured by Hatt in 1931 are among the collections of the American Museum of Natural History.

Herpetological collecting was conducted by the usual employment of eye and ear to locate the animals. A truly vast amount of beach debris (Fig. 5) was turned over in seeking specimens, and on five of the smaller islands literally every stranded log and bit of flotsam of any size was scrutinized. Night hunting, with headlight, was done on most of the islands.

Bird collecting was done chiefly with gun, though a few items were obtained by netting and otherwise.

The small mammals were secured with Sherman live-traps, variously baited. Larger mammals were shot. Records of tracks and scats were made when possible.

The Cranbrook-University of Michigan expeditions were very largely dependent on the courtesy of the United States Lake Survey, the United States Coast Guard, and their representatives, for transportation between the islands, and it is our wish to thank the following gentlemen in those organizations for the help they gave: Mr. Sherman Moore; Mr. C. R. McKechnie; Mr. Deto; Mr. O. Smith. The Manitou Island Association generously provided several facilities through the friendly interest of its President, Mr. William R. Angell, and its representatives, Messrs. Tracy Grosvenor and Ed McKee; the lightkeepers on two of the islands, South Fox and South Manitou, were also ever helpful on our visits.

Mrs. Helen T. Gaige, Dr. Norman Hartweg, and Miss Grace Orton, all of the University of Michigan, have our thanks for assistance in studying the herpetological collections.

Dr. Milo Quaife made several valued suggestions relating to the historic material and so to him we are indebted, as we are for similar help from Dr. F. Clever Bald.

To the several individuals who supplied us with original data, here first published, we owe special thanks. Among these are Drs. Max Minor Peet and Olin S. Pettingill, Jr., whose records from the Beaver group are included in the chapter on birds, and Mr. Sherman Moore, whose notes, historical and zoological, were used.

Except for Chapter 6, "The Birds," by Josselyn Van Tyne, the major responsibility for compiling, synthesizing, and editing the reports and preparing the general sections was that of Robert T. Hatt, but all of the numerous problems encountered have been discussed among the several authors, and each has reviewed the general sections, as well as those pertaining to his special field. The herpetological section was compiled by Hatt from the reports of Stuart, Pope, Grobman, and Hatt. The ornithological section, prepared by Van

Tyne, is based on his own work and the original reports of Staebler, Case, and Hinshaw. Responsibility for the evaluation and tabulation of the field observations on birds is: 1937 — Hinshaw; 1938 — Van Tyne; 1939 and 1940 — Staebler. The mammal section is largely the work of Hatt. Geological data was extracted from published and manuscript reports by Stanley.

The editor has deviated from current practice in the matter of capitalization of the non-technical names of animals in order to have the whole harmonious with the section on birds, in which group the names are commonly capitalized. He considers this defensible on the grounds that it makes location of the animal names easier than it would otherwise be.

Since the itinerary (Table 1) indicates the composition of all of the field parties of 1916 - 1944, it has been possible to condense the paper considerably by omitting from most records the names of the individual field observers.

The photographs are all by members of the expeditions except for the aerial views (Figs. 12, 14, 16, 20, 23, 24, 27, 28, and 29), which are from the files of the Agricultural Adjustment Administration.

The editor is grateful to Paul McPharlin for assistance in the designing of this book.

Table of Contents

Chapter 1.	Introduction	Page 1
Chapter 2.	Geological history	11
Chapter 3.	Cultural history	23
Chapter 4.	The islands described	31
Chapter 5.	The amphibians and reptiles	54
Chapter 6.	The birds	69
Chapter 7.	The mammals	115
Chapter 8.	Modification of habits	137
Chapter 9.	Factors of distribution	140
Appendix:	List of the vertebrate faunas arranged by islands	157
Bibliography		167
Index		172

Descriptive List of Illustrations

Figure *Facing page*

Frontispiece: Herring Gull — Title

1. Facsimile of the first page of the Strang report — 2
2. Loading on the east shore of North Fox Island — 4
3. Van Tyne and Morrill skinning birds — 4
4. Tracks of a large toad walking in sand — 5
5. Driftwood on North Fox Island — 5
6. Western shore of South Fox Island — 12
7. Unforested top of old shingle beach, on Trout Island — 12
8. Former town of Crescent, North Manitou Island — 13
9. Logging camp on South Fox Island — 13
10. Beaver Island, as seen from the fire tower — 20
11. Miller's Marsh, Beaver Island — 20
12. Aerial photograph of Gull Island — 21
13. Juniper heath on Gull Island — 21
14. Aerial photograph of Hat and Shoe Islands — 28
15. Tern nesting colony on Shoe Island — 28
16. Aerial view of North Fox Island — 29
17. North Fox Island's gravelly eastern shore — 29
18. Broad wet beach on the northwest shore of North Fox — 36
19. Pismire Island — 36
20. Aerial photograph of South Fox Island — 37
21. South Fox Island's west shore — 44
22. Dried organic matter on the beach of South Fox Island — 44

Figure		Facing page
23.	Aerial photograph of South Manitou's eastern plain	45
24.	Aerial photograph of South Manitou's southwestern quarter	45
25.	South Manitou's sand dunes	52
26.	Virgin forest on South Manitou Island	52
27.	Aerial photograph of Squaw Island	53
28.	Aerial photograph of Whiskey Island	53
29.	Aerial photograph of Trout Island	53
30.	Pools behind beach bars on Trout Island	60
31.	Ant nest on Trout Island	60
32.	Boulder pavement on the shore of North Fox Island	61
33.	Leopard Frog on South Manitou Island	61
34.	Garter Snake on South Manitou Island	68
35.	Great Blue Heron nest on Shoe Island	69
36.	Willow Thrush nest on South Fox Island	69
37.	Site of Duck Hawk's nest on South Fox Island	76
38.	Duck Hawk's nest on South Fox Island	76
39.	Herring Gull nest in wet area, Gull Island	77
40.	Young Herring Gulls hiding in beach drift, Gull Island	77
41.	Hatching Herring Gull, Gull Island	84
42.	Young Herring Gulls in nest, Gull Island	85
43.	Nest of a Woodland Deermouse, on North Manitou Island	85
Map		33

List of Tables

Table		Page
1.	List of islands studied with dates of collecting and names of collectors on the Cranbrook-University of Michigan parties	4
2.	Related studies on these islands	6
3.	Altitudes of present and recent beaches—Fox Islands	16
4.	A chronological listing of selected events indicative of changes in the island region	26
5.	Size, area and shore line length of the islands	30
6.	Birds breeding on the adjacent mainland though not on the islands	71
7.	Distribution of breeding birds which are restricted mainly to the larger islands	72
8.	Breeding birds restricted to Beaver Island and certain small islands	73
9.	Species occurring as transient migrants on the adjacent mainland though not recorded on the islands	74
10.	Casual occurrences of non-breeding birds during the breeding season	74
11.	Deer mortality on North Manitou Island	134
12.	Correlation of faunal variety with ecological diversity	147
13.	Correlation of faunal variety (birds and bats omitted) with ecological diversity	147
14.	Correlation of faunal variety with ecological diversity in relation to area	149
15.	Relative abilities of the several land vertebrates to invade islands	153
Appendix: List of the vertebrate faunas arranged by islands		157
List of abbreviations		157

Personnel of the Cranbrook-University of Michigan Expeditions

ROBERT T. HATT, Director, Cranbrook Institute of Science; Collaborator, Museum of Zoology, University of Michigan.

JOSSELYN VAN TYNE, Curator of Birds, Museum of Zoology, University of Michigan; Trustee, Cranbrook Institute of Science.

LAURENCE C. STUART, Assistant Biologist, Laboratory of Vertebrate Biology, University of Michigan.

CLIFFORD H. POPE, Curator of Amphibians and Reptiles, Chicago Natural History Museum.

GEORGE M. STANLEY, Associate Professor of Geology, University of Michigan.

ARTHUR E. STAEBLER, George Reserve Fellow, University of Michigan.

ARNOLD B. GROBMAN, Assistant Professor, Department of Biology, University of Florida.

THOMAS D. HINSHAW, formerly of the Division of Birds, Museum of Zoology, University of Michigan.

RALPH E. MORRILL, formerly Assistant, Division of Birds, Museum of Zoology, University of Michigan.

LESLIE D. CASE, formerly Assistant, Division of Birds, Museum of Zoology, University of Michigan.

WILLIAM JEWELL, student in 1937 at the University of Michigan.

1. Introduction

INSULAR FAUNAS have long been of great interest to naturalists, and their study perhaps contributed more than any other phase of zoology to the foundation of the doctrine of organic evolution. It was the peculiar distribution of the fauna of the Galápagos Islands which stimulated Charles Darwin's (1858, 1859) civilization-changing train of thought; the distribution of animals in the Malay archipelago which independently led Alfred Russel Wallace (1858, 1880) to propound a theory similar to Darwin's.

The reasons that islands have often provoked original thought or provided data for productive analysis are several, but foremost is that the segregation afforded by islands speeds differentiation. A second reason is that island existence has often altered the habits of species and their ecologic associations principally through changes in interspecific pressure. The patterns of mainland habits and segregations are thus the more readily understood.

It has not, however, required equatorial conditions to make islands good targets for faunal analyses, since within our Great Lakes, insular studies have proven quite productive. The first study* was that of the rebel Mormon prophet and self-crowned king, James Strang, who in 1855 published a report on the natural history of Beaver Island, Lake Michigan. His philosophic comments were, however, not concerned with the land vertebrates, and his report is of interest only because it was first, because it contributed a few early records, and because of the colorful background of its history, best given in reports by Quaife (1930) and Riegel (1935). Adams and colleagues in 1909 published a classic work on Isle Royale, which in many respects remains a model for other interpretive and fact-establishing surveys. N. A. Wood (1911) reported on the birds of the Charity Islands, Lake Huron, observing direct ratios between island size, ecologic diversity, and the size of his bird lists; and further, that

---

*Thurlow Weed (Mansfield, 1899, pp. 209, 212-213) visited North Manitou July 3 and 9, 1847, and observed, "It is not even inhabited by animals. I saw none of the feathered race. Reptiles are seldom seen."

predators were few because of an inadequate food supply. H. H. T. Jackson (1920), analyzing the mammalian populations of the Apostle Islands in Lake Superior, suggested that winter inactivity was a prime determiner of island distribution, since such species as did surmount the water barriers either were those which were active in the winter and roamed widely, were animals more or less active in winter and frequently found in driftwood on the beach, or were strong swimmers.

The score of islands along the northeast shore of Lake Michigan offer an interesting set of conditions for analysis of varied biologic problems, because they range from small gravel reefs to Beaver Island, with over 50 square miles of land surface. The islands vary in character from those which have but one or two definable habitats to one with almost as great ecologic diversity as the mainland. In degree of isolation they vary from Fisherman's Island and Grape Island, which are islands only at times of high water, to the Fox Islands, which are separated from the nearest mainland by 17 miles of open water, much of it 300 feet deep, and a minimum of 10 miles of continuous water by an inter-island route to the mainland. True, this isolation is but seasonal, for the ice bridges all the inter-island waters in cold winters. Even the seasonal isolation appears to have been largely eliminated for a time by geologically recent lowering of the lake.

These islands have, of course, long attracted the attention of scientists and naturalists, and scattered records of their findings are in the literature, as attested by the accompanying synoptic listing (Table 2). It was not until 1937, however, that the first concerted effort was made toward a faunal survey of the group as a whole.

Beginning in the field season of 1937, the Cranbrook Institute of Science undertook the study of the land vertebrates of representative islands in eastern Lake Michigan. Though the Institute met the major part of the field expenses and some salaries, the University of Michigan shared in no less important degree through the grant of time of many members of the expeditions and the care of collections.

In the first season explorations were made on the Fox Islands by Messrs. Hatt (mammals), Pope (reptiles and amphibians), Stanley with Jewell assisting (geology), and on North Manitou by Pope.

In 1938, a party of zoologists made studies on all the smaller

NINTH ANNUAL REPORT OF

MISCELLANEOUS CORRESPONDENCE

ON

NATURAL HISTORY.

Some Remarks on the Natural History of Beaver Islands. Michigan.

BY JAMES J. STRANG.

SAINT JAMES, BEAVER ISLAND, *December* 7, 1853.
Secretary of Smithsonian Institution:

I have prepared for your use the following lists of animals, plants, &c., found upon the "Beaver Islands," in Lake Michigan, which I beg to submit to you. I am aware that these lists are quite imperfect, but hope they will serve some useful purpose until better can be prepared.

Truly and sincerely, yours,
JAMES J. STRANG.

DOMESTIC ANIMALS.

Horses, oxen, sheep, swine, dogs, cats.

WILD ANIMALS.

Foxes, red, quite numerous.

Foxes, black, scarce; silver grey, very rare. Some hunters assert that these are the same variety, the colour only distinguishing the sex. The silver grey is the most valuable fur in market, a single skin being priced at more than fifty dollars.

Hare, or rabbit. Two species, large and small.

Chipmunk, or red ground-squirrel.

Otter, very scarce.

The beaver are extinct. Caribou, or reindeer, range as far south as here, but visit the islands only on the ice, and very rarely. Elk are found on the east shore, and bears on both. American deer are found as near as Green Bay and Manistee river, *piloting civilization.*

BIRDS.

Geese, brant, duck (numerous varieties), loons, gulls (two varieties), crows, hawks, (several varieties), woodcock, pigeons, blackbird, robin, redheaded woodpecker, snipe, snowbird, pewee.

FISHES.

In some of the small streams on the mainland "brook trout" are found in abundance. Most of the streams are destitute of them, but abound in other fish, the names of which I do not know.

---

1. *The first published report on the natural history of the Beaver Islands was that of Strang in 1855. This is a facsimile of the first page.*

islands of the Beaver archipelago and to a lesser extent on Beaver Island. This party consisted of Hatt (mammals, reptiles, amphibians) and Van Tyne with Morrill assisting (birds).

In 1939, Staebler and Case collected birds on the Fox Islands.

In 1940, the Manitou Islands were studied by Hatt (mammals, reptiles, amphibians) and by Staebler and Case (birds).

In 1941, the herpetology of Beaver Island and High Island was studied by Stuart and Grobman.

In 1944, Hatt returned to South Manitou Island for a brief check on earlier data.

TABLE 1

LIST OF ISLANDS STUDIED, WITH DATES OF COLLECTING AND NAMES OF COLLECTORS ON THE CRANBROOK-UNIVERSITY OF MICHIGAN PARTIES

BEAVER ISLAND
    1937 — June 9-July 22; Hinshaw, Morrill.
    1938 — June 14-15; Hatt, Van Tyne, Morrill.
            July 11-12; Hatt, Van Tyne, Morrill.
            July 18-26; Hatt.
    1939 — June 9-19; Stuart, Grobman.

GULL ISLAND
    1938 — June 15-22; Hatt, Van Tyne, Morrill.

HAT ISLAND
    1938 — July 7-11; Hatt, Van Tyne, Morrill.

HIGH ISLAND
    1938 — June 23; Hatt, Van Tyne, Morrill.
    1939 — June 14; Stuart, Grobman.

HOG ISLAND
    1938 — July 11; Hatt.

NORTH FOX ISLAND
    1937 — June 27-July 2; Hatt, Pope, Stanley, Jewell.
    1939 — June 28-July 5; Staebler, Case.

NORTH MANITOU ISLAND
    1916 — Two days, dates uncertain; Hatt.
    1931 — August 17-20; Hatt.
    1937 — July 6-10; Pope.

2. Transportation to the less accessible islands was sometimes furnished by the U. S. Coast Guard. Loading on east shore of North Fox Island, July 2, 1937. R. T. Hatt.

3. The insect nuisance occasionally required work behind a net. Van Tyne and Morrill skinning birds. Squaw Island, July 4, 1938. R. T. Hatt.

4. Tracks contributed to distribution records. Tracks of a large toad walking in sand. South Fox, June 24, 1937. R. T. Hatt.

5. Turning over driftwood in search of snakes and mice was arduous. North Fox, June 28, 1937. R. T. Hatt.

INTRODUCTION 5

NORTH MANITOU ISLAND—*continued*
    1940 — June 15-16; Staebler, Case.
              June 17-19; Hatt, Staebler, Case.
              June 20-24; Hatt, Staebler.
              June 29-July 5; Case.
              July 2-5; Hatt, Case.
              July 6; Hatt.

PISMIRE ISLAND
    1938 — July 11; Hatt.

SHOE ISLAND
    1938 — July 7, 10; Hatt, Van Tyne, Morrill.

SOUTH FOX ISLAND
    1937 — June 21-27; Hatt, Pope, Stanley, Jewell.
              June 30; Stanley, Jewell.
              July 1; Pope, Stanley, Jewell.
    1939 — June 16-28; Staebler, Case.
              July 17-19; Staebler.

SOUTH MANITOU ISLAND
    1940 — June 7-13; Staebler, Case.
              July 6-10; Case.
              July 10-16; Hatt.
              July 30-August 1; Staebler.
    1944 — August 30-September 1; Hatt.

SQUAW ISLAND
    1938 — June 29; July 2-7; Hatt, Van Tyne, Morrill.

TROUT ISLAND
    1938 — June 22-27; Hatt, Van Tyne, Morrill.

WHISKEY ISLAND
    1938 — June 27-July 2; Hatt, Van Tyne, Morrill.

Table 2

RELATED STUDIES ON THESE ISLANDS

A Chronological Listing.

1847. Thurlow Weed (Mansfield, 1899, pp. 209, 212-213), whose boat stopped at North Manitou for wood, went to the interior of the island but saw no mammals or birds. He remarked that reptiles were rarely seen.

1847-1856. James Jesse Strang, rebel prophet of the Mormon Church, established a large colony of his adherents on Beaver Island, and the most colorful part of the history of the upper lake concerns his actions. His paper (1855. See also Fig. 1) on the natural history of the Beaver group contains few usable records.

1894. Members of the staff of the temporary limnological station at Charlevoix collected in High Island harbor and around Beaver Island, studying the Whitefish. A storm caused them to spend one day on Beaver Island, where some collecting was done, as reported in Ward (1896) and Walker (1896). None of this concerned the vertebrate faunas.

1896-1897. Charles L. Cass visited Hat Island and the gull and tern colony on Shoe Island. He apparently published nothing about the birds he observed there, but Caspian Tern and Herring Gull eggs that he took are now in several museum collections, and Amos Butler (1898, p. 573) reported that Cass found Ring-billed Gulls nesting "on the Beaver Islands." (See also *Bull. Mich. Ornith. Club*, 1, 1897, p. 32; Barrows, 1904, p. 78.)

1903? Before 1904 Samuel M. Coulter studied the plant ecology of the swamps of North Manitou, as cited in the bibliography.

1904. Walter Barrows spent the week of July 8-13 on "the Beaver Islands." He published (1904) a list of 53 species of birds he found there but unfortunately referred only a few of the records to particular islands. He apparently spent a good deal of time on Beaver Island, but he also visited at least Gull, and presumably (July 11) Shoe, islands.

1914? Earlier than 1915 Frank R. Taylor visited the Manitous, Beaver, High, and Garden islands to investigate the occurrence of beaches of glacial lakes. His results are incorporated in Leverett and Taylor's (1915) monograph.

1916. Robert Hatt (1924) paid a brief visit to North Manitou Island noting a few animals.

1917. George D. Fuller, of the University of Chicago, made botanical studies of sand dunes on Beaver, High, and South Fox islands in September, as reported in his paper of 1918. The collections made were deposited in Chicago Natural History Museum.

1919-1926. Sherman Moore of the United States Lake Survey, while engaged in charting the Beaver archipelago, made numerous observations on the fauna, which he has generously made available for this report.

1922. W. S. McCrea (Lincoln, 1924a, p. 38; 1924b, pp. 6-7) banded gulls and terns on Gull (July 16), and on Hat and Shoe (July 29) islands.

Henry T. Darlington, of Michigan State College, spent about a week in September on Beaver Island and a half day on Garden Island, collecting plants, as part of the Land Economic Survey then in progress and published a summary of the survey (1940).

1922-1929. Norman A. Wood spent June 14-17, 1922, June 20-25, 1925, and May 1-15, 1929 (the last with James H. Wood and W. B. Tyrrell), on Beaver Island. He published only two brief notes (1931, 1943) on these expeditions, both concerned mainly with Holboell's Grebes.

1923. Marion and Fisherman's islands' mammals and birds were studied by a party from the University of Michigan. Lee R. Dice has reported (1925a) on the mammals of Marion Island; J. Van Tyne (1925) on the birds of Marion and Fisherman's islands.

1923-1925. Frederick C. Lincoln (1924a, 1926) visited the Beaver group with McCrea, July 20-29, 1923, and July 18-30, 1924, to band gulls and terns; Lincoln (1926, p. 242) paid a visit there in 1925.

1925. Walter E. Hastings, N. A. Wood, and Frank N. Wilson visited the Beaver group to photograph and band birds.

1927. Walter E. Hastings, W. Bryant Tyrrell, and W. B. Purdy visited Hat and Shoe islands June 29.

1927-1931. William I. Lyon visited Shoe Island to band Caspian Terns (Lyon, 1927; Ford, 1931).

1928. Edward H. Hyer and James H. Wood visited Beaver Island in May, obtaining specimens for the University of Michigan and the Grand Rapids Public Museum.

1929. W. Bryant Tyrrell, then of Cranbrook, visited Hat Island July 3 to photograph the nesting colony of Great Blue Herons and to band gulls. He also visited Shoe Island and made notes on conditions there.

1931. Robert Hatt collected a few mammals, reptiles, and amphibians on North Manitou Island, August 18-20, for the American Museum of Natural History.

Margaret Canby Reis studied the flora of Beaver Island under the auspices of the Cranbrook Institute of Science. These collections are in the herbarium of the Institute.

1932. Victor H. Cahalane and James H. Wood, for Cranbrook, collected birds on the Beaver Islands from at least May 14 to 28.

1933-1937. The late Frank N. Blanchard, of the University of Michigan, made several trips to Hog, Garden, and Hat islands for herpetological studies which are at present being prepared for publication by Frieda Cobb Blanchard. Some of his ornithological students also went on these trips, but so far as is known their reports are not published.

1934-1941. F. E. Ludwig (1942, 1943) and C. C. Ludwig banded birds at most of the gull and tern colonies of the Beaver group from 1934 to 1941.

1937. The birds of Beaver Island were studied by Thomas D. Hinshaw and Ralph E. Morrill, of the Museum of Zoology, University of Michigan, as part of the Museum's general study of the avifauna of the State.

1937-1944. Sister M. Marcelline Horton, of Aquinas College, Grand Rapids, spent vacations in each of these years, except 1939, at Saint James on Beaver Island. These periods ranged from May 28 to October 14. In that time she was able to collect plants extensively over Beaver Island and made one-day stops on High Island and Garden Island. Her specimens are in the herbaria of Aquinas College and of the University of Michigan.

1938. George M. Ehlers, of the University of Michigan, made a geological reconnaissance of Beaver, Squaw, and Garden islands with a view to determining the age of the rocks exposed on them. This survey was extended by his studies of 1943.

1940. Calvin Goodrich (1941), at that time Curator of Mollusks in the Museum of Zoology, University of Michigan, spent two weeks of July collecting on Beaver Island and made brief stops on Whiskey Island and Garden Island, on each of which some specimens were collected.

Olin S. Pettingill, Jr., on the summer staff of the University of Michigan Biological Station, visited Hat Island in 1940 and made records quoted in part in our report.

1942. A partial fisheries survey of some of the lakes on Beaver Island was made by Walter R. Crowe of the Institute of Fisheries Research, Michigan Department of Conservation. Lakes visited (August 4-7) were Barney's, Fox, Genesareth, Font, and Green's. Mr. Crowe's report, which includes temperature, oxygen, vegetation, and bottom data and is concerned chiefly with fish stocking practices, is not published but is on file in the Department.

1943. Kenneth K. Landes and George M. Ehlers, of the University of Michigan, but for the Michigan Department of Conservation, surveyed the sub-surface geology of the Mackinac Straits region and during the project visited North Fox Island, Ile aux Galets, and all of the Beaver group. Their report was issued in 1945.

1945-1946. Karl F. Lagler, of the Department of Zoology, University of Michigan, conducted a survey of the inland-water and shore fishes of the islands in Lake Michigan under the joint auspices of the Rackham Fund, University of Michigan, and the Institute for Fisheries Research of the Michigan Department of Conservation. Collections with related ecological observations were made as follows: Beaver Island, August 9-19 and 21-22, 1945; High Island, August 19-20, 1945; North Manitou Island, August 23-26, 1945; South Fox Island, August 8, 1945; South Manitou Island, August 26-29, 1946.

2. Geological History

THE BED-ROCK of the islands is largely masked by heavy glacial and recent deposits. Rock outcrops do, however, occur on most of the islands of the Beaver group at or just below lake level. These are mainly dolomites, limestone, or sandstone, containing Upper Silurian to Middle Devonian fossils. Ehlers (1945) has assigned these to the Detroit River, Bois Blanc, Garden Island, and St. Ignace formations. These rocks conspicuously determine the shore character of some of the northern islands through their resistance to erosion.

The only aspect of the geological history which concerns this report, however, is the postglacial. If the distribution of the faunas cannot be satisfactorily explained on the basis of modern conditions it becomes important to know how old the islands are, how long it has been since they emerged from the larger glacial lakes, and whether since that time they have been connected with the mainland or with one another.

Stanley's study of conditions on the Fox Islands was part of this survey and an extension of his earlier studies of the glacial history of the Great Lakes area. The history of South Fox may be considered typical of each of the higher islands of the group, though all would differ in detail in relation to their geographic position, surrounding water depth, and present as well as former heights. His summary of the history of these islands, quoted from manuscript, follows:

"The Fox Islands were still covered or surrounded by ice during the formation of the Manistee moraine and as the glacier was withdrawing from the Lower Peninsula of Michigan. The veneer of ferruginous gravel, poorly washed and assorted, which generally caps the till bluffs of South Fox Island, seems the result of working by small ponded or draining waters while ice was still at hand. It scarcely suggests the activity of large waves.

"South Fox became an island after the glacier had melted back and left an open expanse of water surrounding it. Hardy plants may have colonized it while stagnant ice still lingered on its shores. Judging from the geographical position of South Fox and the extent of the principal Algonquin shoreline for miles to the north, the emergence probably occurred about the time of that early stage of Lake Algonquin when drainage was through the Trent Valley. However, there are no data from the island itself to confirm this, nor is it known positively that the Michigan basin was even occupied by that lake.

"South Fox was for certain an island in the greater Lake Algonquin during its two-outlet stage and the formation of the strong Algonquin shoreline, and by this time the glacier had receded 100 miles or more to the north. This may have been 1,000 years after the Fox islands area became ice free. Of the other mid-Lake Michigan islands, only Beaver and the Manitous (and possibly High Island) were then existent. South Fox Island was then some four miles long and stood fully 100 feet above the Lake.

"Although the formation of the Algonquin shoreline on South Fox Island had been accompanied by a rising lake level, as everywhere south of the Trent Valley, due to the broad tilting effects of the postglacial uplift, drainage of Lake Algonquin was eventually turned from Trent Valley to Port Huron, and thereafter the tilting caused a further gradual emergence of South Fox Island, amounting to some 25 or 35 feet.

"Further emergence occurred repeatedly at intervals, as the glacier abandoned various valleys leading eastward from Georgian Bay, and caused the lake to fall to successively lower levels. A number of lower Algonquin stages thus followed. They are, in order, Wyebridge, Penetang, Cedar Point, Payette, and there must have been later ones, of which little is yet known. North Fox was probably awash during the Wyebridge stage. At the Cedar Point stage, the lake had fallen to about the present shores of the Fox Islands; during the Payette stage the water was about 35 feet lower. The very lowest level of the lake was reached long after the Payette stage and apparently when the ice had entirely melted out of the North Bay-Mattawa valley and this most northerly outlet channel was in full use. *The water fringing the Fox Islands was then probably over 200 feet lower than at present.* There is evidence for this, as also for the lower Algonquin stages, in reports on beach studies of Georgian Bay and Lake Superior (Stanley, 1936, 1937). No beaches for these stages were noted on the Fox Islands, because the general terrain

6. South Fox was an island in glacial Lake Algonquin. Its western shore is eroded by waves, and sand from the bluffs is brought southward and deposited along the beach in the foreground, then blown over the flat at the south neck of the island to be prograded along its eastern shore. June, 1937. G. M. Stanley.

7. The tops of old shingle beaches from higher lake levels remain unforested on Trout Island but their sides support a dense growth of cedar and fir. June 25, 1938. R. T. Hatt.

8. Some old lumber towns such as Crescent on North Manitou Island have completely disappeared today. Summer, 1916. R. T. Hatt.

9. While buildings of abandoned settlements, such as this logging camp on South Fox, remain standing, they furnish shelter and nesting sites for several species of birds and a few mammals. June 26, 1937. R. T. Hatt.

there is not adapted to record falling stages and because thick woods and blown sand hinder observation. However, the near region is not without some evidence to confirm these much lowered lake levels. A submerged and winding river valley in the Mackinac Straits region connects the Lake Michigan basin with the basin of Lake Huron, far below the present level (Stanley, 1945).

"While knowledge is not yet sufficient to make more detailed statements, some geographic consequences of the extremely low level may be at least approximated, since they may have allowed certain animals and plants to reach these islands which would not otherwise have done so. The islands of the Beaver group were connected with lower Michigan through the region of Waugoshance Peninsula. The Manitou Islands were connected with one another and with Leelanau County. North Fox Island was probably land-tied by way of the Beavers. On the other hand, South Fox may have continued as an island, though less isolated than at present, and much larger. It embraced the present South Fox shoals and extended to the north and south for three times its present length. The deep four-mile gap which now separates it from North Fox Island was certainly much narrower, and may even have been land-bridged. All these relations seem probable when one considers the water 150 feet lower than now between Squaw Island and Point Patterson, at the west end of the submerged Mackinac valley; and also by taking into account the increasingly lowered effect farther south, inasmuch as the major part of the post-Algonquin deformation of the region had not yet taken place.

"The lakes were brought back to near the present aspect through further slow uplifting in the north. By elevating the North Bay-Mattawa outlet, this gradually raised the lake level until overflow again took place at Port Huron, and it was then that the well known Nipissing shoreline was developed. It is very marked on both the Fox Islands. North Fox stood only about 10 or 15 feet above water at this time.

"Most of the postglacial uplift had already taken place before formation of the Nipissing shoreline, but some very moderate tilting occurred thereafter and raised the shoreline above the present lakes by amounts which reach a maximum of 100 feet in the far north part of Lake Superior. It is only 40 feet at the Fox Islands. It is generally considered that this latest movement was a slow gradual process, but there is evidence in the Algoma shoreline that may have been interrupted.

"The Algoma shoreline on the Fox Islands is approximately half way, vertically, between the Nipissing and the present. Its fine development as an eroded terrace and bluff, especially along the east coast of South Fox Island, where it strongly resembles the Nipissing, is good grounds for considering that it was made by a transgressing water level. Also the peculiar situation of the highest Algoma gravel ridge not far north of the lighthouse on South Fox Island, unconformably cutting off slightly lower beaches, at least hints at the same conclusion. This may have been only the result of remarkably high water for a year or so, as occurred in 1917-1918 and 1929. It might also have been due to a temporary reverse in the tilting which had been taking place and which later was renewed. It would be an interesting matter for future geological study to discover the true explanation for the strongly developed Algoma beaches.

"Whatever the cause for this advance, the lake then very gradually withdrew after the Algoma shoreline was formed, the last slight tilting took place, and perhaps 1,000 or 2,000 years elapsed until the present time."

To summarize: The larger islands emerged from glacial lake Algonquin in its early stages and became available to hardy plants and such animals as may have remained near the front of the glacier. It is deemed improbable that any species now inhabiting the islands was among the first populations to invade them. The water dropped, in many stages, to a point probably 200 feet below present lake levels. Under these conditions all the islands, possibly excluding South Fox, would have been connected with the mainland. The highlands of this period were restored as islands by gradual rise in lake levels owing to tilting in the north, and in the end all the present small islands and much of the area of the large islands were again covered with water by Lake Nipissing, which represented the last great rise of the lake.

The question must be considered whether some part of the modern faunas of the higher islands could date back to the pre-Nipissing period when the present island areas were united to the mainland.

HEIGHT OF PRESENT AND RECENT BEACHES

Stanley has contributed the following observations:

"As a chronological study, geology is always aided by formations which link the present with the immediate past. The writer found some interest on the Fox Islands in accumulating data on the heights of active beaches above the present water, and those recent nearby beaches which seem to date back a few years into the historic period of the region.

"A positive indication of age of a beach is the presence of vegetation. Some herbaceous plants appear on a beach almost immediately after the water recedes. Shrubs, such as osier, and ninebark, may follow in a few years, then poplar or cedar may appear. When trees a foot in diameter cover the beach, it would seem to have been formed at least 40 or 50 years ago. Bare gravelly beaches gradually accumulate a dark coating of lichens when no longer molested by the waves, and contrast with the brilliance of fresh gravel.

"A layer of driftwood over or in back of a beach indicates naturally that the time since it was formed by the waves is insufficient for complete decay of the woody material. One does not usually have to go far back from the lake to leave the driftwood zone. In all cases this was found to comprise nailed or sawed planks, slats from boxes, or other fashioned sticks (Fig. 5), such as might date from some period well within the last half century. Most driftwood of greater age than this, or certainly driftwood antedating commercial enterprise on the lake, has totally disintegrated.

"During the course of running levels in to the much higher ancient beaches of the islands, a number of observations were made upon the beaches near the present shore, and these are summarized in Table 3.

"The incompleteness of this table is due to the fact that a full succession of beaches is not to be found everywhere along the shore. What is deposited at one point has usually been eroded from nearby. Where erosion rather than deposition has been the rule, only the latest erosion level may be observed, and then only if there is a fairly marked cliff or bluff cut by the waves. A few conclusions may be drawn from the data.

"1. Around the Fox Islands (and similar shores) beaches are formed generally not more than 7.5 feet above lake level, and in most cases much less.

TABLE 3
ALTITUDES OF PRESENT AND RECENT BEACHES — FOX ISLANDS
(in parenthesis, height in feet above water level—578.7 above sea-level—of June, 1937)

A Locality	B Modern storm beach, or beaches probably of recent years	C Beaches abandoned for several years	D Highest or oldest identifiable beach of modern era	E Latest beach which may antedate modern era
SOUTH FOX				
North shore near base of northwest point	585.0 (6.3) Gravelly beach on terrace cut into fore-dune			beaches enclosed by fore-dune 10-15 feet higher 586.0 (7.3) Gravel beaches discordant with present shore which truncates them at right angles
West shore, .75 mile north of lighthouse	583.6 (4.9) Sandy beach at base of high bluff			
West shore 500 feet north of lighthouse	583.0 (4.3) Sandy beach along fore slope of fore-dune			
East shore near lumbertown piling	581.3 (2.6) Sandy beach on prograded plain	584.7 (6.0) Beach covered with bleached and rotted driftwood. 585.9 (7.2), 587.1 (8.4) Gravel beaches with rotted drift logs behind a fore-dune sand ridge	587.1 (8.4) Beach mentioned to left	
North shore at east end of high bluffs	582.4 (3.7) Storm beach at base of high bluff			

GEOLOGICAL HISTORY 17

North shore, .5 mile east of northwest point	584.0 (5.3) Gravelly storm beach line at base of high bluff				
NORTH FOX Point on northwest shore	Boulder-paved terrace for 150 feet back from water, with small grasses and shrubs a foot or so in height	583.9 (5.2) Gravel ridge, accumulation of bleached driftwood, boxes, etc. on beach and in swale; cedars up to 4 inches on beach. 585.5 (6.3), 586.0 (7.3) Higher beaches with much rotted driftwood	587.0 (8.3) Gravel ridge circling the base of point at edge of woods; a 9-inch balsam, 12-inch and 14-inch cedars on beach, and a 26-inch spruce in swale; no driftwood		587.8 (9.1) Flat terrace back in woods with bluff 6 feet high. This strand runs at an angle to the present shore and is truncated by the 584.7 bluff. Farther south the Algoma and Nipissing shorelines are similarly truncated
300 feet south of last		584.8 (6.1), 585.6 (6.9) Gravel beaches with bleached driftwood and drifted saw logs	586.9 (8.2) Beach in edge of woods with 12-inch cedar and 14-inch paper birch trees		
500 feet still farther south	Bouldery flat for 150 feet back from water	583.9 (5.2) Gravel beach with bleached driftwood	584.7 (6.0) Base of low bluff at edge of woods		

TABLE 3 — continued
ALTITUDES OF PRESENT AND RECENT BEACHES — FOX ISLANDS
(in parenthesis, height in feet above water level—578.7 above sea-level—of June, 1937)

A	B	C	D	E
Locality	Modern storm beach, or beaches probably of recent years	Beaches abandoned for several years	Highest or oldest identifiable beach of modern era	Latest beach which may antedate modern era
West shore, 1 mile north of triangulation tower	Broad, bouldery, flat		583.7 (5.0) Gravel beach line with many bleached and rotted drift logs, at base of 30-foot bluff	
West shore, .5 mile north of tower	580.7 (2.0) Gravel beach	581.3 (2.6) Beach grown to some grass. 581.7 (3.0), 583.6 (4.9) Older beaches	587.0 (8.3) Base of 40-foot wave-cut bluff —not very recent	
West shore, by tower	581.0 (2.3) Broad, sandy beach formed probably within a few weeks	581.7 (3.0), 582.6 (3.9) Gravel beaches with drift logs	586.9 (8.2) Now a beach swale behind a fore-dune ridge (592.8), filled with aged driftwood and at base of low wave-cut bluff	595.7 (17.0) Algoma gravel beaches at top of bluff
West shore, .25 mile south of tower			585.3 (6.6) Gravel beach with aged drift logs	587.7 (9.0) Base of wave-cut bluff in woods
West shore, 500 feet north of south point	Broad, boulder flat	584.4 (5.7) Large accumulation of drift logs		588.2 (9.5) Base of shore bluff in back of low fore-dune. No driftwood observed, but this feature may belong in column D

GEOLOGICAL HISTORY 19

Southwest side of south point	East side of south point (Obtained with data above in a continuous section across south point)	East shore, near south end, by abandoned cabin	East shore opposite triangulation tower
...Terrace on bluff in young woods	587.5 (8.8) Beach with absolutely no driftwood, grassed but no trees 589.3 (10.6) Beach with young trees	587.4 (8.7) Terrace at base of 9-foot wave-cut bluff in woods behind cabin	596.3 (17.6) Cut terrace back in woods
...Gravel beach with lichens and aged driftwood	587.9 (9.2) Beach with some rotted driftwood including sawed boards	587.4 (8.7) Strong gravel beach directly in front of cabin at edge of woods. This beach perhaps belongs in column to right, though there is driftwood on it	589.1 (10.4) Highest line of driftwood on strand; blown sand ridges behind it
...Gravel beach with rotted driftwood and lichens	585.4 (6.7), 587.8 (9.1) Beaches of lichen-covered gravel, with much accumulated, rotted driftwood	584.3 (5.6), 584.7 (6.0) Strong gravel ridges in front of cabin, gravel with lichens, abundant and much rotted drift logs and boards, and tin cans rusted nearly to pieces	586.5 (7.8) Strong beach of lichen gravel with rotted driftwood. 588.2 (9.5) Highest beach of pure gravel. Wagon tracks (associated with abandoned cabin) on these beaches cross over them down to where they have been obliterated by the waves that formed the 586.0 beach
	585.9 (7.2) Highest ridge of fresh gravel, washed back over rotted drift logs	Bouldery flat for 100 feet back from water	581.3 (2.6), 580.8 (2.1) Beaches of fresh gravel 581.6 (2.9) Base of low bluff, cut perhaps in 1937. 585.3 (6.6), 586.0 (7.3) Beaches of fairly fresh gravel behind low bluff

"2. Vegetation, aged driftwood, lichen-covered gravel, etc., distinguish various beaches which were formed several years ago, at levels up to about ten feet above the present lake. Some of these were probably formed during the high lake levels of 1929, 1917-1918, 1908, or other years of high water. Although many of these beaches of a decade or two ago are higher than any of the very recent beaches, elevation alone is hardly a method of differentiation. Variation in shore topography causes a range of several feet for beaches that might be built during a single year, and seasonal fluctuations are also to be considered.

"3. Certain beaches found at elevations only eight to ten feet above the present lake are probably much older than the lichen-covered beaches, perhaps a century or two, as required by their position in forest, beneath or behind artificial structures, or as seems indicated by their discordance with the present shore, and absence of any driftwood. In level, they differ immaterially from beaches of the past decade.

"4. Though the uplifting process which has so widely splayed out the ancient strandlines of this region appears to be continuing slowly at the present time, it has not effected any permanent change sufficient to eclipse the secular fluctuations of the lake which amount to some five feet."

DISTRIBUTION OF ROCKS

That the distribution of rocks and rock types is indicative of the extent of wave action, present and past, is shown by Stanley's observations which follow.

"Wave action along the shore and the resulting clean and unweathered rocks to be found there, render it ideal for noting the various types of rocks, or for collection of interesting pebbles. Pre-Cambrian types from the north are to be found in abundance, as elsewhere in Michigan, all imported by the glacier. Limestones are very common on the Fox Islands and may have been derived from closer sources. In fact the large amounts of limestone gravel to be found in some of the beaches lead to the suspicion that ledges of the Paleozoic rock may exist below water close offshore, or shallowly

10. Beaver Island's extensive hardwood forests give a mainland character to the island. View southward from the fire tower. June, 1939. L. C. Stuart.

11. Miller's Marsh, Beaver Island, was rich in Painted Turtles, Spring Peepers, Bull Frogs and Leopard Frogs. Note the sedges and pond lilies in the foreground, the floating mat and islands in the background. June, 1939. L. C. Stuart.

12. Gull Island, though small, has a varied shore and cover. Dark areas towards the south are largely cedar forest; hardwood forest bands the center. Towards the north is reverted field and near the tip a small patch of balsam and poplar forest. The north end is at the right. July 15, 1938. Agricultural Adjustment Administration.

13. A heath well carpeted with creeping juniper occurs north of the point on the east shore of Gull Island. June 22, 1938. R. T. Hatt.

buried somewhere nearby. Dark green porphyries with creamy white feldspar phenocrysts are common erratic types here, as also are the reddish Keweenawan porphyries and amygdaloids, and Lake Superior sandstones. Jasper conglomerates were rare, two being found on North Fox Island, but none on South Fox.

"Occasional clinker pebbles were seen, such as might have floated ashore from passing vessels. Rounded pebbles of coal were found along certain desolate beaches where it would seem only logical that they had been cast up by the lake. It is of course possible that they might be ferried ashore by cakes of ice. On the other hand, it may be no idle speculation to think of them as being washed up by waves from far offshore where dumped by passing steamers or fish tugs. Their low specific gravity might enable the waves to propel them landward for some distance along the lake bottom. Accurate data concerning instances of this sort in the Great Lakes would be welcomed.

"An interesting observation was made from high up on the north shore of South Fox Island. Elevation enables one to see easily the great number of boulders which litter the bottom for some distance offshore. The boulders are not scattered purely at random, but are aggregated in clusters. Apparently they have been thrust hither and thither by the shove of lake ice, and have been gathered into piles, each pile having gradually become a buttress sufficient to break the movement of the ice, and so accumulate more lodged boulders."

In the opinion of Mr. Sherman Moore of the United States Lake Survey the knotted distribution of boulders, which Stanley attributes to action of ice and water, may be attributed to their having fallen from a formerly existent bluff face at a period of wave action during high water. In the instance of the boulders at the north end of South Fox Island, it is pointed out that the present highlands doubtless once extended a considerable distance north and west and that when lake storms cut away the bluffs, boulders held therein were loosened and rolled down to the bottom where, he believes, there would be some tendency to form rows and piles. Moore's opinion is based on the presence of knots of boulders as much as 40 feet below the surface, where, in his opinion, the lake level never descended.

"In view of the powers of waves and winds that occur along the shore," writes Stanley, "it is interesting to see occasional electric light and radio bulbs tossed up by the waves and stranded unbroken. Six in all were observed, and most of them, incidentally, rested on bouldery or coarse gravel beaches."

3. Cultural History

THE HISTORY of the islands has followed this general sequence of periods: emergence, development of plant cover, animal and aboriginal occupation, exploration and exploitation by whites, agricultural development, and recreational reversion. Historians have, however, largely neglected the story of these outposts. The cultural history of the islands and the island region is of paramount importance to this study because of the numerous modifications imposed by man, both on the natural cover and on the land vertebrates themselves.

The fauna may be considered as having been in balance with the aboriginal human population. With the advent of the French, however, came the fur trade and its reduction in the numbers of some species and extirpation of others. As the lands were deforested or cleared for farms, animals of mature forests withdrew, the larger game and wild pigeons disappeared, but prairie species moved into the territory. Finally man, intentionally and otherwise, introduced several species to the islands and provided suitable conditions for others through the shelter of his buildings.

That the islands, from before the time of the whites, were known to the Indians, whose bark canoes provided easy passage to them when ice did not bridge the channels, is indicated on North Manitou and Beaver at least by the occurrence of flint arrows and stone axes. Lawler (1938, p. 297) reports "numerous mounds" about the latter. A village of Ottawas was reported on Beaver Island in 1763, and that same year the Ojibways transferred prisoners from Mackinac to Beaver. In 1832 Father Baraga established a mission on this island. High Island was occupied by Indians at the time the Mormons settled on Beaver. Two Indian burying grounds are known on Beaver Island, and one on Garden Island is still in use. The Fox Islands and the smaller islands of the Beavers probably held no Indian families for very long, since opportunity for their occupations of hunting, fishing, and herb gathering would have been too limited. The Manitou islands are reputed to have been held sacred and not used for ordinary purposes. There were no Indians resident there in 1847 but they came occasionally for trade.

Indian settlements on the islands today have little permanence; a few families may move in one year and be gone the next. In 1916 there was a small group living in shacks in the interior of North Manitou. In 1938 the only islands occupied by the Indians were the Beaver Islands; most of them lived in Saint James and on High Island, where three families were engaged in fishing. Most of the islands bore some evidence of Indian visits. On Whiskey Island Indians had peeled a large number of birches, removing sections about 30 inches wide from trees 4 to 10 inches in diameter. On Squaw Island a fragment of cattail matting was found. One hears numerous accounts of the Indians hunting for herbs on the islands. These present-day movements of the Indians, however, would only be of significance to this study if there were indication that they introduced animals on the islands or exterminated others, and of neither circumstance is there a shred of evidence.

The French at the time of their seventeenth century explorations of the Lakes probably used the islands as stepping stones as they worked southward, but few vestiges of that period remain—perhaps only the names, now translated, such as Beaver Island (Ile du Castor), or corrupted, as Skilligallee (Ile aux Galets). At the time of the Mormons, however, Strang reported many evidences of French farming, and evidence does point to occupation of Beaver Island before 1650. The few families of French name now on the islands or nearby mainland represent nineteenth century migrations from eastern Canada.

The fur trade affected this area particularly during the period from 1670 to 1830, when trading posts were active on Mackinac Island. A building yet standing on Beaver Island is said to date from the early part of the nineteenth century and to have served as quarters for the American Fur Company. By this time the beaver must have been largely gone from the island and the post served by mainland sources of supply.

The period 1840-1880 was one of great shipping activity on the lakes, and numerous sailing schooners plied their waters, taking up lumber, fish, and agricultural products from the islands, and delivering supplies to the residents: 1,006 schooners were registered in

1857; even more were on the waters in 1875. From about 1850, steam vessels were common on Lake Michigan, and for many years thereafter, the demand for cordwood was extremely heavy. Much was cut on the islands during this period and sold to the steamers at $1.75 per four-foot cord. On the Manitous, where wharves were in use in 1847, and on South Fox, lumber villages were set up, piers and railroads laid out. Extensive deforestation certainly changed the status of some of the land animals, but of prime importance to animal distribution, small animals during this era had their best opportunity to move from one island to another—as stowaways on boats and as passengers on the driftwood, most of which originated at this time. Wrecks were frequent, and much of both cargo and vessel became flotsam. Around South Manitou alone are remnants of some 50 wrecks, and the islanders told us that at one time they could live the year around on salvage from the vessels. Many of the buildings were erected from lake-salvaged lumber. In this period, too, reaching a climax about 1880, large rafts of logs were moved about the lakes and when storms broke these up, the beaches were strewn with wood that later furnished excellent cover for many small animals.

The Beaver Islands appear to have been surveyed before 1853, for John Farmer published a map that year (Karpinski, 1931, p. 277) which carried on an inset, "Map of Beaver Isles from Actual Survey, scale of 6 miles to an inch." The first federal survey in the area was done under Captain J. N. Macomb, of the Topographical Engineers, in 1854 and 1855. The resulting chart was issued by the War Department in 1857.

Largely in the steps of the lumbermen, but occasionally as pioneers (on Beaver Island the French farmed in the seventeenth century and the Mormons, by reoccupation, in 1847), the farmers moved in, clearing important sections of all the larger islands and planting them to grains, potatoes, and fruit trees. Religious colonies of farming people, as related elsewhere, took up land on Beaver Island and High Island. Improvement in mainland transportation facilities, however, spelled the doom of most of the farms by making operation of the lake ships, which served the mainland ports as well as the islands, unprofitable. Today, cultivated farm lands, except on Beaver Island, are all but gone, and the old homesteads are disappearing rapidly.

The tourist and recreational values of the islands are slowly being realized, though only on North Manitou and Beaver Islands have these become an important economic factor. In the instance of North Manitou, where the interest and control are centered on hunting, the animal populations have been much altered.

TABLE 4

A CHRONOLOGICAL LISTING OF SELECTED EVENTS INDICATIVE OF CHANGES IN THE ISLAND REGION

1612. Brulé probably discovered Lake Huron about this time, eight years before the landing of the Pilgrims at Plymouth.

1615. Father Joseph LeCaron made the first recorded discovery of Lake Huron, which was the first of the Great Lakes to be seen by a white man.

1632. Champlain's map of the Great Lakes (showing ,however, little accurate knowledge of the area).

1634. Nicolet in his search for a passage to the Indies discovered Lake Michigan.

1641. Two missionaries from Ste. Marie (near the present city of Midland, Ontario) preached to 2,000 Indians at the Sault.

1658. Thirty-one French fur traders passed through upper Lake Michigan to the Wisconsin shore, returning to Quebec in 1660 with 60 canoe loads of furs.

1665-1675. Allouez, Marquette, and Joliet explored the upper end of Lake Michigan and gave it the name of Michigan or Illinois.

1669-1670. The missions of St. Ignace and St. Francis Xavier, at Green Bay, were founded.

1672. The Beaver Islands were shown, unnamed and grossly inaccurate, in a map in the Jesuit Relations. This was founded in great part on the explorations of Marquette, Joliet, and Allouez.

1679. LaSalle's ship, the *Griffin*, loaded with furs, was lost with all hands, probably in a great storm that struck a few hours after they left Green Bay.

1742. A Jesuit mission was established at present Cross Village and exerted a strong influence over the Ottawa in the Beaver Island region.

1744. Bellin's map, in Charleviox's *Histoire et description generale de la Nouvelle France,* shows "I. du Castor," probably the first recorded name for a Lake Michigan island.

1755. Kitchen's map of this date used the name "Caster's Island," and Mitchell's map has "Beaver I.".

1761. The British occupied Fort Michilimackinac on the Straits.

1763. Following the Ojibway massacre of the English garrison at Mackinac City, three captives were being transported to the Beaver Islands when a band of Ottawa took them away from the captors. This indicates Indian use of the islands at that date.

1779. His Majesty's sloop *Felicity* was sent on a tour of Lake Michigan, and on the return voyage from Milwaukee it stopped in the lee of North Manitou Island. About this same time the sloop *Archangel* was also assigned to service on Lake Michigan. Though there were several European establishments on the west shore of Lake Michigan at this time, the eastern shore was virtually unsettled.

1796. Mackinac Island was transferred to the Americans, to remain in their possession except for a brief interlude, 1812-1815, until today.

1797-1798. The extent of commerce in the upper Lakes is indicated by the fact that the North West Company then built a lock at the Sault, providing a depth of about two feet. Lake traffic was, however, confined essentially to the fur trade and the maintenance of government posts.

1808. The Mackinaw Company, British owned, maintained a post at Mackinac, to be succeeded in 1816 by the American Fur Company, operated by Astor. This became the chief agent of the fur trade in upper Lake Michigan.

1821. *Walk-in-th-Water*, the first steam-propelled boat in the Lakes, entered Lake Michigan on a trip to Green Bay. She, and her successor, the *Superior*, made occasional trips thereafter.

1825. The opening of the Erie Canal initiated the period of rapid colonization of the Lake Michigan area.

1830. The fur trade reached its peak.

1831. Baraga was sent as a missionary to L'Arbre Croche, now Cross Village, and in 1832 established a mission on Beaver Island.

1832. The real start of steamboat navigation on Lake Michigan, with its attendant great demand for firewood, dates from the Black Hawk War of this year.

1835. North Manitou Light was established (followed in 1839 by the South Manitou Light; 1850—Ile aux Galets Light; 1851—Beaver Island Light; 1853—Cat Head Point Light; 1867—South Fox Light).

1837. Regular steamboat service was established on Lake Michigan, and in this decade much of the shore was settled, but Leelanau County was still Indian country, with villages at Leland and near present-day Omena.

1841. The first propeller ship entered the Great Lakes. More economical of fuel, this type quickly replaced the sidewheelers.

1843. Margaret Fuller, the author, visited the woodcutters on the Manitous.

1846. Nicholas Pickard settled on North Manitou Island and supplied wood for steamers. The lightkeeper and two fishermen completed its population. At this time there are said to have been two or three families on South Manitou supplying a wooding station. There were yet no white residents on the nearby mainland and Mackinac was the nearest village. South Fox Island was also inhabited about this time, and by 1854 had a population of Mormons and other Caucasians.

14. Hat and Shoe Islands are important nesting areas for gulls and terns. The shoal southwest of Shoe Island was covered by a few inches of water in 1938. August 4, 1938. Agricultural Adjustment Administration.

15. Shoe Island supports nesting colonies of Caspian and Common Terns in years when it is not covered by the lake. July 7, 1938. R. T. Hatt.

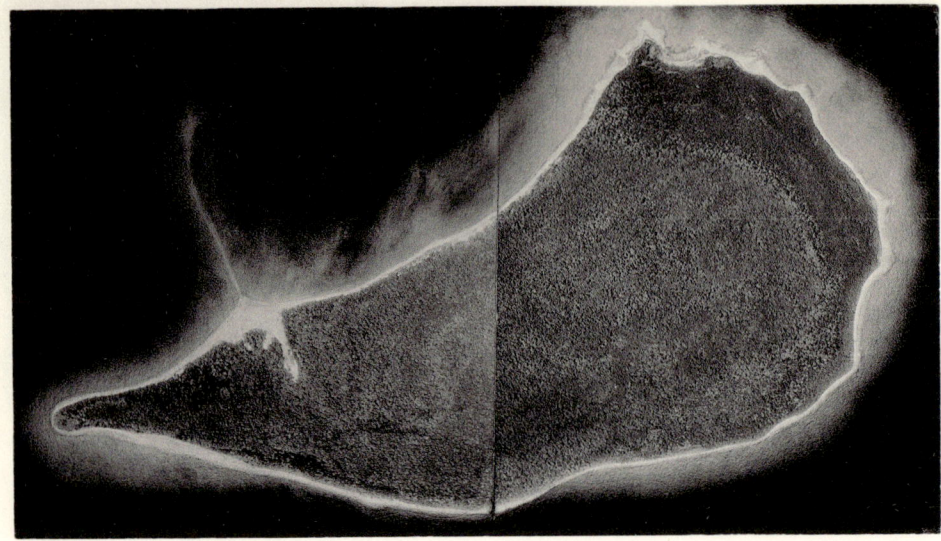

16. North Fox Island is largely low and forested. Its one active sand dune lies in back of the beach spit on the western shore. North is to the right. July 15, 1938. Agricultural Adjustment Administration

17. North Fox Island's gravelly eastern shore. The lowest two or three water marks were made as wave action was abating from a storm a day or so before the picture was taken. The next higher marks were probably made during the current spring. The highest bank of gravel to the left is of the higher beaches, probably of 1917-1918 or 1929-1930. 1937. G. M. Stanley.

1847. Strang's band of Mormons started its settlement of Beaver Island, and within two years about 50 families were established there. A sawmill was started at the present site of Traverse City. Elk Rapids, on the mainland, also had its first settlers.

1853. Farmer's map was published, showing the Beaver Islands from actual surveys. Antoine Manseau set up a mill at Leland, and by 1859 a dock was established here for the wood business. Glen Arbor was also settled.

1854. The steamer *Westmoreland* was wrecked near Sleeping Bear Point.

1856. Strang was murdered and the Mormons driven from their island kingdom.

1860. This year, by account of Quaife (1944, p. 164), "there were on all the lakes 1459 ships of which 1122 were sailing vessels, 335 steamers and propellers." The number of sailing vessels decreased from 1868, and in 1922 there were but 86 in service. All of these are probably out of service in 1947.

1863. Northern Michigan was thrown open to settlement by the homestead laws.

1868. A dock existed at Glen Arbor on Sleeping Bear Bay.

1869. An iron smelter was established on the Leland shore and operated for several years.

1872. Traverse City had its first railroad service.

Table 5

Size, Area, and Shore Line Length of the Islands

Compiled from large-scale Field Sheets of the U. S. Lake Survey.

Island	Square Miles	Acres	Shore Line in Miles
Beaver Island	58.4	37,385.6	41.6
Bellow Island	0.009	5.5	0.4
Fisherman's Island	0.016	10.2	0.7
Garden Island	7.8	4,914.6	20.7
Gull Island	0.4	270.1	3.4
Hat Island	0.025	16.0	0.6
High Island	5.8	3,692.8	12.5
Hog Island	3.9	2,530.0	16.0
Marion Island	0.4	243.8	2.8
North Fox Island	1.4	894.7	5.5
North Manitou Island	20.4	13,056.0	20.6
Pismire Island	0.004	2.5	0.3
Shoe Island	0.005	3.2	0.3
South Fox Island	5.4	3,392.0	11.8
South Manitou Island	7.9	5,030.4	12.6
Squaw Island	0.1	75.5	1.6
Trout Island	0.2	115.2	1.8
Whiskey Island	0.2	129.2	2.0

4. The Islands Described

THE ISLANDS CONCERNED have a more moderate climate than the mainland. Summer temperatures at Saint James, Beaver Island, do not get as high, nor winter temperatures as low, as at the shore stations (Charlevoix and Traverse City) on the nearby mainland. The Beaver Island weather records also indicate less rainfall for that island than for shore stations in this area and Mackinac Island. The annual difference amounts to six inches.

BASSETT ISLAND.
This is a peninsula from Marion Island, its north end isolated in periods of high water. Its area is less than two acres.

BEAVER ARCHIPELAGO, BEAVER GROUP, BEAVER ISLANDS, AND THE BEAVERS.
These terms are used here, and often elsewhere, to include the following islands: Beaver, Garden, Grape, Gull, Hat, High, Hog, Pismire, Shoe, Squaw, Trout, and Whiskey.

BEAVER ISLAND (*Isle du Castor* at least as early as 1744; often called "Big Beaver" in distinction to the Beaver Islands).
Figures 1, 10, 11.

Beaver Island, the largest in Lake Michigan, has diversity of topography and cover rivaling the mainland. It has 58 square miles of surface, and on this there are eight lakes and ponds with a total surface of 6.5 square miles. Its maximum elevation above the lake is about 200 feet, but the greater part does not exceed 80. In general it lacks the bold bluffs and areas of blowing sand encountered on others of the larger islands. "Mount Pisgah" is, however, a well marked captured dune, and back from the west shore is a complex of small dunes. The shores vary from broad to narrow, and are variously sandy, marshy, shingled, or, in one place, of bedrock. The land rises gradually to the higher areas of the interior. The glacial drift and sand areas have no marked drainage pattern,

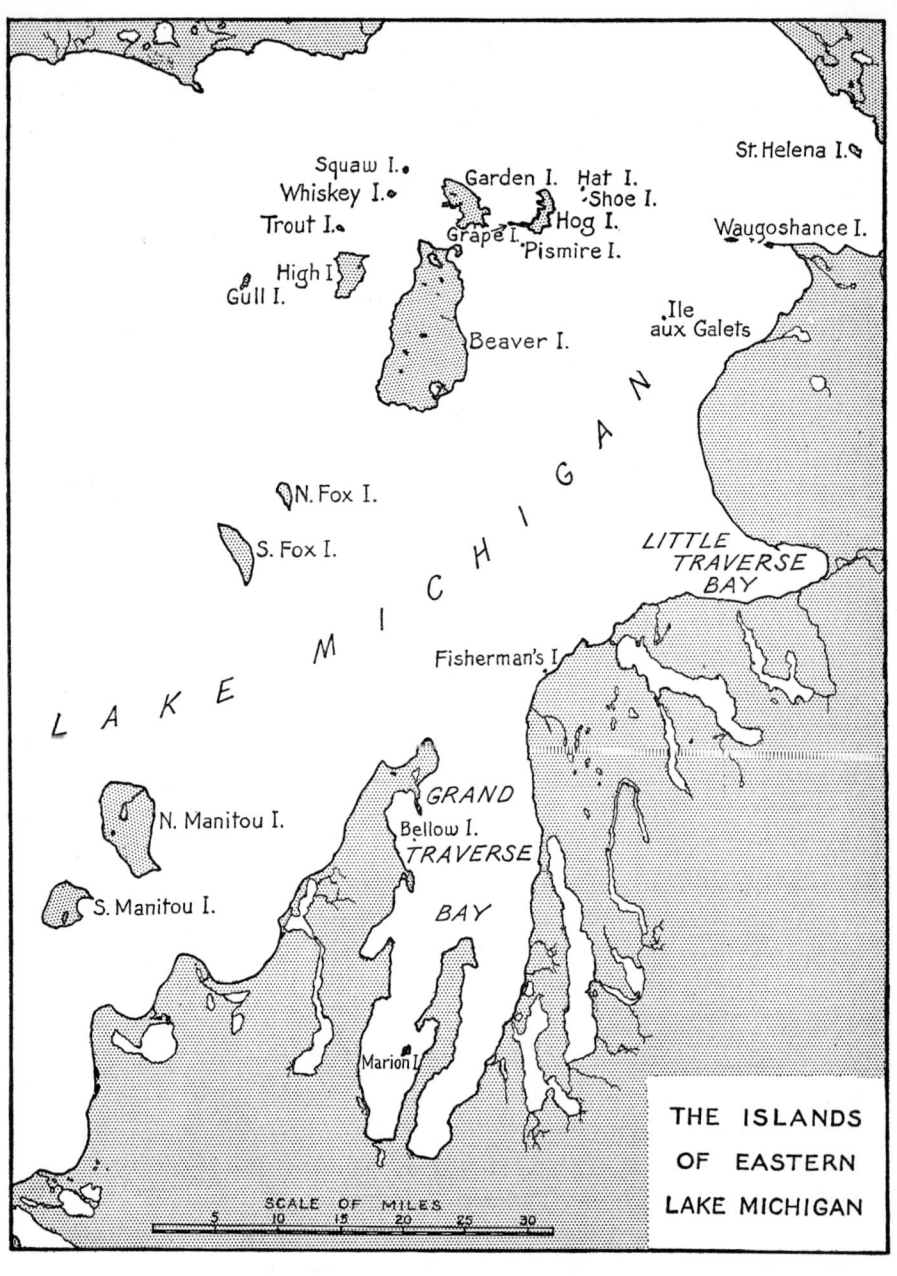

though a few small streams are swift flowing and have high banks, either open or forested.

The lakes are shallow, some with firm sandy shores and bottoms, as the north sides of Font Lake and Lake Genesareth, others with boggy shores and soft bottoms, abundantly vegetated, as Barney's Lake and Miller's Marsh. The lakes are surrounded by open meadows, hardwood forests, or occasionally, cedar bogs.

The town of Saint James lies along the center of the crescent of the good harbor at the northeast corner of the island. Roads make all but the central western shore and a large area in the south-central section easily accessible.

The vegetation of Beaver Island, as has been suggested above, approaches the diversity of the mainland and, like that flora, has been considerably modified by lumbering, with its subsequent fires, and by agriculture. The extent of modification is indicated by Darlington's (1940) note that in a week's field work he observed 75 non-native species.

The climax forest here is beech-maple, but by 1939 what may have been the island's last virgin timber was scheduled for early removal. Typical plants of this forest type on the island are listed by Darlington. Extensive areas of sandy soil near Saint James and behind Point Lapar are characterized by forest in which red pine and red oak predominate. Where moist areas border this, spruce, fir, hemlock, arbor vitae, and birch become more prominent.

Bog conditions are found around the borders of some lakes and marshes, particularly at Egg Lake, where Darlington reports a floating mat with typical sphagnum associates. Cedar swamps are found in areas of peaty soil.

The grasslands, represented by pastures, meadows, and stump-land, occupy a relatively small part of the island.

The climate of the island, as compiled by the Weather Bureau (Darlington, 1940, p. 32) shows a growing season 14 per cent longer than mainland Emmet County, Michigan, at approximately the same latitude. Over a 22-year period the average yearly temperature was 42.8 degrees F., with extremes of 97 degrees (May 1) and –28 degrees (December). The average annual rainfall was 24.66 inches, with maximum in October and minimum in March.

The Ojibway and Ottawa Indians were apparently occupants of the Beaver Islands at the time of the first explorations by whites. No records exist of the first white settlement on Beaver Island, but the archipelago was mapped roughly by 1672. There are evidences of some early French occupation and cultivation, possibly before the mid-seventeenth century, but this colony did not survive, and when some two hundred years later the Mormons settled, the cultivated lands were only party discernible. In the interim, however, trappers, traders, and missionaries visited the island, and the American Fur Company had a building at the harbor about 1830. Strang noted that the beaver were no longer present in 1855. The population under the Mormons built up to 1,300 or, by some estimates, to as much as 2,600, but after these people were driven off their lands the population never again grew large. Today there are about 600 permanent residents, engaged in farming, fishing, church or government service, and the trades of the town of Saint James.

Bellow Island (also called Gull Island, Trout Island).
Bellow Island is a five-acre gravel bar in Northport Bay, Leelanau County. On it is a summer residence, said to have proven unusable by reason of the colony of Herring Gulls which nest on the island. It has not been visited by us. It is recorded (Leach, 1902, p. 81) that the first settlers at Northport held a Fourth of July picnic on Bellow Island in 1849.

Big Beaver. See Beaver Island.

Crane Island (Ehlers, 1945, p. 80). See Waugoshance Island.

Fisherman's Island.
This is a 10-acre patch of wooded ground, lying very close to the mainland of Charlevoix County, that is an island only in times of high lake level. Even in those summers when it is separated from the main shore by a narrow strip of water, its isolation is meager and it would be inaccessible to few vertebrate animals. The winter ice bridge, of course, prevents the isolation from being more than seasonal. Some records were made here August 7-10, 1923, by Van Tyne and A. S. Warthin, Jr.

Ford Island. See Marion Island.

Garden Island.
Garden Island, a large member of the Beaver group, was not visited by any of our expeditions, and because we have no original data on

it, it is not fully described. Aerial photographs show it to be largely forest-covered, though reports have it that no beech or hemlock is present. Minor lumbering operations have been conducted in some years. Some 200 Indians are said to have lived on the island until about 1879, and their clearings were widespread in the early part of that century. In recent years Indian dead have been placed in the island's old cemetery, one of those with wooden shelters covering the graves. Garden Island has had a few white person's farms on it; one of them was occupied from at least 1880 to 1923, but in 1938 the land was uninhabited. Newspapers in December 1946 reported that a family was then moving to the island to establish a permanent home.

GRAPE ISLAND.
This island was not an island in 1938, but was well connected by beach with Hog Island. The peninsula, of which the "island" forms a tip surmounted by a few large pines, is paralleled by many other east-west boulder reefs, clearly discernible in aerial photographs.

GRAVEL ISLAND. See Shoe Island.

GULL ISLAND, Northport Bay, Leelanau County. See Bellow Island.

GULL ISLAND, Charlevoix County. Frontispiece; Figures 12, 13, 39-42.
Gull Island, lying 6.5 miles west of High Island and 15 miles south from the nearest mainland shore, is separated by the widest water channel of any of the islands. It has an area of 270 acres and a shore line of 3.4 miles. The top of a sand ridge is 10 feet above the lake, and it is unlikely that any point exceeds 15.

Its beaches, particularly along the south and west, are broad and bouldery and carry well developed lines of drift. Willows of small size are abundant on the middle beach of the western shore. The southern end of the island is grown to arbor vitae. About 50 acres of mature hardwoods occur on the central wooded section, and this forest on the east blends into an area of pine and arbor vitae. The smaller forested area at the northern end of the island is of balsam and poplar trees, which here seem to die and rot at an earlier than usual age. Heath areas cover a large proportion of the island. That which separates the northern and southern forests is a grassy area with a great amount of shrubby cherry growth and much poison ivy. The heaths of the upper beaches, best developed on the eastern point, are characterized by a solid mat of procumbent juniper and reindeer moss, through which a few balsams and mountain ashes appear. One small heath (possibly an old clearing) occurs in dense forest. Herring Gulls nested here, though the young needed to walk through 100 yards of forest to reach beach and water.

The island's name is the clue to its faunal character, but it is less strictly a gull island than some of the small ones whose ratio of beach to forest is greater. The fauna is quite depauperate, there being but one amphibian, no reptiles, and but three mammals known.

Gull Island is not now inhabited, though it is frequently visited by fishermen. At its northern tip is an unattended light. Three fairly recently made fishermen's cabins were on the south shore, and foundations of three earlier structures were found.

HARBOR ISLAND.

Such an island, intermediate in size between Hat Island and Ile aux Galets, has been listed (Anon., 1902). It could only be present-day Pismire Island or an island formerly existing where there is now shoal water, south and east of Saint James Harbor, Beaver Island. The name has also been applied to Marion Island.

HAT ISLAND. Figures 14, 35.

Hat Island lies 2.5 miles east of Hog Island and 15 miles from the nearest mainland. It is 16 acres in area and has a shore line of about .6 miles. Its greatest height above lake level must be less than 20 feet. Approximately half the area is beach, mostly a coarse shingle thrown up from the limestone visible as an outcrop just offshore. The center of the island is covered with a young forest, varying from a thick growth of arbor vitae, through cherry scrub, to a dense stand of white birches.

The vertebrates of the island in late July 1938 were confined to the birds, though a single Hare bone was found. It was the site of a large colony of Herring Gulls, whose nests occupied much of the beach, and of Great Blue Herons, which nested in the low trees.

Hat Island has probably never been inhabited for long, though the base of a fisherman's shack was found on it. The U. S. Lake Survey established a triangulation point on the island in 1920. In

18. Broad wet beaches on the northwest shore of North Fox are favorable habitats to Water Snakes and toads, which were found here. 1937. R. T. Hatt.

19. Pismire Island's cover is now confined to shrubs and herbs. July 11, 1938. R. T. Hatt.

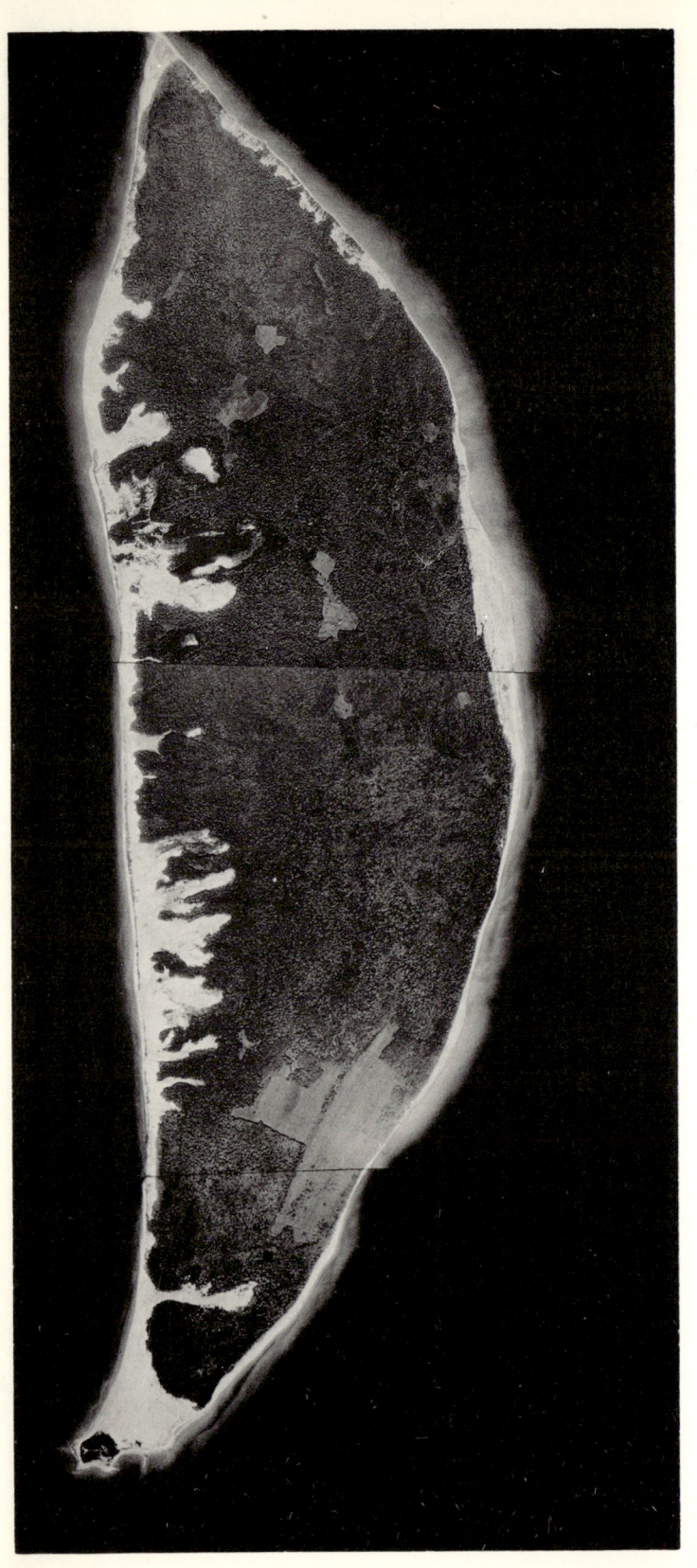

20. South Fox Isla[nd]

the late war Hat Island was used as a bomb target by the U. S. Navy, and it is reported that a crater has been blown in its center.

Hat Island is not a pleasant place for human abode. Our tent, on a coarse shingle beach, was exposed most of the day to a hot sun. Around us were a thousand gulls, young and adult, loudly screaming day and night. The corpses of hundreds nearby added their stench to the other odors of the colony. Swarms of house flies and biting dog flies plagued us. There was no place to bathe, as the water everywhere about the island was fouled by the numerous birds. No drinking water was available, except such as one could dip out of the lake a long way offshore, which act, owing to rough water, a heavy boat, and a rocky shore, was in itself not always easily accomplished.

High Island.

High Island, which lies almost four miles west of Beaver Island, exhibits much the same physiographic features as South Manitou. It has a high (240 feet) western bluff that is being torn away by the waves produced by the prevailing westerly winds; a low eastern shore with a crescentic-shored small natural harbor; a small interior lake. Owing to the limited opportunity of examining the island, it is not, however, possible for us to give an accurate original delineation of its character. The dunes on the west side and their flora are described by Fuller (1918). Hardwood forest covers much of the surface, but about 500 acres have in past years been cleared and planted to grains, potatoes, and fruit trees. The elevation here is 85 feet above the lake. There are numerous buildings along the bay shore of the island, which furnish home sites to birds.

High Island is said to have been settled by the Mormons at the time Strang's colony flourished on adjacent Beaver Island. More recently (1912-1928), the House of David, a religious sect with its headquarters at Benton Harbor, Michigan, established a colony of about 500 persons here and developed the agricultural and forest resources. Most of the dwellings date from this period. At the time of our visit there were three Indian families in residence, and the men operated a commercial fishing boat. A Roman Catholic chapel was on the island and was in good condition, with the altar decorated and vestments in place for the occasional visits of a priest who served such island outposts.

HIGH ISLAND GRAVEL BAR.

This bar lies a few hundred yards northeast of the northeastern point of High Island. In 1938 it was but inches above lake level and had a surface probably not exceeding 100 square yards. It appears on the U. S. Lake Survey chart of the Beaver Islands (Chart No. 79, edition of 1935), although in years of high water it is probably but a reef. At the time of our visit it served as a nesting site for a small colony of Caspian and Common Terns.

HOG ISLAND.

Hog Island, a large island of the Beaver group, was not visited by our parties except for brief contact with the southern shore. It is described as being largely low and wet, with thick forests of black ash. Parts of the northeast shore, at least, are 30 feet above the lake, and here a clearing and a hut were visible from Hat Island. Aerial photographs show broad flat shores on the west, with many long ridges of rock and boulders extending NW-SE into the dangerous channel between this and Garden Island. The island has the reputation among Beaver Islanders of being heavily populated by snakes, and it does seem probable from the topography that Water and Garter Snakes might be abundant on at least the western shore.

ILE AUX GALETS (The light has been officially named by the corrupt anglicization "Skilligallee" since at least 1906, and the island is always thus known in the upper Lakes, though its original name, meaning Pebble Island, is retained on Lake Survey Charts).

This island lies 5.5 miles off the Emmet County shore, about quarter way to Beaver Island. As shown by the survey of 1901, it is a triangle with concave sides, and measures 580 feet from the NW point to the SE base and 425 feet from the NE side to the SW point. Its height above the lake is about six feet. The island is a bed rock exposure with a topping of gravel and sand. Coast Guard descriptions and a photograph indicate almost no vegetation. The island is, of course, dominated by the light tower and associated buildings. No vertebrates are known to breed here, but it doubtless is a stopping place for birds traveling across the lake.

ISLE LE GALET (Anon., 1902. Also Landes, Ehlers and Stanley, 1945, p. 4). See Ile aux Galets.

THE ISLANDS DESCRIBED

LITTLE HAT ISLAND. Some published accounts have used this name for Shoe Island.

MARION ISLAND (More commonly known as Ford Island since its acquisition by Mr. Henry Ford in 1917. In the late nineteenth century it was known as Island No. 10 and by 1902 was called Harbor Island).

The island, not visited by the 1937-1944 expeditions, is described by Dice (1925a) as follows:

"Marion Island, which comprises 215 acres, is slightly oblong in shape, and is located in the western branch of Grand Traverse Bay, an arm of Lake Michigan. To the north is a small peninsula, called Bassett Island on some maps, which perhaps may be separated by water from the main part of Marion Island during heavy winter storms, as it is joined only by a low neck of land.

"A high hill with a very steep bluff to the northwestward occurs on the northern portion of the island. All the exposures examined are of glacial drift. The shores in general are rocky, although sandy shores occur in a few protected places.

"Although the water is mostly quite shallow near the shores there is little development of aquatic vegetation, probably owing to the heavy waves which frequently beat upon the island. In a somewhat protected bay near the northeastern part of the island there are some patches of bulrush growing in the water a short distance from shore, and the shore here and in a few other protected situations is bordered by a growth of bulrushes and common rushes. In general, however, the beach has only a scanty growth of vegetation or none at all.

"In the low depression between Marion Island proper and 'Bassett Island' there is a small development of marsh, growing on wet muck mixed with gravel. A few other such marshy areas are found in protected situations on the upper beach.

"The island is covered, with the exception of the narrow beaches and the marshy areas just noted, with a splendid growth of hardwood timber. The dominant species of trees in this forest vary in different parts of the island, part being dominated by Norway pine, part by white birch, part by beech, but most by hard maple. Although many of the trees in this forest are of good size, the forest itself is not mature, and the longer-lived trees are far from their maximum growth. It is probable that the present forest is not more than 100 years old; it may not be more than 75 years old. Probably the original forest was destroyed by fire or cutting in the early part of the last century."

In 1839 Henry R. Schoolcraft, who was then Indian Commissioner for the region, visited Marion Island to consider its suitability for an Indian school.

NORTH FOX ISLAND (also called Little Fox). Figures 2, 5, 16-18, 32.

North Fox Island lies 28 miles due west of Charlevoix. Its nearest neighbors are South Fox Island at 4 miles and Beaver Island at 9.5 miles. From the triangulation tower on the island may be seen Gull, High, Beaver, South Fox, North Manitou Islands, and much of the eastern shore from the north side of Little Traverse Bay south to Sleeping Bear. North Fox is roughly triangular in outline, widest at the low and bouldery northern end. The island is barely over two miles long, scarcely a mile across at the widest. It reaches a height of but 178 feet above the lake.

The beaches are generally wide and rocky except along a portion of the west shore where sand predominates. Typically they are from 50 to 150 feet wide.

"Like South Fox," Stanley (MS) observes, "North Fox is receiving some addition of beach materials along the east shore and is subjected to erosion on the west. Dunes are developed on the west shore and are being pushed eastward, but their perched situation is not conspicuous here as on South Fox, since the bluffs are less imposing. Considerable recession of the west shore is indicated however by the extensive bouldery shoals. On the other hand, the water is deep close to the eastern shore and power boats may be nosed up on the beach. Excepting for wind blown sand, North Fox is very low. Maximum elevations of 46, 51, and 55 were noted for summits of non-aeolian deposits in the middle of the island or along the west shore bluffs. In places, the till surface seems to decline eastward from the tops of the bluffs, and probably the highest parts of the original island have already been eroded away by the lake. Lake Algonquin covered the spot with fully 50 feet of water, and there is no Algonquin beach, but Nipissing and Algoma shorelines are well marked.

"On the west shore opposite the triangulation tower is a pronounced cusp in the shore which continues for some distance out into the lake as a submerged shoal. It seems as though the cusp of the shore in this vicinity has been a neutral point representing a balance between the northward and southward driven longshore currents, and therefore the dumping ground for beach drifted materials. The proximity of the great sand dunes seems fairly attributable to this neutral point where the waves discharge their burden, the sand being eventually taken by the wind and added to the dunes which east of the cusp form the summit of North Fox Island."

The communities of the island are few, limited to forest and beach. At the southern end there is a growth of large hardwoods, chiefly hard maple. Most of the rest of the island is covered with a dense young forest of arbor vitae, balsam, spruce, hemlock, quaking aspen, white birch, ash, and moose maple. None of the trees are large, very few attaining a diameter of six inches. Along its edge the forest is almost exclusively coniferous. Birch and balsam compose the bulk of growth in the center. Along the southern beach the conifer fringe is narrow but at the northwest is broad and shows clearly in the aerial photograph (Fig. 16). Pines, conspicuous on the other large islands, are absent on both the Fox Islands except for a few large white pines just north of the big sand blow on North Fox. The more valuable timber has been cut from North Fox, but no clearings remain.

A considerable area of the lower beaches, especially at the north end of the island, is low and wet and supports a good growth of rushes and sedges. Here, in pools between the boulders are adequate breeding grounds for frogs and toads. More driftwood is found along the middle and upper beaches (Fig. 18) than is commonly encountered on the islands, and under it is ample shelter for deer-mice, snakes, and toads. On the upper beaches grow some thickets of small birch, red osier, and poison ivy. At the south end is a small heath of bearberry (*Arctostaphylos*).

Except for a brief period of lumber operations the island has probably remained uninhabited, and no traces of occupancy are found except for one cabin, a triangulation tower, and a horse skeleton. Attempts to exploit the island as a skunk ranch or gravel deposit have had little effect on the island's history.

NORTH MANITOU ISLAND.   Figures 8, 43.

North Manitou is second in size to Beaver Island. It differs considerably from that island in having less diversity of aquatic habitats and in having less of its land under cultivation. In greatest length North Manitou is 7.4 miles; in breadth but 4.2 miles at the wider, northern, end. It is isolated by a 3.75-mile channel from South Manitou and by 17 miles of water from South Fox. Nearest point on the mainland is Pyramid Point, Leelanau County, at 7 miles. Leland, from which comes regular mail service, is 12 miles by boat.

The margins of the island vary. High bluffs and sand dunes are characteristic of the southern, northern, and northwestern shores; low land or moderate banks occur elsewhere. In the northwest corner are about two square miles of very rugged forest-covered sand dunes. Most of the central area is flat or gently rolling, but towards the south are hills, some of them probably being 200 feet or more in elevation above the lake.

Though all of the island has been lumbered at one time or another, as attested by the logging roads which lead everywhere, much of the cutting was selective, and mature hardwood forest is encountered in many places. Beech, hard maple, black birch, and hemlock are dominant trees. Along the high dunes large arbor vitae are often found, and they are common, too, about the lakes. Red and white pine stands occur chiefly along the southeastern shore.

Cultivated lands or deserted fields probably do not exceed 1,000 acres.

Inland water of the island is confined to two lakes, an intermittent stream draining the larger of these, another small stream entering the small lake, and a few small marshy areas such as that at the site of the old lumber town of Crescent, now known as the "West Side." There are wet forested areas north and west of the larger lake and many undrained pockets, especially in the northwest sector, which are temporary catch basins and may serve as breeding areas for salamanders. Beach pools are occasional along the north shore.

The larger lake is named Lake Manitou. It is located in the north-central sector, is slightly in excess of one mile long and about a half mile broad. The forest crowds to its shores in most places, and many trees fall into the water. There is very little free beach. The west shore is dominantly weedy.

The smaller lake, called Tamarac, is on the west side of the island, and it is difficult to locate owing to dense growth surrounding it. It is about 150 yards across and circular in outline. The lake bears a fringe of tamarack and is largely surrounded by a wet arbor vitae forest. A small stream drains into the lake, and there is an intermittent drainage away from it which, however, disappears in the soil without attaining Lake Michigan. A quaking bog extends as a shelf into part of the lake. Coulter (1904) has given an excellent description of this area.

As early as 1846, steamers were stopping at the island for wood. That year, before the opposite mainland was settled, besides the lumbering operations personnel, there were two fishermen and a lightkeeper. In 1847 Weed (Mansfield, 1899, pp. 209, 212-213) visited the island and described its forest as of maple and beech. There were then some 40 men employed in cutting and hauling wood, and one family lived there. During the lumbering period the island had a network of railroads, wagon roads, and trails. Later, docks were at Crescent (Fig. 8) on the west side, where some 300 people lived, and at North Manitou, where the Coast Guard Station was located. Crescent was abandoned prior to 1916, and today but one farm dwelling and a large barn mark the site of the village. The town of North Manitou survives as the headquarters of the Manitou Island Association, and here there is a small hotel, post office, residences, farm buildings, etc. Some 30 persons stay here through the year, and many more come in the summer for recreation or cherry picking. In deer season there is an influx of hunters. The light tower at the southern end was abandoned about two decades ago and later was undermined by the lake. The Coast Guard Station was deserted soon after the lighthouse.

Today the island is all but completely owned by the Manitou Island Association, which operates it for its cherry orchards, lumber, and deer herd.

NUMBER 10. An early name for Marion Island.

PISMIRE ISLAND. Figure 19.

A small island lying midway between the southern tips of Hog and Garden Islands. In 1938 its area was about two acres, about half of which would disappear with a foot's rise in lake level. The highest point was but 10 feet above the lake. All but one of the few trees which once grew on the island had died, probably as a result of changed lake level. The dead trees were arbor vitae, the survivor a black ash. Two-thirds of the surface was covered with shrubs, the balance with herbaceous growth. Other than a triangulation tower and the base of a former camp, there are no man-made structures on the island.

Pismire appears to be entirely a gravel bar, formed long enough ago to have acquired some soil. Several similar, but smaller, islets are in formation directly to the west.

The island in 1938 was used as a nesting site by Herring and Ring-billed Gulls (the latter in the lower southern quarter of the island only), a few Black Ducks, one pair of Great Blue Herons, and a pair of Crows. It was visited by a number of Starlings which flew over to Hog Island as the expedition boat touched shore.

The island is said to take its name from the same Middle English word, but, though ants were not obvious on the island, a foul smelling mire did exist at the southern end.

RABBIT ISLAND. Squaw Island bore this name about 1902.

ST. HELENA.
Lying close to Michigan's Upper Peninsula and distant from the islands studied, it is not considered in this report.

SHOE ISLAND. (Also called Gravel Island. Is it called Shoe Island because it is "below" Hat Island, or because it is shaped somewhat like a shoe?). Figure 14.

This is a large gravel bar, omitted from many maps. It was only some four feet above lake level in 1938 and largely submerged in 1939. In 1929 Tyrrell found the bar all but under water and few birds on it. Shoe Island lies 2.5 miles east of Hog Island and .5 miles south of Hat Island. An equal distance south of Shoe Island is another gravel reef exposed at low lake levels. The island has neither trees nor bushes, but is thinly coated at the highest point with cinquefoil, etc. It bore no driftwood in 1938.

It is, so far as known, used as breeding territory only by gulls and terns.

21. South Fox Island's west shore is largely backed by a precipitous bluff surmounted by sand dunes. June, 1937. G. M. Stanley.

22. Pasteboard-like sheets at the water's edge are the result of layers of organic material being deposited on the beach where they shrink and curl as they dry. Such material is found in places along the northwest shore of South Fox Island, where quiet waters, behind shallow bouldery shoals, are frequently roiled with organic material. Animal tracks are sometimes well preserved in this material. June, 1937. G. M. Stanley.

23. South Manitou's eastern plain is marked by a series of strongly developed and parallel fossil beach bars marking stages in recession of the lake. The inland lake appears in the lower center. Agricultural Adjustment Administration.

24. The shore of South Manitou's southwestern quarter is marked by high bluffs topped by sand dunes which rapidly encroach on the forest. This is shown larger scale than Figure 23. July 15, 1938. Agricultural Adjustment Administration.

SKILLIGALLEE. See Ile aux Galets.

SNAKE ISLAND. A reef near Pismire Island. (Lyon, 1927, p. 182.)

SOUTH FOX ISLAND (also called Big Fox).
                                    Figures 4, 6, 9, 20-22, 36-38.
South Fox, most isolated island in Lake Michigan, is large enough for some farming, but its cover is not diversified and the fauna does not approach the mainland fauna in richness. The island lies due west of Charlevoix but, with North Fox and the Manitous, it is administered by Leelanau County. Nearest islands are North Fox at 4 miles and North Manitou at 17 miles. The nearest point of the mainland is Cat Head Point, on the Leelanau peninsula, at 16.5 miles.

South Fox is long, narrow, and slightly crescentic. The southern end tapers to a long point, and the northern end, pointed too, is more blunt. The island, which trends NNW to SSE, is about 5.5 miles long and nearly 2 miles wide. The west shore of South Fox Island is a long, curving line of tall shore cliffs. Slightly concave, this coast faces WSW, and is severely buffeted by the westerly storms. The northeastern and western shores rise abruptly from the narrow beach to sand cliffs and dunes of impressive height.

Stanley has described the island in these words:

"The great cliffs are eloquent of the erosion that has taken place and the soundings on the lake chart indicate that the island has been eaten away almost a mile in places, perhaps much more. This is implied also by the concentrates of boulders, over shoals near the northwest point. A survey was made to the top of a bald peak less than two miles north of the lighthouse, showing it to have an elevation of 334 feet. This appeared to be the highest point of the Fox Islands, but a few timber-covered peaks farther north may reach to about the same or slightly greater elevations. About four miles north of the lighthouse there is a system of deep gullies dissecting the island into a veritable 'badlands' to be traveled only in the gully bottoms. Several cold springs occur where these gullies debouch upon the beach. The gullies are a marked variation of the general topography of the Fox Islands. The largest has a maze of dank growth near its mouth, but farther up it clears into a narrow, winding channel, lined with cedars and carpeted with grass and moss and an occasional clump of yellow lady-slippers.

"Viewing the bluffs from the water (Fig. 6), one's eye is immediately taken by the nearly horizontal line which strikes along their entire length. Above this line only sand is found. Beneath it the material is generally glacial till. Being more compacted than the sand, the till stands out in conspicuous shoulders. It furnishes a stony floor on which the dunes have been built up or pushed back in broad apices. At practically all points of close examination, the floor exhibits a marked soil line which consists of a thin grey layer of sunbaked organic material, much like a piece of heavy pasteboard, overlying a weathered zone of till or ferruginous gravel. Some of the best exposures showed five or six feet of poorly assorted and poorly rounded sandy gravel on the till, the upper foot of gravel having the brown ferruginous stain. The soil line is characterized also by an abundance of dune buried trees and snail shells. Evidently there was a considerable period of weathering on the original surface of the island here before the dunes covered it. It seems probable too from this that the island then extended much farther west, for the advancing front of the dunes was surely some distance in from the shore, if one can judge at all by the existing dunes.

"In addition to the soil line which sets off the bulk of the dunes along the west shore from the coarser deposits on which they are perched, younger soil lines were found at higher levels amongst the dunes themselves, marking stages in their growth. These were especially prominent along the troughs or 'blows' which lead eastward up to the peaks of the higher dunes. All these old soil lines are marked by much dead timber, the buried forests reappearing on the west slopes of the dunes in the trail of their eastward march. Many perched dunes facing the west shore are heavily littered with this wood which is bleached and hard, and heavily pitted by flying sand.

"Strong wave erosion has been attacking also the north shore of South Fox. For a mile and a half eastward from the northwest point, there extends a long line of bluffs like those on the west shore. Then the shore turns more to the southeast and has a different character, with low, broad beaches. Whereas lake attack, resulting in recession or truncation of the island, has dominated the west and north shores, upbuilding by deposition along the beach has had more effect on the east shore. Only very locally does the east shore show any recent erosion. Multiple beach ridges parallel the water for great distances, and small foredunes are common. The only considerable piles of sand occurring on the east shore are near the south end of the island where they have migrated right across from the west shore.

"The Plank farm is situated on a well developed Nipissing bar, extending north and south, parallel to and slightly concave toward the present shore. Shortly to the west, the ground falls away into a deep trench or ditch with sharp banks. It has evidently been incised into the surrounding formations after they were abandoned by the lake, yet the method of its cutting is an enigma inasmuch as it has no outlet or escape for water except by underground seepage. It follows neatly the curve of the Nipissing bar, throughout its length of about half a mile. Witnesses stated that this trench is occasionally filled with water. At the south end, the trench is squarely blocked off by high, sharp, arrested dunes which are strung in parallel order from west to east marking the tracks of ancient sand blows across the island."

Forest lands cover about 90 per cent of the island, abandoned farm land less than 5 per cent, of which the greater part is in a single piece of about 140 acres. Beaches and dunes account for the balance. There are no lakes or pools except for the wet trough described above, no streams except the outlets of a few springs along the west shore.

Along the lower eastern shores are dense growths of hemlock, arbor vitae, aspen, and birch. Most of the interior is covered with hardwoods, chiefly hard maple, beech, and birch. In the north-central interior is a large tract of virgin hardwood timber where some trees scale over 30 inches. The crests of the cliffs are covered with an impassable tangle of arbor vitae, spruce, and yew, but along the southwestern shore the crests are usually large bare sand dunes. The beaches of the western and northeastern shores are narrow and sandy, whereas the southeastern beaches are wide and often stony.

Occupants of this island are first mentioned in 1846. By 1854, it is reported both Mormons and other Europeans were here.

Man greatly changed the natural cover of South Fox. Between 1900 and 1926 there were six farms on the island. Surviving evidence shows that horses, oxen, dairy cattle, hogs, and poultry had been kept at some of these. One report has it that in 1905 pigs were feral on the island which that year had no human occupants. It is probable that the most recent farms were deserted at the time ship service to the lumber camps stopped and the docks deteriorated. The largest clearing, about 140 acres, is the former John Oliver Plank farm along the southeastern shore. In the north-central interior are two farms of 100 acres or so and a third farm of about 40 acres. There are four or five additional clearings scattered about the interior and along the eastern shore, but they are all of 10 acres or less. Parts of some clearings were planted to orchard trees, but none of the open areas show tendency to revert to forest.

A lumber camp of fair size was operating on the eastern shore from 1918 to 1926, and although the clearing is not large, a considerable number of deserted buildings remain (Fig. 9). Of a shingle mill once located along the mid-eastern shore, no trace remains except a sawdust pile, where snake collecting proved good. Here the 1937 party made its camp.

All farms had one or more buildings on them, many of log construction. Many birds use these as nesting sites. In addition to the farm buildings there are ruins of two cabins at the north end.

In recent years South Fox has been inhabited only by the four lighthouse attendants, and they leave in the winter. Their post is considered one of the most lonely lights on the lake, for now almost the only visitors are fishing boats which occasionally lie behind the island for respite from the wind. These men in 1937 and 1939 had a genuine interest in the animals of the island and have aided in the establishment of a large colony of Purple Martins by erecting two houses for them. Clearly the work of man on South Fox has proven beneficial to the animal life of the island. Buildings, fields, sawdust piles, even driftwood, have been man-wrought shelters greatly increasing the populations of some species if not indeed making their very existence there a possibility.

Deer are said to have been introduced on the island about 1915 by Mr. Plank and to have built up a herd of about 40 by 1925. At this time Mr. Plank moved from the island and deer have apparently been wiped out.

SOUTH MANITOU ISLAND.   Figures 23-26, 33-34.

South Manitou Island, southernmost of the islands of the eastern lake, is a thick, flat-backed crescent, of almost eight square miles.

Like South Fox and High islands, it has a high (480 feet) western edge, faced with steep clay bluffs, the product of long years of highland erosion by pounding waves of the southwestern storms. These high bluffs are surmounted over much of this length by a large perched dune. The eastern or lee slope of the highland is abrupt towards the south, but northward of mid-island it gently slopes to the central low area of the lake and swamp. From this point to the eastern bay shore there is a long series of old beach lines, or bayhead bars (Fig. 23), formed at successive stages of lake retreat. These merge gradually into the beach of the present fine bay. The north end of the island is also marked by a moderate east-west ridge of blown sand.

The island habitats are, in the main, the sandy to bouldery beaches; the open sand dunes; hardwood forests of the captured dunes and higher central and western parts of the island; marshes (of restricted extent) in the center; conifer forests of the eastern half of the island varying from arbor vitae with balsam to open jack pine. This latter is unique among the islands; on no other is the species found. Cleared lands, largely reverted to meadow with bramble and sumac, occupy about 20 per cent of the island, mainly in the center. Lesser communities are the cattail marsh and sedge shores of the inland lake, and an area of about 50 acres of virgin arbor vitae (Fig. 26) and hardwood. This latter, in a pocket behind the dunes of the southwest corner, contains many fine trees, some scaling up to four feet.

The inland lake, which appears nameless, is about 1.5 miles long and one quarter as wide. It has no outlet. Its beaches, for the most part narrow and sandy, are interrupted on the southwest by a small area of cattail marsh and on the north by a flat reed-sedge area. Forest borders most of the beach, and there are no dwellings along the shores.

Because of its fine harbor and good forests, South Manitou was among the first of the islands settled. By 1839 it was the site of a lighthouse. What its aboriginal population was is not known to us, and in 1847 when a Mr. Barton had a wharf here, there were no Indians. In the late nineteenth and early twentieth centuries it was a fueling station. Cordwood (at $1.75 a full cord) was widely cut, and only scattered patches of forest skirting the dunes escaped the ax.* The effect on the flora and hence on the fauna was, of course, cataclysmic, and the forest fires, of which there were several in this period, increased the transformation of the forests.

Following the period of cutting, most of the central area of the island was farmed and, at least during the period of the War of 1914-18, proved quite profitable. Since then, lack of adequate transportation and other factors have largely done away with farming. Today only two real farms are maintained on the island. Its only exports are Rozen rye, here raised for seed, and beef. Its 70 or so non-farming residents are mainly associated with the Coast Guard and the Lighthouse Service. Until the Second World War the bay served as summer headquarters for five naval training boats operating in the upper Lakes, and this was an economic asset to the island colony but probably little affected the island fauna.

Despite abandonment of farming there are relatively few deserted buildings about the island. Some buildings have been demolished and in others the owners remain, gaining a little livelihood from miscellaneous services to the Federal community.

SQUAW ISLAND (Called Rabbit Island in 1902). Figure 27.

Squaw is a small island, the farthest to the northwest of any in the Beaver archipelago. It is 2 miles from Whiskey Island, 3 from Garden, and 9 from the nearest mainland shore in the Upper Peninsula. Its land area is approximately 75 acres, a little over half of which is forested. Roughly a quarter is in heath or field, a quarter in beach. Its highest point is about 15 feet above lake level.

The forest is of arbor vitae, balsam fir, and birch. The trees attain a maximum height of about 50 feet. Between the forest edge and the water there is almost no sandy beach but a broad shelf of limestone boulders on which grow thickets of alders, willows, and herbaceous plants. The north shore borders a shallow cove where there is a good cattail growth. An abandoned lighthouse and attendant structures now used as a summer home, occupy a portion of the grassy northern end of the island.

The faunal character of the island in 1938 was largely given by the nesting colonies of Herring Gulls, Ring-billed Gulls, Common

---

*Many of the remaining large trees were felled in the great storm of November 11, 1940, in which the barometer dropped 100 points in 22 hours, unequalled in the 70 years of recording on this island.

Terns, and Great Blue Herons. In 1939, however, according to Dr. F. E. Ludwig's report, there were no nesting gulls or terns, owing to the higher lake level which flooded much of the flat beach.

TEMPERENCE (sic) ISLAND.

An island between Waugoshance Island and Waugoshance Point, designated on the Landes-Ehlers' (1945) map.

TIM'S ISLAND.

A small satellite of Hog Island, lying along its east shore. Designated by this name on the Landes-Ehlers' (1945) map.

TROUT ISLAND (See also Bellow Island). Figures 7, 29-31.

Trout Island is the southernmost of the tier of three similar-sized islands extending northward above High Island. Of its 115 acres, about 90 are forested. The shore in 1938 was broad, flat, generally of cobble. Driftwood was abundant, particularly on the south shore. Beach pools were well developed on the north shore, and cattail and reed growth was adequate to provide nest sites for several pairs of Red-wings. The island rises by a series of concentric ridges, fossil beaches from periods of higher lake levels, to a height of about 15 feet. On the southeast corner of the island there are 20 major shore-line ridges between the present lake level and the forest edge. From the north shore there are five strongly marked fossil beaches with glades between. The crests of these beaches are of hard-packed shingle and tend to remain free of trees, thus forming natural clear pathways through the forest that grows on the shoulders of the ridges. The depressions between the ridges are also free of trees, and here are grassy or mossy glades looking well suited to meadow mice and deer, which were, however, not there.

The forest of the island is mainly of balsam and arbor vitae, with scattered birch and poplar and an occasional tamarack. Hardwoods are quite lacking, as are heath associations. Ground hemlock is abundant in the woods.

The island at the time of our visit had the remnants of a single dwelling, once a well built summer home. It had been stripped of the doors, windows, and plumbing and was a draughty place in which to camp, but one furnishing a good concrete floor and a tight roof. A remnant of an ice house yielded one interesting salamander record.

The major faunal character of Trout Island was the paucity of vertebrate species. This is more fully discussed beyond. The superabundance of ants, to which the faunal peculiarity is there attributed, constitutes an interesting problem in itself, for which we offer no solution. The size of some of the mounds testifies that this was no temporary affair of the season we touched the island. The first day on the island Hatt wrote: "Never before have I seen ants so numerous, so universally distributed, or with so many huge nests. On the beach these are of small pebbles, on the forest floor of general woods debris. Some nests are fifteen feet across and two feet high. On the upper beach every bit of driftwood has a flourishing colony."

VIRGIN ISLAND. Whiskey Island was so called in 1902.

WAUGOSHANCE ISLAND. Also called Wobbleshanks; Crane Island.

This island lies immediately off the point of the same name in Emmet County, to which it is connected *via* "Temperence Island" by shoal water. It has not been considered in this report.

WHISKEY ISLAND (See Virgin Island). Figure 28.

Whiskey Island is a roughly rectangular island in line with Squaw and Trout islands from which it is separated by channels of two and four miles respectively. It is an island possibly 50 feet above lake level which may have started as a growing gravel bar in Lake Nipissing or subsequently. Its 130 acres are about 90 per cent forested. The beach varied in 1938 from about 30 feet to a 100 feet in width. Extending more than a mile into the lake from the island's northeast point is a narrow ridge of boulders, many of which break the surface and provide perching places for the gulls. Here too, far from shore, we resorted to bathing to escape the plague of mosquitoes and flies for which we remember the island.

There is some bedrock exposure on the western half of the island which, from fossils and calcite-filled vugs we collected, was found to be of the St. Ignace formation.

The forest was characterized by a large area of broad-leaved trees on the western half of the island, birch, poplar, black ash, and moun-

25. South Manitou's western highland carries magnificent perched dunes. The distant land is North Manitou Island. July 12, 1940. R. T. Hatt.

26. A virgin forest in the southwestern sector of South Manitou contains cedars four feet in diameter. July 12, 1940. R. T. Hatt.

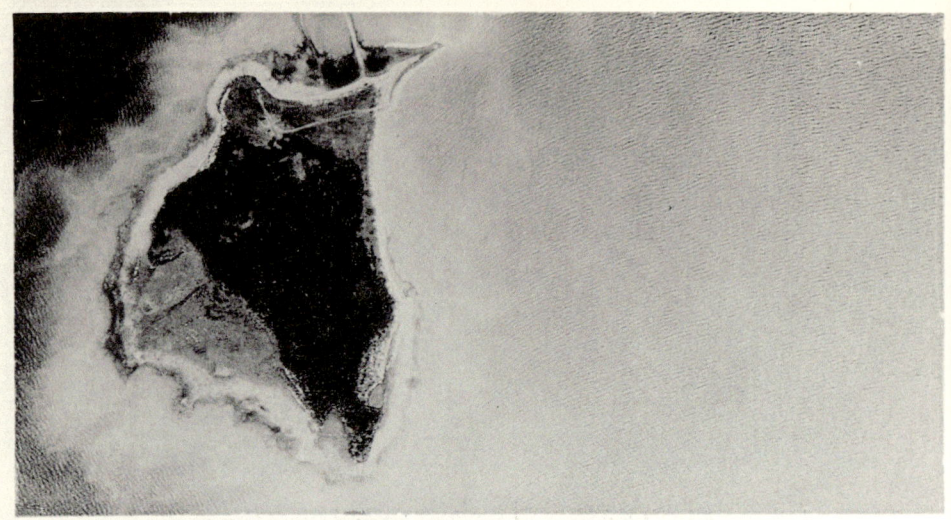

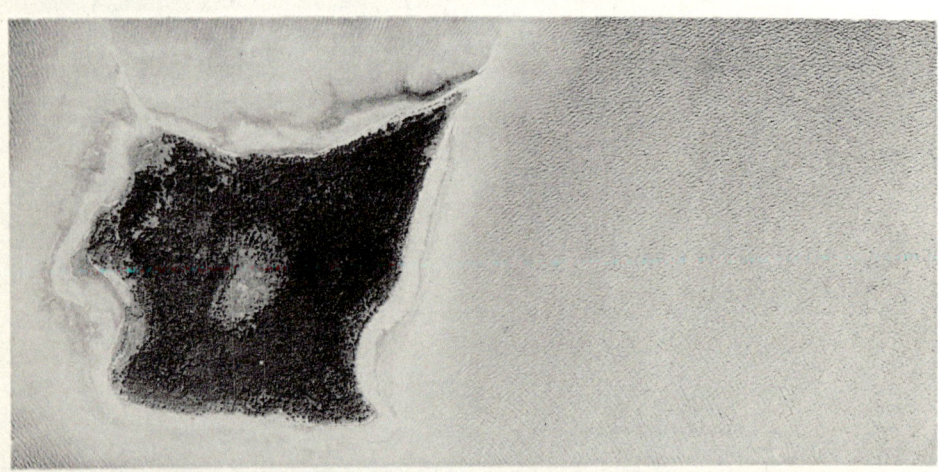

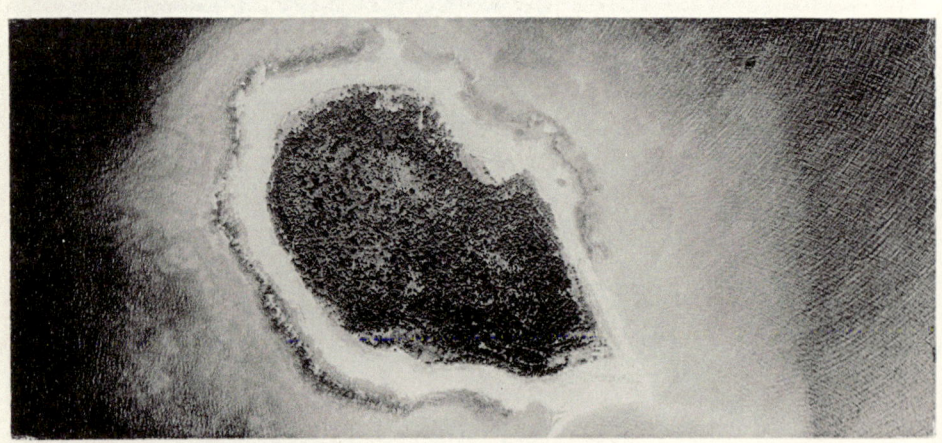

27. Squaw Island, 28. Whiskey Island, 29. Trout Island.
All same scale. All photographed July 15, 1938. Agricultural Adjustment Administration.

tain ash being dominants. Elsewhere the forest was of arbor vitae and balsam, much as on Trout Island. A clearing in the higher central part of the island appears to have been man made, though the island's only habitation was a small emergency cabin by the lake shore, evidently occupied by Indians at one time. Many birches on the island had sections of their bark removed, presumably for basket making. One tree stump measured three feet in diameter.

The shores were in the main flat and broad, with little plant growth. A small cattail marsh supported a little colony of Redwings.

5. The Amphibians and Reptiles

As WITH other island faunas, the herpetological one is but a depauperated mainland fauna, its composition determined by the availability of breeding sites and other cover, the ability to traverse the barrier of the large open lake, and, seemingly in a few instances, the ability to meet interspecific competition where enemy populations are concentrated.

The records are believed to be reasonably complete for these animals, though chance operates here as much as with other vertebrates. For example, two records of the Spring Peeper and one of the Tree Frog would not have been made if we had not chanced to hear the animals singing on one of the rare evenings when conditions were right. The single Wood Frog record on Beaver Island was an accidental acquisition. The only Jefferson's Salamander record was obtained on the rarest chance when one of us dug fully through the sawdust at the site of an old ice house. Records of collecting hours for amphibia and reptiles were kept only by Pope, who reports about 36 hours collecting on South Fox and about 24 hours on North Fox.

The spotty distribution of several species is not altogether explainable on the basis of available information. Thus, the Redbacked Salamander might be expected to find conditions favorable on Gull, High, Trout, and Whiskey islands. It may have lacked opportunity to reach these islands; have escaped our search for it; or, on the smaller islands, have lacked suitable breeding sites, owing to the scarcity of rotting logs.

As to the geographical aspects of the islands' fauna, it is observed that the species represent merely a selected mainland fauna that to all appearances has been derived from the southern peninsula of Michigan through accidental or occasional means of dispersal rather than through direct connection with the mainland. Supporting the statement that the islands are inhabited by a reduced mainland fauna, it may be noted that only about one-half the forms known from the mainland were found on the islands. Though it is certain that we have by no means completed the islands' species-list, we were unable to find on the larger islands such common mainland species as Jefferson's Salamander, Red-bellied Snake, and the Green Snake.

That the islands' herpetofauna has been derived from the southern rather than from the northern peninsula of Michigan, is evidenced by the presence of the Ribbon Snake and the Milk Snake, unknown from the latter region. The plastral pattern of the Painted Turtles of Beaver Island is the sole indication of any northern or western element, and even in these specimens the typical southern peninsula type of carapace is present. Further evidence supporting an eastern origin of the fauna of the islands is to be found on comparatively small High Island, which, lying several miles to the west of Beaver, is in a favorable position to receive any derelicts from the west or north. Despite the abundance of suitable habitats, the Ring-neck Snake, the Water Snake, and the Red-backed Salamander, all three exceedingly abundant on Beaver Island, were not observed on High Island. The apparent absence (except for the salamander on Squaw Island) of these same species from other Beaver group islands on which adequate collecting was done further suggests the accidental. It may be noted that all were present on North Fox Island, an island smaller in size than High Island and no better suited to their needs.

The island faunas are somewhat irregular and show the "hit-and-miss" composition indicative of "accidental" dispersal. Furthermore, all of the faunal elements of the islands are of a type that could readily traverse channels of water. The aquatic types, such as frogs and turtles, need hardly be mentioned, but purely terrestrial forms, such as the Red-backed Salamander, Milk Snake, and Ring-neck Snake, require some explanation. All three of these are commonly found in logs along the mainland shore and, moreover, deposit their eggs in logs. Though it might prove difficult to conceive of the adults surviving a stormy journey from the mainland to the island, it requires little imagination to conceive transportation of eggs in drifting logs. This consideration of habits may explain the absence from many islands of the ovoviviparous terrestrial forms, the Red-bellied Snake and the upland oviparous Green Snake.

There is fairly strong evidence supporting "accidental" entrance of the fauna onto the islands, but Stanley points out that Beaver Island was, in all probability, connected to the mainland through an extension of the Waugoshance Peninsula westward from the mainland during the Algonquin-Nipissing interval. This being the case, we might well expect the Beaver Island fauna to be essentially like the mainland fauna, rather than in the impoverished condition that exists today. Two hypotheses seem to explain the observed discrepancies. Either the fauna now present on the mainland had not had sufficient time, following the glacial retreat, to invade northern Michigan and thus utilize the extended peninsula, or ecological conditions on the island areas or the "bridge" were unsuited to the dispersal or survival of many species. It is entirely possible that some species utilized a "bridge" whereas others were transported or swam across the channel between the islands and the mainland. Certain features of differentiation in the Beaver island fauna seem to favor the "bridge" hypothesis. With so little knowledge of the habits of the fauna and even less of palaeogeographic conditions, we can do no more than present evidence in support of each hypothesis and await more ample data before arriving at any definite conclusion.

As suggested above, a portion of the fauna of Beaver Island shows a tendency towards differentiation, and this feature is of some importance in solving its origin. Since this phenomenon is discussed in greater detail in the annotated list of species, it is sufficient to note here that the Red-backed Salamander, Milk Snake, and Water Snake differ slightly from the mainland forms, whereas the rest of the fauna has remained typical. It is indicated that for the three atypical forms isolation has been effective over a period of time sufficient to permit differentiation or that the populations are derived from few individuals, whereas other species are either genetically more stable or have been receiving a constant infiltration of "new blood" from the mainland. It is surprising, however, that so aquatic a form as the Water Snake should show differentiation if the island is constantly receiving additional stock from the mainland, but the Water Snake does not lay eggs, and possibly few adult individuals cross long stretches of open water. This would admit of a random drift of species characters under isolation. The other two variant populations are of egg-laying species and with them, the chance for re-introductions would seem greater. It is such anomalies as these that make it difficult to draw firm conclusions regarding the age and the mode of origin of the island fauna. It should be reiterated, however, that the presence of even slight differentiation argues for the fauna's origin through the utilization of the Waugoshance "bridge." More complete differentiation in the future seems improbable, as the rising of the land north of the "hinge line" will cause a gradual decrease in the width of the channel and permit a more ready means of communication between the island and mainland faunas.

ANNOTATED LIST

THE AMPHIBIANS

Newt
Triturus viridescens viridescens Rafinesque

Beaver (spn.).*

This salamander was taken in small numbers and at only one locality, Green's Lake. In the surrounding hardwood forests several specimens of the terrestrial stage were found, while a number of the aquatic stage individuals were noted in the shallow, vegetation-filled water of Green's Lake. A single individual of the terrestrial stage was discovered in a hardwood forest about a mile from Green's Lake. The material at hand is not adequate for diagnosis of degree of possible intergradation with *T.v. louisianensis*, which occupies the Wisconsin shore of Lake Michigan.

Red-backed Salamander
Plethodon cinereus cinereus (Green)

Beaver (spn.); N. Fox (spn.); N. Manitou (spn.); S. Fox (spn.); S. Manitou (spn.); Squaw (spn.).

Red-backed Salamanders were common on North Manitou, North and South Fox, and Beaver islands. Specimens were found on Squaw but not on Trout or Gull islands. The apparent absence from Trout and Gull islands suggests accidental methods of distribution, since suitable habitats were abundant and *P. cinereus*, laying its eggs on land, is independent of lakes and pools.

The species was found throughout the wooded sections of Beaver Island. It showed a marked preference for hardwood areas, however, and occurred only sparingly in mixed pine and hardwood forests, whereas only an occasional specimen was found in the wetter arbor vitae forests. It was most common in decaying hardwood logs, though a few individuals were discovered in the humus on the forest floor.

Ten specimens from Squaw Island were found in decaying logs in a dry meadow where the sun struck the logs in full force.

---

* For list of abbreviations see page 156.

On both North and South Fox, the red phase predominated. On the former, 75 consecutive minutes of collecting yielded 15 individuals, all with red backs; on the latter, some 90 consecutive minutes of search resulted in the discovery of 18 specimens, all of which belonged to the red phase (though the backs of 2 or 3 had a little gray mixed with the red).

On Beaver Island no individual in the gray phase was collected or seen.

A good many data on the numbers of red and gray individuals are now available and show that the ratio of one to one, although usual, is by no means universal. Either phase may predominate, and there is no apparent rhyme or reason in the distribution of one type as predominant. Though Blanchard (1928b, pp. 157-158) reported an approximately 50-50 ratio between the gray and red phases in southern Michigan, northern Michigan collections which he studied (1928a, p. 45) showed a five to one preponderance of the red-backed phase. Both Burger (1935) and Reynolds (1937) give considerable further information on this subject.

On June 9 Stuart and Grobman found an egg cluster on Beaver Island guarded by a female, but the great majority of the females still retained the eggs in the body cavity. This indicates that the laying period probably reaches its height about the middle of June, a period that checks fairly well with Blanchard's report (1928a, p. 45) for northern Michigan. An egg cluster and an adult salamander with it were collected June 22 on North Manitou. Two egg clusters were found on South Fox, one on June 22, the other a day later. Two more were discovered June 29 on North Fox.

Jefferson's Salamander
Ambystoma jeffersonianum (Green)

Trout (spn.).

Two specimens of Jefferson's Salamander were recovered from sawdust at the site of a former ice house on Trout Island. Since the likelihood of finding such animals during brief summer field work is remote, the absence of records on other islands does not mean that the species is not there, but the slight weight of evidence does suggest accidental distribution.

The only possible breeding place for the ambystomas on the smaller islands would be beach pools, and these vary with storms and lake levels. Beach pools on Trout Island, in 1938, existed within 100 yards of these salamanders.

American Toad
Bufo terrestris americanus Holbrook
Figure 4

Beaver (spn.); High (spn.); N. Fox (spn.); N. Manitou (spn.); S. Fox (spn.); S. Manitou (spn.); Squaw (spn.); Trout (spn.); Whiskey (spn.).

The toads have been more successful in establishing themselves on the islands than have any other amphibians. This may be attributed to their relative independence of water, normal habit of feeding along the beaches, breeding in beach pools, and hiding in beach drift. Opportunity to reach the islands on drift may have been frequent, and once the toads were on the islands they found conditions favorable for survival. Their apparent absence from Gull, Hat, Shoe, and Pismire may possibly be correlated with the high populations of nesting gulls and terns, for, at least on Gull Island, there were suitable breeding sites for toads. Toads emerging after metamorphosing in a beach pool might be quickly devoured by gulls.

On North Manitou, North Fox, Beaver, Trout, Whiskey, and Squaw islands, shallow beach pools seem to be their chief breeding sites. Tadpoles were actually discovered in such pools on Beaver, North Manitou, and North Fox. Probably no other standing water is ever available on some of the smaller islands.

On South Manitou, toads were found around the shore of the inland lake, and in its shallows toad tadpoles were abundant on July 12, 1940. That day a few newly emerged young toads were also found on the shore. Turning over every board and log on the two-mile shore of this lake yielded but four adult toads. On August 30 and 31, 1944, this same area, re-examined, yielded only two adult toads; but in the forest east of the lake, and for as much as one-quarter mile from the lake, toads about one cm. long were present by thousands, foraging in midday over the forest floor. They averaged one to each square yard in a representative area.

Toads are generally distributed throughout Beaver Island in the vicinity of water. Although the species was still mating June 9-18, 1939, tadpoles were also found abundantly, especially in beach pools along the Lake Michigan shore. The species also occurs in abundance in St. James.

A surprising condition of seeming gigantism was encountered in late June, 1937, on South Fox. Here all specimens secured could be classified as large. In one hour's collecting, some 30 specimens were obtained and, carried in the pockets of a hunting coat, they were a truly heavy load. Of 15 specimens saved, all proved to be adult females retaining their eggs well past the normal breeding season. The mean length was 97 mm., the minimum 88 mm., and the maximum 109 mm. The only reasonable explanation is that for several years the lake level had not permitted the formation of suitable beach pools. This would have prevented repopulation during these years. In 1937 there were no beach pools on this island. The tracks of these large toads, crossing the narrow sandy beach between the day's hiding places in the forest edge and the night feeding ground along the water's edge, were for a time a puzzle. The animals never seemed to hop along this route, but walked deliberately, dragging their feet, alternately, in strides of six and a quarter inches (Fig. 4). The trails made by their toes measured up to four and a half inches in width.

The South Fox toads appeared to gain a considerable portion of their food by picking up the insects washed ashore, for jack-lighting at night revealed most of the toads right at the strand line. Stomach contents of two of the specimens were kindly identified for us by Mr. A. W. Andrews.

The following list, annotated as to habitat of the food animal, substantiates this field observation.

Beetles

Carabus serratus Say.   (Carabid)   Damp localities.
Calosoma calidum Fab.   (Carabid)   On beaches and inland.
Amara basillaris (Say).   (Carabid)   Under boards and debris on beaches.
Platynus cupripennis (Say).   (Carabid)   As above.
Chlaenius sericeus Forst.   (Carabid)   Under damp debris and flat stones, in damp locations.
Harpalus opacipennis (Hald.).   (Carabid)   Under logs and boards on lake shores.
Pseudamphasia sericea (Harris).   (Carabid)   Debris on shores.
Omophron tesselatum Say.   (Omophronid)   On shores.

All the above are nocturnal and are considered beneficial.

30. Pools behind beach bars, though temporary, sometimes furnish the only breeding areas for island amphibia. Trout Island, June, 1938. R. T. Hatt.

31. Abundant ant colonies, some of great size, characterize Trout Island and may account in part for its exceptionally depauperate ground dwelling vertebrate population. June, 1938. R. T. Hatt.

32. Spring Peepers on North Fox were found breeding in the margin of Lake Michigan where relatively quiet waters occurred between the boulders of the wave-eroded pavement near the south end. June, 1937. R. T. Hatt.

33. Leopard Frogs were not found on South Manitou in July, 1940, despite thorough search, but were common in August four years later. August, 1944. R. T. Hatt.

Cryptohypnus abbreviatus (Say). (Elaterid)
Byrrhus americanus (Lec.). (Byrrhid)
Porcinolus undatus (Melsh). (Byrrhid) Found on sandy ground under boards and logs.
Three wing covers of three species of carabids, not complete enough to be identified.

Miscellaneous

Camponotus herculaneus subsp. *pennsylvanicus* var. *noveboracensis* (Fitch). (Carpenter ant)
Vespa maculata L. "heads" only. (Wasp)
Vespa maculifrons Buy. (Wasp)
Bug, spiders, millepedes.

Tree Frog
Hyla versicolor versicolor Le Conte

Beaver (voi.); Trout (voi.).

Tree Frogs were heard June 14, 1939, on Beaver and June 25, 1938, on Trout, but no specimens were secured. This amphibian is easily overlooked except during rainy weather at the height of its breeding season.

Spring Peeper
Hyla crucifer crucifer Wied
Figure 32

Beaver (spn.); Gull (voi.); N. Fox (spn.); N. Manitou (voi.); Trout (spn.).

Specimens were secured on Trout and North Fox islands, and one was heard June 21 in a beach pool on Gull Island, and one in a swale, June 19, on the west side of North Manitou. The two collected on North Fox called early in the night of June 27 from the rocky beach at the southernmost tip of the island, where a quiet pool of water continuous with Lake Michigan was broken up by boulders and clumps of grass. As on North Fox, there were but two singing individuals in the beach pool on Trout Island, and both of these were secured.

A single adult was taken in a hardwood forest near the southern end of Beaver Island, whereas all others collected were found (breeding) in Miller's Marsh and in a swampy backwater of the same. Neither eggs nor tadpoles were collected in Miller's Marsh, but a tadpole believed to be of this species was found with the tadpoles of toads, in a beach pool along the Lake Michigan shore. Other Spring Peepers were heard singing at Font Lake, Beaver Island.

Wood Frog
Rana sylvatica cantabrigensis Baird

Beaver (spn.); N. Manitou (spn.).

This amphibian was not rare along the stream that feeds Tamarac Lake, North Manitou.

On Beaver Island but one specimen was secured. This was collected in 1938 along a small, cold stream running through a stand of mixed hardwood and evergreens, not far from the shore of Lake Michigan below Point Lapar.

Bullfrog
Rana catesbeiana Shaw

Beaver (spn.); N. Manitou (spn.).

Bullfrogs literally swarmed in Tamarac Lake on North Manitou. Innumerable small individuals played in the shallow water covering the quaking bog of the lake's border, and adults called from its center in the bright mid-morning light of July 6. A swampy arbor vitae forest surrounds the lake. Young Bullfrogs were also common in the stream that feeds the lake, and tadpoles were collected here in 1931.

No adult Bullfrogs were secured on Beaver Island, but several tadpoles of the previous year were taken in Green's Lake. Adults were heard singing in Miller's Marsh, Font Lake, and Fox Lake.

This frog is probably absent from the smaller islands because of its thoroughly aquatic habits and long larval life. It cannot, apparently, survive in Lake Michigan itself but requires permanent ponds, small lakes, or sluggish streams.

Green Frog
Rana clamitans Latreille

Beaver (spn.); N. Manitou (spn.).

Green Frogs were not uncommon in Manitou Lake and the stream that feeds Tamarac Lake of North Manitou. None were seen in Tamarac Lake itself, where Bullfrogs were so abundant. Competition with this larger species probably explains such scarcity in, or absence from, this lake. A few Green Frogs were encountered in a swale just behind the beach at the northeastern corner of North Manitou. On Beaver Island a single specimen of the Green Frog was secured from the pond of a dammed stream in which the Water Snake occurred in great numbers.

This frog, like the Bullfrog, depends on permanent bodies of water, although it is less aquatic and has a shorter larval existence than the Bullfrog. Proof of the Green Frog's absence from the smaller islands would not therefore be surprising.

Leopard Frog
Rana pipiens pipiens Schreber
Figure 33

Beaver (spn.); S. Manitou (spn.).

What seemed a most thorough search for frogs was made around the lake on South Manitou in 1942 without result, and it was concluded that even though frogs were reported as present in earlier years they were no longer there. This conclusion was belied, however, when in late August 1944 Leopard Frogs were found in hundreds there. This clearly shows the danger of drawing conclusions from few samples. All but one of the animals observed in 1944 were, however, about one and one-quarter inches long, and probably all of these were from eggs laid that season.

The Leopard Frog is apparently widespread on Beaver Island, in the vicinity of water. Tadpoles of this species were secured at several localities.

THE REPTILES
Snapping Turtle
Chelydra serpentina serpentina (Linnaeus)

Beaver (spn.); N. Manitou (obs.); S. Manitou (rpt.).

A large snapper was digging in the beaver lodge in Tamarac Lake, North Manitou, June 19. The South Manitou report, given by two residents, was of a very large individual that came ashore from Lake Michigan a few years ago and was caught near the lighthouse. There is also the report of another Snapping Turtle on the beach of the mainland, near Leland, but in general the Lake Michigan shores are poorly suited to these animals.

Although the Snapping Turtle is said to inhabit most of the lakes on Beaver Island, we found definite evidences of it only at Font

Lake. No specimens except a skull were secured, but tracks and nests on the dunes at the north end of Font Lake indicated that it is relatively abundant. Several nests were discovered on these dunes, and from one of them we took four dozen eggs. The abundance of tracks and nests indicated that the egg-laying season was at its height, in mid-June. The species apparently reaches a large size on the island. Although we may discount some of the exaggerations of the residents, we measured the tracks of one specimen and found the width from foot to foot to exceed 30 cm.

Painted Turtle
Chrysemys picta marginata Agassiz

Beaver (spn.); High (rpt.); S. Manitou (spn.).

A Painted Turtle was covering her eggs in the sand of the upper beach, 25 feet from the margin of South Manitou's lake, at 3:40 p.m., July 12. Seven eggs were in the pocket, which was three to five inches deep. Two other turtles were nearby, possibly in search of nest sites. All four of the Beaver Island specimens were females; three were secured on land, about a hundred yards from the nearest water. Of the three secured on land, none contained eggs, indicating that they had probably deposited the eggs and were returning to their native lakes.

Though we secured only four specimens of the Painted Turtle on Beaver Island, it is reported that the species is abundant in most of the lakes on the island. Dr. Norman Hartweg, who examined our specimens, has informed us that, though all possessed a typical *marginata* carapace, three had plastrons very similar to the *bellii-marginata* intergrades of the northern peninsula of Michigan. This is the only Upper Peninsula or Wisconsin influence noted in the island herpetofauna.

Ring-neck Snake
Diadophis punctatus edwardsii (Merrem)

Beaver (spn.); N. Fox (spn.); N. Manitou (spn.); S. Fox (spn.); S. Manitou (spn.).

This snake was frequently encountered on both Manitous, on both Fox islands, and on Beaver Island but was not seen on any of the others. It was collected in or under dead wood and only in the three following types of situation:

1. Driftwood lying along the zone of union of beach with forest or other forms of dense interior vegetation. All (approximately 30) North Fox specimens discovered were living in this beach habitat, as were a few of those from South Fox and North Manitou.
2. Dead wood of man-made clearings. Most of the South Fox Ring-necks (about 25), as well as four from North Manitou, were uncovered in such places.
3. Decayed wind-fall logs extending from bank to bottom of Manitou Lake, North Manitou. Nearly every log examined along the lake's border held either snake or slough, and in one a nest of five eggs was discovered (July 7). Thus, these snakes lived in a fringe habitat that was adjacent to the woods, well exposed to the sun for some of the time, and in part actually over the lake. Such an unusual situation perhaps affords protection from certain enemies. Search in logs in the woods surrounding the lake failed to reveal signs of these snakes, except in a log lying on the edge of a small clearing.

The above data are in agreement with the results of Blanchard's Michigan work in Emmet and Cheboygan counties east of the Fox Islands. Blanchard (1937b) concluded that Ring-neck Snakes commonly lay their eggs in logs exposed to the sun, and he wrote of numerous adults and eggs found in beach logs. He did not state what part of the beach the snakes frequented, but our observations indicate a strong preference for the uppermost border. Food is undoubtedly most abundant here, and there is greater safety from the action of high water and storms.

Unlike the Milk Snake and Water Snake, the Beaver Island population of *Diadophis* shows no tendencies toward differentiation. On the island this species was abundant in decaying logs and beneath boards in open meadows and cut-over land. Most of the females contained fully developed eggs, and often several snakes were found beneath the same board or log, but no nests or eggs were discovered. This indicates that copulation had already taken place and that the females were preparing to deposit their eggs. This time of laying coincides fairly well with Blanchard's observations (1927, 1930, 1937b) on the same species in northern Michigan.

Water Snake
Natrix sipedon sipedon (Linnaeus)

Beaver (spn.); N. Fox (spn.); Squaw (spn.); Whiskey (spn.).

The apparent absence of this snake on the Manitou islands is not understood. There is abundant suitable cover for them, but the residents do not know of them, and extensive search failed to locate a single specimen. A total lack of streams and ponds does not deter this reptile, however, for it takes readily to beach existence and was abundant on two of the small islands. On Whiskey Island, particularly, it was inordinately abundant, a score of specimens being secured in the first half hour on the island, and about that many being seen in every day's collecting activities on the island. In strong contrast to this abundance, not a single specimen was seen during equally intensive collecting on nearby, and similar, Trout Island. As elsewhere discussed, the only possible explanation which occurs to us is the preëmption of virtually all hiding places on Trout Island by innumerable ants.

Though we collected a relatively small series of this form on Beaver Island, it was by far the most abundant snake there. It is generally distributed throughout the aquatic and aquatic-margin habitats and was especially abundant in open meadows adjacent to the shore of Lake Michigan on the eastern side of the island. At one locality, a sunny bank along the outlet of Lake Genesareth, it occurred literally by the hundreds, and it was impossible to step without disturbing at least one specimen.

The specimens from Beaver Island show, as do those of the Milk Snake, a tendency toward a high number of dorsal scale rows, and a relatively low number of abdominals. This latter character is of considerable geographic importance, as noted at the start of this chapter. Wisconsin specimens recorded by Clay (MS) show an abdominal range of 140-151 in females, as compared with 139-147 in Michigan females. The averages for these two groups are 143 and 145, respectively. Females from Beaver Island range from 129-139 and average 136.

Of further interest is the pattern of these specimens, as there is a distinct tendency for the larger specimens to approach the pattern of *Natrix s. insularum* Conant and Clay. These two authors (1937, pp. 3-5) have divided the Lake Erie populations into patterns "A-

D," ranging from typical *insularum* (A) to typical *sipedon* (D). In three of our specimens, all longer than 940 mm., two exhibit pattern "B" and one pattern "C." Our other specimens, all under 905 mm. in length, show the typical *sipedon* pattern.

This ontogenetic change is interesting because the approach of Beaver Island *sipedon* to *insularum* does not imply relationship. Conant and Clay (*ibid.*, p. 2) show that the peculiar pattern of *insularum* is definitely not ontogenetic.

Red-bellied Snake
Storeria occipitomaculata (Storer)

Squaw (spn.); Whiskey (spn.).

Red-bellied Snakes were found only on Whiskey and Squaw islands, five on the former, three on the latter. All were under beach drift. One of those secured on Whiskey Island was under a log with four Water Snakes and three Garter Snakes.

Ribbon Snake
Thamnophis sauritus sauritus (Linnaeus)

Beaver (spn.); N. Manitou (spn.).

With an abundance of suitable habitats on Beaver Island, it is surprising that this species should be so rare. We found but a single specimen and that near a water-filled ditch along the road. Frequent stops at this locality and diligent search in the adjacent meadow, which contained several small ponds, failed to reveal others. The specimen had 157 ventral scutes, which is the lowest number recorded in 15 Michigan specimens (157-169; average, 164.3). Only one specimen of this snake was secured on North Manitou.

Garter Snake
Thamnophis sirtalis sirtalis (Linnaeus)
Figure 34

Beaver (spn.); High (spn.); N. Fox (spn.); N. Manitou (spn.); S. Fox (spn.); S. Manitou (spn.); Squaw (spn.); Trout (spn.); Whiskey (spn.).

Six Garter Snakes were secured on South Manitou; one was under a board on the shore of the inland lake, three were in dry grass near the lake, and two in a grassy swale a quarter of a mile from the lake. Others were seen along the field borders and in a barn. The four specimens secured on Trout, Whiskey, and Squaw islands were all under beach drift of the Lake Michigan shore. A South Fox Island specimen was in an old pile of sawdust in which Ring-neck Snakes were also found, and two more were found under a board in a dry field, along with two more Ring-neck Snakes.

Two Beaver Island females (lengths, 740 and 768 mm.) contained embryos.

One North Manitou Garter Snake was collected in the act of devouring a dead and maggot-infested young bird. Green Frogs were seen nearby, so other food was certainly available to the snake.

This species was not uncommon on Beaver Island. It was generally observed in the vicinity of water and was most frequently taken from beneath boards in open meadows. As in the Water Snake, this form shows a slight reduction in the abdominals when compared with mainland specimens.

Milk Snake
Lampropeltis triangulum triangulum (Lacépède)

Beaver (spn.); High (spn.); N. Fox (spn.); Whiskey (spn.).

A Milk Snake was found on the western side of North Fox near the northern end. It was coiled under a driftwood log lying about 100 feet from the lake along the upper border of the beach at the edge of the woods that almost completely cover the island. Another was taken in a log lying on the beach of Whiskey Island. Three specimens were collected from beneath boards in open meadows on Beaver Island, not far from the Lake Michigan shore. All finds indicate a preference for beaches and the region of their union with woods. Snakes of this kind, however, are not easily found, so generalizations based on the results of such brief collecting should not be given much weight.

The three specimens of this species that Stuart and Grobman collected on Beaver Island are interesting in possessing the maximum of dorsal scutes recorded by Blanchard (1921, pp. 190 and 199). In all three the dorsal scale formula is 21-23-21-19. The number of dorsal blotches is also high, ranging from 56 to 62, with an average of 59, as compared with 35-61, and 47, for 61 Michigan specimens recorded by Blanchard (*ibid.*, p. 201). The tail length ratio is also high, individuals exceeding Blanchard's record among 404 specimens.

34. Garter Snakes were the common snakes of the clearings on the larger islands. They were frequently found by turning over lumber on the sites of abandoned farms. South Manitou Island, August, 1944. R. T. Hatt.

35. Great Blue Herons nested high where trees were high, low where there were no suitable tall trees or on the ground where there were no trees. This nest with three large young was on Hat Island in an arbor vitae at a height of about fifteen feet. July 8, 1938. R. T. Hatt.

36. The Willow Thrush is one of the most conspicuous of island birds, but its nests, often in dense growths of ground hemlock (*Taxus canadensis*) are difficult to discover. South Fox Island, June 19, 1939. A. E. Staebler.

6. The Birds*

OUR KNOWLEDGE of the avifauna of the Lake Michigan islands is still far from complete, but enough work has now been done on the Manitou Islands, the Fox Islands,† and the Beaver group to justify an attempt to make some generalizations about it. Unfortunately, it was not possible for the 1937-1940 expeditions to do field work on three islands of the Beaver group — Garden, High, and Hog — and their avifaunas are almost wholly unknown. Therefore, the general statements made below about birds of the "Beaver group" actually refer to Beaver Island and the six small neighboring islands studied. For Bellow, Fisherman's, and Marion islands, which are very small, scattered, and close to the mainland shore, there are few records available. These few are given under the several species in the annotated list, but it seemed best to exclude the islands from the tables and from consideration in the general conclusions on distribution.

The first fact to be noted is that the avifauna of every island studied, and even that of the whole group of islands taken together, is poorer (in number of species) than that of the adjacent mainland. This is in spite of the fact that, unlike most other land vertebrates, all of the birds that now occur on the nearby mainland *could* reach the islands (by flying). It is therefore particularly interesting to find that quite a number of species do not. Species that breed on the adjacent mainland‡ but have not yet been recorded on the

---

*By Josselyn Van Tyne.

†Knowledge of the birds of the Manitou and Fox islands is based almost entirely on the observations and collections of Arthur E. Staebler and Leslie D. Case, Sr., and their data are incorporated here.

‡Our knowledge of the birds of the adjacent mainland of the Lower Peninsula is based on Van Tyne (1925); F. N. Blanchard and Theodora Nelson (MS report on the Douglas Lake region, 1937); Nickell (1943); and specimens and manuscript records in the University of Michigan Museum of Zoology. The northern boundaries of the Beaver group extend within 10 miles of the Upper Peninsula shore, but the avifaunas of the two sides of the Straits of Mackinac are not known to differ significantly.

islands in the breeding season (except for stray non-breeding individuals) are listed in Table 6. Table 7 shows an additional 15 species that occur as breeding species only on the very large Beaver Island. Arranging the islands in the order of size, we find more and more species dropping out as we progress toward the smaller islands. Many species occur on only a few large islands (Table 7), but on the other hand, not a single species occurs exclusively on the small islands. There is, however, one curious exception to this simple correlation between the size of the island and its avifauna: a few species (Table 8) are apparently restricted to the largest island (Beaver) and two or more of the smallest islands.

A small number of transient migrants recorded regularly on the mainland are thought not to migrate across the islands (Table 9). Perhaps some of the following will have to be added to that list: Turkey Vulture, Yellow-bellied Flycatcher, Olive-sided Flycatcher, Gray-checked Thrush, Olive-backed Thrush, Philadelphia Vireo, Black-poll Warbler, Wilson's Warbler, and Rusty Blackbird. Each of these has so far been represented on the islands by only one individual, which may have been a stray rather than the representative of a species regularly migrating through the area.

Barrows (1904, p. 64) commented on the "total absence" of seven species that he failed to find on "the Beaver Islands" although they were "more or less common" on the adjacent mainland, but his six days of field work were an inadequate basis for the conclusion, and all seven species have since been found regularly on Beaver Island.

It is difficult to understand the reason for the (at least apparent) absence of many species from some of the islands. In some cases it seems to be due to a lack of suitable habitat, especially on the smaller islands, but in a great many cases there is no such simple explanation. For example, it would seem that an island with many acres—even many hundred acres—of forest supporting a good population of Oven-birds and Redstarts would also support a population of Least Flycatchers and Wood Pewees. As Lack (1942, p. 15) has pointed out, the small number of a given species that can exist on a small island makes the species very susceptible to accidental extirpation. It may then be several years before the island is recolonized. This is probably the explanation of certain gaps noted in faunas of several of the small islands.

During the four seasons' field work of this study, our parties recorded on some islands during the breeding season stray non-breeding individuals of certain species (Table 10), some of which were breeding in some numbers on other islands but occurred only casually on the islands listed in the table. Most of these casual records were of single individuals found in habitats unusual for the species.

There are a few land birds which are remarkably abundant and widely distributed among the islands. Especially notable are the following: Kingbird, Tree Swallow, Crow, Willow Thrush, Cedar Waxwing, Starling, Oven-bird, Redstart, Red-wing, and Song Sparrow. The presence of the Starling on this list is remarkable evidence

TABLE 6

BIRDS BREEDING ON THE ADJACENT MAINLAND
THOUGH NOT ON THE ISLANDS

Pied-billed Grebe
   Podilymbus p. podiceps (Linnaeus)

*Marsh Hawk
   Circus cyaneus hudsonius
   (Linnaeus)

Ruffed Grouse†
   Bonasa umbellus togata (Linnaeus)

Prairie Chicken
   Tympanuchus cupido pinnatus
   (Brewster)

Florida Gallinule
   Gallinula chloropus cachinnans
   Bangs

Coot
   Fulica a. americana Gmelin

Upland Plover
   Bartramia longicauda (Bechstein)

Black Tern
   Chlidonias nigra surinamensis
   (Gmelin)

Screech Owl
   Otus asio naevius (Gmelin)

Barred Owl
   Strix v. varia Barton

*Alder Flycatcher‡
   Empidonax t. traillii (Audubon)

*Olive-sided Flycatcher
   Nuttallornis borealis (Swainson)

Wood Thrush
   Hylocichla mustelina (Gmelin)

*Olive-backed Thrush
   Hylocichla ustulata swainsoni
   (Tschudi)

Canada Warbler
   Wilsonia canadensis (Linnaeus)

*Slate-colored Junco
   Junco h. hyemalis (Linnaeus)

---

*Occurs on the islands, but apparently only as a transient migrant.
†Leopold (1931, p. 155) has remarked on the absence of this species from many Great Lakes islands.
‡A single individual was seen on Beaver Island July 10, 1904, by Barrows.

TABLE 7

DISTRIBUTION OF BREEDING BIRDS WHICH ARE RESTRICTED MAINLY TO THE LARGER ISLANDS

This table is based in part on breeding season occurrence without actual proof of nesting.

The names of small islands on which there is but a single record of the occurrence of that species are placed in parenthesis.

Garden, High, and Hog islands were not studied.

	Beaver	N. Fox	S. Fox	N. Manitou	S. Manitou	Small Islands
*American Bittern	x					
*Least Bittern	x					
*Wood Duck	x					
Goshawk	x		x			
Sharp-shinned Hawk	x			x		
Red-tailed Hawk	x		x	x	x	
*Red-shouldered Hawk	x					
*Sparrow Hawk	x					
Virginia Rail	x			x		
Piping Plover	x		x	x	x	
Woodcock	x		x	x	x	(Squaw)
Mourning Dove	x		x	x		
Whip-poor-will	x		x		x	
Nighthawk	x		x		x	
Chimney Swift	x		x	x	x	Squaw
Ruby-throated Hummingbird	x	x	x	x	x	(Trout)
*Kingfisher	x					
Red-headed Woodpecker	x				x	(Gull)
*Sapsucker	x					
Hairy Woodpecker	x		x	x	x	(Trout)
Downy Woodpecker	x	x		x	x	
Crested Flycatcher	x	x	x	x	x	Gull and Trout
*Alder Flycatcher	x					
Least Flycatcher	x			x	x	
Wood Pewee	x	x	x	x	x	Gull
*Prairie Horned Lark	x					
Bank Swallow	x		x	x	x	
Barn Swallow	x		x	x	x	Squaw
*Cliff Swallow	x					
Purple Martin	x		x	x	x	
Blue Jay	x	x	x	x	x	
White-breasted Nuthatch	x			x	x	

*Restricted to Beaver Island.

THE BIRDS

TABLE 7 (Continued)

	Beaver	N. Fox	S. Fox	N. Manitou	S. Manitou	Small Islands
*Brown Creeper	x					
Short-billed Marsh Wren	x			x	x	
Catbird	x			x	x	
Brown Thrasher	x		x	x	x	Gull
Robin	x		x	x	x	(Gull), Squaw
*Hermit Thrush	x					
Bluebird	x		x	x	x	Gull
Black and White Warbler	x			x		
Nashville Warbler	x			x	x	Trout
Black-throated Blue Warbler	x	x	x	x		
*Myrtle Warbler	x					
Chestnut-sided Warbler	x		x	x	x	(Trout)
Yellow-throat	x			x	x	(Trout), Hat
Bobolink	x		x	x	x	
Eastern Meadowlark	x		x		x	
Baltimore Oriole	x		x		x	
Bronzed Grackle	x				x	
Cowbird	x		x	x	x	
Scarlet Tanager	x			x	x	
Rose-breasted Grosbeak	x			x	x	(Gull)
Indigo Bunting	x		x	x	x	Gull
Purple Finch	x		x	x		
Goldfinch	x		x	x	x	(Gull)
Towhee	x	x	x	x	x	
*Savannah Sparrow	x					
Grasshopper Sparrow	x		x	x	x	
Vesper Sparrow	x	x	x	x	x	
Chipping Sparrow	x		x	x	x	(Gull)
*White-throated Sparrow	x					

TABLE 8

BREEDING BIRDS RESTRICTED TO BEAVER ISLAND AND CERTAIN SMALL ISLANDS

	Beaver	Gull	Trout	Whiskey	Squaw	Hat
Red-breasted Nuthatch	x	x		x		
Winter Wren	x			x	x	
Yellow Warbler	x	x	x	x	x	
Magnolia Warbler	x		x		x	
Blackburnian Warbler	x	x	x			
Mourning Warbler	x	x			x	x

---

*Restricted to Beaver Island.

Table 9

Species Occurring as Transient Migrants on the Adjacent Mainland Though not Recorded on the Islands

Cape May Warbler
 Dendroica tigrina (Gmelin)

Bay-breasted Warbler
 Dendroica castanea (Wilson)

Pine Warbler
 Dendroica p. pinus (Wilson)

Northern Water-Thrush
 Seiurus n. noveboracensis (Gmelin)

Canada Warbler*
 Wilsonia canadensis (Linnaeus)

Fox Sparrow
 Passerella i. iliaca (Merrem)

Table 10

Casual Occurrences of Non-breeding Birds During the Breeding Season

	Beaver	Gull	Whiskey	Squaw	Hat	N. Fox	N. Manitou	S. Manitou
Turkey Vulture								June 13
Marsh Hawk	May 6-10	June 17-21		July 6				
Sora								July 8
Lesser Yellow-legs				July 2-5				
Semipalmated Sandpiper		June 20						
Arkansas Kingbird							June 20	
Purple Martin		June 21-22		July 8				
Short-billed Marsh Wren						June 30		
Bobolink		June 17						
Western Meadowlark	July 3							
Cardinal								June 13
Clay-colored Sparrow				June 29				
Swamp Sparrow							June 19	

---

*Recorded as a breeding bird, as well as a transient migrant, on the adjacent mainland.

of its hardiness, aggressiveness, and adaptability. Spreading from its point of introduction in the eastern States, the Starling did not reach the mainland shore adjacent to these islands until 1927. By 1938 it had spread to nearly all of the islands, even the very small ones. (The other introduced species, the English Sparrow, is less migratory and much more closely attached to human habitations; it is restricted to the inhabited parts of Beaver and of the Manitou islands.)

There is a wide difference in distribution and abundance among some related birds which might be expected to be more alike in these respects. For example, the Black-billed Cuckoo is quite common and widespread, but the Yellow-billed Cuckoo has been seen only twice—once on North Manitou and once on South Fox. The Crow is abundant and very widely distributed, whereas the Blue Jay has been found only on the large islands and perhaps breeds only on Beaver. The Willow Thrush is common and it nests on most of the islands, but records of the Wood Thrush are entirely lacking, and there is only a single record of the Olive-backed Thrush (on Beaver).

But one certain case of subspecific varation occurs among breeding birds of these islands: the Western House Wren is found on all of the Beaver group, but the Eastern House Wren is the form occurring on the Fox and Manitou islands. As explained in the annotated list beyond, the Red-wings of the islands differ slightly from the mainland population but probably not sufficiently for recognition in the nomenclature.

Certain unusual habits and choices of habitat were noted among the island birds. For example, a Duck Hawk was found nesting directly on the ground on the side of a sand dune on South Fox; Great Blue Herons and Crows were found nesting close to, and even directly on, the ground; Red-wings were nesting in trees and bushes along the shores of many islands which lacked completely the marsh habitat that mainland Red-wings seem to require for nesting; Crested Flycatchers were inhabiting evergreen, as well as hardwood, forest on Gull Island; on Marion Island the Towhees lived deep in the big hardwood forest, a habitat quite unlike the open brush in which they are usually found. Lack (1942, p. 20) also found such "habitat adaptations" among the birds of the small islands about Great Britain.

At least two species have disappeared from the islands in historic times. The Passenger Pigeon (*Ectopistes migratorius*), once abundant throughout this region, is now extinct. The "pigeons" listed by Strang (1855) were doubtless of this species. The Osprey (*Pandion haliaëtus carolinensis*), which has declined sharply in numbers in Michigan in recent years, was noted by Barrows on the Beaver group in 1904 but has not been recorded since on any of the islands.

ANNOTATED LIST

Lesser Loon
Gavia immer elasson Bishop*

Beaver (spn.); Fisherman's (obs.); Gull (obs.); Hat (obs.); N. Fox (nst.); N. Manitou (obs.); S. Fox (obs.); S. Manitou (obs.); Squaw (obs.); Trout (obs.); Whiskey (obs.).

One or two loons were seen about most of the islands studied. In 1939 there were two pairs at North Fox, and a young one "somewhat smaller than a teal" was seen there on July 1. No certainly summer resident specimens were taken on the islands, but three specimens taken June 30, 1928, at Petoskey on the adjacent mainland and specimens taken as late as May 13 (1928) on Beaver Island prove to belong to this subspecies.

Holboell's Grebe
Colymbus grisegena holböllii (Reinhardt)

Beaver (spn).

There is apparently a heavy migration of this grebe during early May, and many are taken in the fishermen's nets. N. A. Wood (1931, p. 617; 1943, p. 88) reported 75 brought in by fishermen at St. James, Beaver Island, May 2-14, 1929.

Horned Grebe
Colymbus auritus Linnaeus

Beaver (spn).

N. A. Wood and W. B. Tyrrell collected several specimens and noted one to 10 Horned Grebes almost daily May 2-15, 1929.

---

*Subspecific names of birds are here used only when specimens from the region have been examined.

37. A pair of Duck Hawks nest on the upper side of the white birch log in the center foreground. South Fox Island, June 20, 1939. A. E. Staebler.

38. The Duck Hawks' nest. There was no construction to it other than a slight hollowing of the ground containing the eggs and shreds of bark from the fallen log. June 20, 1939. A. E. Staebler.

39. Herring Gull nests were built up to a foot in height in wet areas and the same mound used for two or more years as is indicated by the luxuriant growth of cinquefoil on the sides of some nests. Gull Island, June 19, 1938. R. T. Hatt.

40. Young gulls, frightened from their nests often successfully hid in the nearby driftwood. There are two in this photograph. Gull Island, June 19, 1938. R. T. Hatt.

Double-crested Cormorant
Phalacrocorax auritus subsp.

Beaver (rpt.); S. Manitou (obs).

N. A. Wood saw one cormorant at Beaver Island, June 21, 1925. As many as four were seen about fish nets on South Manitou June 11 and July 6-10, 1940. Natives of South Manitou reported that they saw a few every spring and fall but none during the summer.

Great Blue Heron
Ardea herodias herodias Linnaeus
Figure 35

Beaver (obs.); Gull (obs.); Hat (nst.); Hog (rpt.); N. Manitou (obs.); Pismire (spn., nst.); S. Fox (obs.); S. Manitou (obs.); Squaw (nst.); Trout (obs.); Whiskey (obs.).

A few Great Blue Herons were noted, almost always singly, on most of the islands studied. There were breeding colonies only on Squaw Island, where 19 occupied nests were found in 1938, and on Hat Island, where C. C. Ludwig banded 152 young in the years 1936-1941. Lyon (1927, p. 182) had found "some Great Blue Herons nesting" on Hat July 14, 1927, and Tyrrell on July 3, 1929, counted eight nests there with egg complements of five, three, and one. Max M. Peet collected one of two nestlings found on Pismire July 23, 1934. Barrows (1904, p. 78) was told of a nesting colony "of some size" in the interior of Hog.

It was interesting to find that the adults feeding young in the nest on Squaw Island did not hunt their food on Squaw but flew several miles across the lake to another island—usually to Garden, three miles away. We observed the same practice at Hat; the adults there went 2.5 miles to Hog Island for food or even 11 miles to Waugoshance.

American Bittern
Botaurus lentiginosus lentiginosus (Montagu)

Beaver (spn.); Hat (obs.).

On Beaver Island, two were seen at Font Lake and an adult male collected at Barney Lake on July 19, 1937. One was seen on Hat Island by Hatt, July 7, 1938.

Least Bittern
Ixobrychus exilis subsp.

Beaver (obs.).

Several were seen at Barney Lake in 1937 (Hinshaw).

Mallard
Anas platyrhynchos subsp.

Beaver (obs.); Fisherman's (obs.); Gull (obs.).

Several were seen on Beaver by N. A. Wood in 1925 and 1929 and several by Hinshaw in 1937. One was seen at Fisherman's Island August 10, 1923 (Van Tyne, 1925, p. 614). Hatt saw four on Gull Island June 16, 1938.

Black Duck
Anas rubripes Brewster

Beaver (spn., nst.); Fisherman's (obs.); Gull (obs.); Hat (obs.); N. Manitou (obs.); Pismire (obs.); Squaw (spn., nst.); Whiskey (obs.).

Recorded as common on Beaver in 1937; a young bird not yet able to fly was collected July 16. An adult accompanied by a flightless young was seen on Squaw July 4, 1938. One to four Black Ducks were noted on the other islands listed above, but there was no proof of their nesting.

Pintail
Anas acuta subsp.

Beaver (obs.); Squaw (spn., nst.); Trout (obs.); Whiskey (obs.).

N. A. Wood saw three on Beaver, May 7, 1929. Two adult females and several flightless young (one collected, July 2) were seen on Squaw in 1938. An adult male was noted on Trout Island, June 27, 1938. Two adults were seen on Whiskey Island, June 28 and July 1, 1938. These Pintails presumably belong to the subspecies *tzitzihoa*, but no adult males were collected. This species had been previously found nesting in Michigan only in the Saginaw Bay region.

Blue-winged Teal
Anas discors Linnaeus

Beaver (spn.); Gull (obs.); N. Manitou (spn.); Squaw (obs.); Whiskey (obs.).

James H. Wood collected a male and female on Beaver May 23, 1932. Two were seen on Gull Island, June 16, 1938 (Morrill). A female in breeding condition was collected in the swamp on the west side of North Manitou on June 19, 1940. A female was recorded on Squaw (July 3-5), and a male and female were seen about Whiskey Island (June 28 and 29) in 1938.

Wood Duck
Aix sponsa (Linnaeus)

Beaver (spn.).

Several were seen and an immature male collected (July 16) at Green's Lake in 1937.

Redhead
Aythya americana (Eyton)

Beaver (obs.).

N. A. Wood observed the species May 3-9, 1929.

Ring-necked Duck
Aythya collaris (Donovan)

Beaver (spn.).

N. A. Wood collected a female May 2, 1929.

Canvas-back
Aythya valisineria (Wilson)

Beaver (obs.).

N. A. Wood recorded two at Beaver May 3, 1929.

Lesser Scaup Duck
Aythya affinis (Eyton)

Beaver (spn.).

N. A. Wood noted 40 "scaups" on May 3, 1929, and smaller numbers on other dates from May 2 to May 15, 1929. James H. Wood collected a male (May 15) and female (May 23) in 1932.

Golden-eye
Glaucionetta clangula subsp.

Beaver (obs.); Gull (obs.).

N. A. Wood recorded the species on Beaver May 7-10, 1929. Three were seen on Gull Island, June 16, 1938 (Morrill).

Buffle-head
Glaucionetta albeola (Linnaeus)

N. Manitou (obs.).

A male was seen on the small lake on North Manitou June 19 and 23, 1940 (Staebler).

Old-squaw
Clangula hyemalis (Linnaeus)

Beaver (spn.).

N. A. Wood and W. B. Tyrrell preserved eight specimens that had been taken in fish nets near Beaver Island May 2-14, 1929.

American Merganser
Mergus merganser americanus Cassin

Beaver (nst.); Gull (obs.); Hat (obs.); N. Fox (spn., nst.); N. Manitou (spn.); S. Fox (obs.); S. Manitou (spn., nst.); Squaw (obs.); Trout (spn.); Whiskey (obs.).

Hinshaw saw several adults with young at Iron Ore Bay, Beaver Island, June 22, 1937. Staebler collected several downy young about 10 days old from a brood of 10 on North Fox, June 30, 1939. On South Manitou, Hatt collected a small downy young found alone in a clearing, at least a quarter of a mile from the nearest water, on July 12, 1940. Small flocks of males or single females were seen about most of the islands during June and early July, 1938. The largest number noted was at Squaw Island, where a flock of more than 250 was seen on June 29, 1938. Most of these were clearly males, still largely in nuptial plumage. At Trout Island, a flock that sometimes contained as many as 75 (chiefly green-headed males) gathered frequently at the southeast point to preen and bask in the sun on the gravel beach or to feed in the quiet water on the sheltered side of the point. Two males molting into eclipse plumage were collected there June 22, 1938, from a flock of 40 males and 12 females (or eclipse males). On July 1, 1938, at 9 a.m., a flock of more than 50 were found sleeping on a gravel spit on Whiskey Island.

Red-breasted Merganser
Mergus serrator Linnaeus

Beaver (obs.); Gull (obs.); Hat (nst.); Marion (nst.); N. Manitou (obs.); Pismire (spn., nst.); S. Fox (spn., nst.); S. Manitou (obs.); Squaw (obs.); Trout (obs.); Whiskey (obs.).

Seen about most of the islands but usually in smaller numbers than the American Merganser. N. A. Wood noted the species at

Beaver Island June 24, 1925, and May 6-14, 1929. On Hat Island a nest and eight eggs on the ground near the shore was recorded on July 10, 1938; Barrows (1904, p. 78) reports that Charles L. Cass collected a nest there in 1897 and saw several broods of young in 1896. Van Tyne (1925, p. 614) found a nest with 11 eggs on Marion Island on July 24, 1923. On North and South Manitou, Staebler recorded that this species was "as numerous as the American Merganser" in 1940. Max M. Peet collected newly hatched young from a nest on Pismire July 23, 1934. A (presumably incomplete) set of four fresh eggs was collected June 19, and a downy young was taken from a group of three seen July 18, 1939, on South Fox.

Turkey Vulture
Cathartes aura subsp.

S. Manitou (obs.).

Case saw a Turkey Vulture soaring over a large clearing on South Manitou on June 13, 1940.

Eastern Goshawk
Accipiter gentilis atricapillus (Wilson)

Beaver (spn., nst.); N. Fox (obs.); S. Fox (obs.).

Three large young were collected from a nest of four on July 6 and 7, 1937, four miles southwest of St. James, Beaver Island. An adult was seen June 24, 1939, on South Fox, and on July 2, 1939, one was seen flying from North Fox toward Beaver Island.

Sharp-shinned Hawk
Accipiter striatus velox (Wilson)

Beaver (spn.); N. Manitou (obs.).

Reported by N. A. Wood on Beaver June 15, 1922, and May 6 and 10, 1929; Barrows (1904, p. 79) noted one on Beaver the second week in July 1904; and James H. Wood collected a male there May 23, 1932. One was seen on North Manitou June 20 and one on July 7, 1940.

Cooper's Hawk
Accipiter cooperii (Bonaparte)

Beaver (obs.); N. Manitou (obs.); S. Manitou (obs.).

N. A. Wood saw one on Beaver Island May 10, 1929. In 1940, one was seen on North Manitou on June 15 and 18; one on South Manitou on June 13.

Red-tailed Hawk
Buteo jamaicensis subsp.

Beaver (obs.); N. Manitou (obs.); S. Fox (obs.); S. Manitou (nst.).

Observed on Beaver June 15 and 16, 1922, and May 7, 1929, by N. A. Wood; a few times in June and July, 1937, by Hinshaw and Morrill. On June 24, 1939, two adults were seen over the virgin hardwood on South Fox. In 1940, adults were seen over both Manitou islands, and on June 13 a nest with young was found on South Manitou.

Red-shouldered Hawk
Buteo lineatus subsp.

Beaver (obs.).

One was seen at Iron Ore Bay, June 30, 1937.

Broad-winged Hawk
Buteo platypterus platypterus (Vieillot)

S. Manitou (spn.).

In 1940 Hatt saw one on July 12, and a male was collected on June 13.

Northern Bald Eagle
Haliaeetus leucocephalus washingtoniensis (Audubon)

Beaver (nst.); Gull (spn., nst.); Hat (obs.); Marion (nst.); N. Fox (obs.); N. Manitou (nst.); S. Fox (nst.); S. Manitou (obs.); Squaw (obs.).

On June 20, 1937, a nest was noted near Mt. Pisgah on Beaver. In June, 1938, there was a nest 35 feet up in a maple tree on the high west shore of Gull Island. The eagles were apparently preying on the young Herring Gulls of the colony there and were mobbed by the adult gulls whenever they came near the nesting grounds. On June 15, Van Tyne flushed an adult male eagle from among the gull nests. The bird had apparently been slightly wounded (perhaps by fishermen who had visited the island a few days before) and could not fly very well. Gulls immediately mobbed it and forced it down on the water about 150 yards offshore. The gulls did not attack the eagle while it was on the water but circled about and twice resumed their attacks when the eagle started to rise. Thereupon the eagle began to swim, using its partly folded wings to force itself forward in a series of spurts. The eagle gradually became more waterlogged; it sank deeper and probably was not then able to rise.

It was collected when it reached the shore. Robert L. Baird (1931, p. 308) has reported a Bald Eagle swimming, but the practice is apparently a rather rare one. The Gull Island specimen measures: Wing, 545 mm.; Tail, 259 mm. A Bald Eagle in immature plumage, observed on Hat Island, July 7-9, 1938, was apparently feeding regularly on young Herring Gulls. There was a nest on Marion Island in 1923 (Van Tyne, 1925, p. 617). The eagles that had a nest on the northern end of South Fox (1939) were also noted about North Fox. In 1940 two nests were found on North Manitou, and a third was reliably reported. An eagle was found eating a young Herring Gull on Squaw Island, July 5, 1938.

Marsh Hawk
Circus cyaneus subsp.

Beaver (obs.); Gull (obs.); Squaw (obs.).

N. A. Wood noted the species on Beaver on several days (May 6-10, 1929). An adult male was seen repeatedly on Gull Island, June 17-21, 1938. Two were seen flying westward over Squaw July 6, 1938.

Osprey
Pandion haliaëtus subsp.

Beaver? (rpt.).

Barrows (1904, p. 79) reported one seen on (presumably) Beaver Island the second week in July, 1904, and was told that they "nest regularly on the islands."

Duck Hawk
Falco peregrinus anatum Bonaparte
Figures 37, 38

S. Fox (spn., nst.).

A pair was found nesting on the ground on the side of a dune; the two eggs were hatching on June 20, 1939. This is the first definite nesting record of the Duck Hawk for the Lower Peninsula.

Eastern Sparrow Hawk
Falco sparverius sparverius Linnaeus

Beaver (spn.).

N. A. Wood reported this species on Beaver June 20, 1925, and James H. Wood collected a female there May 6, 1929.

Ring-necked Pheasant
Phasianus colchicus subsp.

Beaver (sgn.).

The occurrence of the Ring-necked Pheasant on Beaver Island was indicated by feathers found in a marshy area one mile west of Sandy Bay on June 28, 1937. There were also many tracks in that region, but no pheasants were actually seen.

Virginia Rail
Rallus limicola limicola Vieillot

Beaver (spn.); N. Manitou (spn., nst.).

Victor H. Cahalane collected a male on Beaver May 19, 1932. The species was quite common in a swamp on the west side of North Manitou in 1940; breeding specimens were collected there June 17 and 18 and a set of eight eggs taken on June 18.

Sora
Porzana carolina (Linnaeus)

Beaver (rpt.); S. Manitou (spn.); Squaw (spn., nst.).

N. A. Wood reported a Sora on Beaver June 16, 1922. Case collected an adult non-breeding male on South Manitou, about 400 yards from the inland lake, on July 8, 1940. In the little marsh on Squaw Island, Morrill collected an adult female July 2, and found an egg on July 4, 1938.

Belted Piping Plover
Charadrius melodus circumcinctus (Ridgway)

Beaver (rpt.); N. Manitou (spn.); S. Fox (spn.); S. Manitou (obs.).

Barrows (1904, p. 79) reported a female Piping Plover, thought to be nesting, at St. James, Beaver Island, the second week in July, 1904. His subspecific determination of the live bird in the field (as "not *circumcincta*") cannot be taken seriously—we now know that in both races the breast band is much less developed in the female than in the male. Staebler and Case saw many and collected several on South Fox in 1939. On North Manitou seven adults were seen and a breeding adult collected July 2, 1940; only two were noted on South Manitou.

41. Hatching Herring Gull. Gull Island, June 19, 1938. R. T. Hatt.

42. Young Herring Gulls. Gull Island, June 19, 1938. R. T. Hatt.

43. Nest of a Woodland Deermouse. It was constructed entirely of floss and seeds from pods of the common milkweed and was under an overturned bushel basket which it nearly filled. North Manitou Island, June 23, 1940. A. E. Staebler.

Killdeer
Charadrius vociferus vociferus Linnaeus

Beaver (spn., nst.); Gull (spn.); N. Fox (spn.); N. Manitou (spn., nst.); S. Fox (spn.); S. Manitou (spn.); Squaw (nst.); Trout (obs.); Whiskey (obs.).

N. A. Wood reported a nest with eggs on Beaver June 25, 1925; the species was plentiful there in 1937, and a downy young was collected July 18. At least two were seen on Gull Island in 1938. In 1939 several were seen on North and South Fox islands and one collected on each. A few were noted on both North and South Manitou, and a downy young was collected on North Manitou June 15, 1940. At least five were seen on Squaw Island, and a nest with eggs was observed on the edge of the Common Tern colony, July 4-6, 1938. Two were seen on Trout Island and three pairs on Whiskey Island in 1938.

American Woodcock
Philohela minor (Gmelin)

Beaver (obs.); N. Manitou (obs.); S. Fox (obs.); S. Manitou (obs.); Squaw (obs.).

Single Woodcock were noted on Beaver Island June 18, 28, and July 3, 1937. Staebler saw Woodcock on North Manitou June 17, 18, and 22, 1940; Hatt saw several on South Manitou July 11, 1940. At least three were seen on South Fox July 17-18, 1939. Morrill saw one on Squaw Island July 3, 1938.

Wilson's Snipe
Capella gallinago delicata (Ord)

Beaver (spn.).

Noted by N. A. Wood on Beaver Island May 6, 9, 10, and 12, 1929; one collected there by James H. Wood May 7, 1929.

Spotted Sandpiper
Actitis macularia (Linnaeus)

Beaver (spn.); Garden (rpt.); Gull (spn., nst.); Hat (spn., nst.); Marion (nst.); N. Fox (obs.); N. Manitou (spn.); S. Fox (spn.); S. Manitou (spn., nst.); Squaw (spn., nst.); Trout (spn.); Whiskey (spn., nst.).

Barrows (1904, p. 78) reported a "pair to every mile or two of beach" on Beaver Island; several specimens have been taken there. Lincoln (1926, p. 241) banded a Spotted Sandpiper on Stony Reef close to the west shore of Garden June 26, 1924. There were at least five pairs on Gull Island in 1938; nests with eggs were found June 16 and 18; an incubating bird collected June 19 proved to be a female. O. S. Pettingill, Jr., reports three nests with eggs (one set hatching) on Hat Island July 1, 1940. The species was common on Marion Island in 1923, and young well able to fly were seen July 24 (Van Tyne, 1925, p. 615). There were about two pairs on North Fox and four pairs on South Fox in 1939. A nest with eggs was found on South Manitou June 13, 1940; the species was rather common there and on North Manitou. In 1938, on Squaw Island, a nest with eggs was observed July 3-7. The set in another nest was completed July 5, 1938; the incubating adult was collected July 6 and proved to be a male. There were at least five adults on Trout in 1938; the same number was observed on Whiskey Island, and a downy young was collected there June 29.

Eastern Solitary Sandpiper
Tringa solitaria solitaria Wilson

Beaver (spn.); S. Manitou (spn.).

N. A. Wood reported this species on Beaver Island May 10, 12, and 15, 1929; James H. Wood collected one there May 11, 1929. Hatt saw one at the inland lake on South Manitou July 11 and collected one there July 12, 1940.

Greater Yellow-legs
Totanus melanoleucus (Gmelin)

Beaver (spn.).

N. A. Wood and James H. Wood collected three on Beaver May 6-14, 1929.

Lesser Yellow-legs
Totanus flavipes (Gmelin)

Beaver (spn.); S. Manitou (obs.); Squaw (spn.).

In 1929 N. A. Wood collected three on Beaver and recorded flocks of 20 to 40 from May 2 to 10, smaller numbers from May 11 to 14. Three were seen on the inland lake on South Manitou July 31, 1940. An adult female, first noted on Squaw July 2, 1938, was collected July 5.

Least Sandpiper
Erolia minutilla (Vieillot)

Beaver (spn.).

V. H. Cahalane collected a male on Beaver May 19, 1932.

Semipalmated Sandpiper
Ereunetes pusillus (Linnaeus)

Gull (spn.).

An adult female was collected June 20, 1938, from a group of three seen on Gull.

Herring Gull
Larus argentatus smithsonianus Coues
Frontispiece, Figures 39-42

Beaver (spn.); Bellow (spn., nst.); Fisherman's (nst.); Gull (spn., nst.); Hat (spn., nst.); N. Fox (obs.); N. Manitou (obs.); Pismire (nst.); Shoe (nst.); S. Fox (obs.); S. Manitou (nst.); Squaw (nst.); Trout (nst.); Whiskey (nst.).

This is the common gull of the whole Lake Michigan area and occurs around all of the islands. The islands on which it is known to nest are indicated above. The largest colonies are on Bellow, Gull, South Manitou, Squaw, and Hat islands, but few reliable data are available on actual numbers. It is apparent, however, that the numbers fluctuate greatly from year to year for reasons that are little understood. Eaton (1934) and Gross (1940) have described and mapped the banding returns from these Beaver Island group colonies. Strong (1923, p. 613) listed the breeding colonies of Lake Michigan as known in 1923.

Ring-billed Gull
Larus delawarensis Ord

Beaver (obs.); Fisherman's (rpt.); Hat (spn., nst.); Pismire (nst.); Shoe (nst.); S. Manitou (obs.); Squaw (spn., nst.); Trout (obs.); Whiskey (spn.).

As F. E. Ludwig (1943) has shown, this species has passed through an interesting cycle in the Great Lakes region. The early records indicate that Ring-billed Gulls nested there in some numbers in the 1890's; then they disappeared entirely from the Great Lakes as a breeding species, but about 25 years later, began to re-occupy the region. The earliest record we find for the Beaver Island group is Butler's (1898, p. 573) statement that Charles L. Cass reported this species "breeding on the Beaver Islands." However, Barrows in 1904 (p. 66) "searched in vain" for it about the Beaver group. Ring-billed Gulls resumed nesting there in 1935. Ludwig (1943) found them first on Pismire in 1935, then on Hat (in 1936), and on Shoe (in 1937). Finally in 1938 a colony of more than 150 pairs was found on Squaw Island. Several Ring-bills were noted about Beaver Island during the summer of 1937. A. S. Warthin, Jr., saw one at Fisherman's Island August 8, 1923 (Van Tyne, 1925, p. 613). Four immature birds were seen by Staebler on South Manitou July 30 to August 1, 1940. Three adults were observed at Trout Island June 26, 1938. As many as 55 Ring-billed Gulls, presumably from the nesting colony on nearby Squaw Island, were seen feeding along the shore of Whiskey Island June 27-July 1, 1938.

Common Tern
Sterna hirundo hirundo Linnaeus

Beaver (spn.); Garden (nst. rpt.); Hat (nst. rpt.); High (spn., nst.); Pismire (nst.); Shoe (spn., nst.); Squaw (spn., nst.); Trout (spn.); Whiskey (nst.).

The Common Tern nests on the six small islands (or their adjacent reefs) indicated above, and during the breeding season it is rather closely confined to them. The species was not noted at Gull (1938), the Fox (1939), or the Manitou (1940) islands. Common Terns were numerous on Beaver Island in 1937, but no nesting colony was found. Lincoln (1926, p. 241) reported a colony of about 300 pairs on Stony Reef, close to the west shore of Garden Island, on July 18, 1924. Data in the egg collection of the Chicago Academy of Sciences record that Charles L. Cass found "several hundred Herring Gulls and Wilson [Common] Terns nesting on Hat Island on July 11, 1896." Hatt found more than 200 nests on a low bar northeast of High Island on June 23, 1938. Lyon (1927, p. 182) reported a colony of 300 to 400 on "Snake Island," a reef near Pismire, on July 14, 1927. A few Common Terns nest with the Caspian Terns on Shoe Island, and the Ludwigs banded between 7 and 74 there yearly from 1934 to 1938. There was a colony of about 200 pairs on Squaw Island in 1938. A few individuals were seen about Trout Island, June 23-25, 1938. On June 29, 1938, Hatt found a lone nest with two eggs on Whiskey Island.

Caspian Tern
Hydroprogne caspia (Pallas)
Figure 15

Beaver (spn.); Fisherman's (obs.); Gull (obs.); Hat (spn., nst.); High (spn., nst.); N. Fox (obs.); N. Manitou (obs.); Pismire (nst.); Shoe (spn., nst.); S. Fox (obs.); S. Manitou (obs.); Squaw (obs.); Trout (obs.); Whiskey (spn.).

The Caspian Tern is regularly seen about all of the islands of northern Lake Michigan, but in the area covered by this report it is known to nest only on Shoe Island (called "Little Hat Island" in some published accounts) and on a low bar northeast of High Island. The first ornithologist known to have visited Shoe Island was Charles L. Cass, who collected a number of sets of eggs there July 1, 1896. Apparently Barrows (1904, p. 65; 1912, p. 58) visited Shoe Island July 11, 1904. Banding young terns at this colony was begun by Lincoln (1924a, p. 40) in 1923 and has been carried out almost every year since. As many as 782 have been banded there in one year, and the total number banded is now over 6,000. In years of exceptionally high water (e.g., 1929) Shoe Island has been largely covered, and the terns have then moved to nearby Hat Island to nest. The record of the Caspian Tern banding at Hat has been published by Lincoln (1924a, 1924b), Ludwig (1942), and Lyon (1927). In 1938 about 200 pairs of Caspian Terns nested on the low bar off the northeast point of High Island, adjacent to the Common Tern colony. Since the island extended not more than 12 inches above water level (which was low that year), the terns would not be able to nest there in years of high lake level.

Mourning Dove
Zenaidura macroura subsp.

Beaver (obs.); N. Manitou (obs.); S. Fox (obs.).

Seen frequently but in small numbers on Beaver in 1937. Three were seen on North Manitou, June 16-20, 1940. One was seen on several occasions June 19-25, 1939, on South Fox.

Yellow-billed Cuckoo
Coccyzus americanus subsp.

N. Manitou (obs.); S. Fox (obs.).

Noted on North Manitou June 17, 1940. One was seen June 25, 1939, on South Fox.

Black-billed Cuckoo
Coccyzus erythropthalmus (Wilson)

Beaver (spn., nst.); Gull (spn.); N. Manitou (spn.); S. Fox (obs.); S. Manitou (spn.); Squaw (obs.); Trout (obs.); Whiskey (spn.).

Common on Beaver in 1937; a nest with two young and one egg was found nine miles south of St. James June 15. On Gull, one was collected June 18, and two seen June 21, 1938. Fairly common on South Manitou and abundant on North Manitou in 1940. Two were seen on South Fox on July 18, 1939. At least one was seen on Squaw, July 4 and 5, 1938. Several were seen on Trout June 22-25, 1938. One was collected and others seen on Whiskey Island June 27-July 1, 1938.

Horned Owl
Bubo virginianus subsp.

N. Manitou (obs.).

One was seen on North Manitou June 17, 1940.

Eastern Whip-poor-will
Caprimulgus vociferus vociferus Wilson

Beaver (obs.); S. Fox (spn.); S. Manitou (voi.).

Seen several times on Beaver in 1937. In 1939 a number were heard and two collected (June 25) on South Fox. Several heard on South Manitou July 31, 1940.

Eastern Nighthawk
Chordeiles minor minor (Forster)

Beaver (spn.); S. Fox (voi.); S. Manitou (voi.).

Common on Beaver in 1937 (two collected July 14, 15). One heard on South Fox June 25, 1939; several heard on South Manitou June 12, 1940.

Chimney Swift
Chaetura pelagica (Linnaeus)

Beaver (spn.); Gull (obs.); N. Manitou (spn.); S. Fox (spn.); S. Manitou (spn.); Squaw (obs.).

Common on Beaver in 1937 (adult female collected July 1). Two were seen on Gull June 18 and 19, 1938. Common on North and South Manitou, 1940; a female, collected on South Manitou June 11, had been banded at Glasgow, Kentucky, September 3, 1939, by F.

Everett Frei. Common in 1939 on South Fox, where they were nesting on the interior walls of the abandoned buildings; a breeding male, collected June 18, had been banded August 27, 1938, at Nashville, Tennessee, by John B. Calhoun. Two seen on Squaw June 29-July 6, 1938, were probably nesting in the abandoned lighthouse buildings.

Ruby-throated Hummingbird
Archilochus colubris (Linnaeus)

Beaver (obs.); N. Fox (obs.); N. Manitou (spn.); S. Fox (spn.); S. Manitou (spn.); Trout (obs.).

Common on Beaver in 1937. A few observed on the Fox islands in 1939. A male was collected on South Fox June 17, 1939. Fairly common (and was collected) on both Manitou islands in 1940. One seen on Trout June 24, 1938.

Kingfisher
Megaceryle alcyon subsp.

Beaver (obs., nst. rpt.); Marion (nst.); S. Manitou (obs.).

Barrows (1904, p. 79) reported the Kingfisher abundant on Beaver Island and saw young just able to fly at Font Lake on July 10, 1904. The species was not uncommon there in 1937. It was common and nesting around the shores of Marion Island, July 23-28, 1923 (Van Tyne, 1925, p. 618). Hatt saw Kingfishers on South Manitou, August 31, 1944.

Northern Flicker
Colaptes auratus luteus Bangs

Beaver (spn., nst.); Gull (obs.); N. Fox (obs.); N. Manitou (spn.); S. Fox (spn.); Trout (obs.).

Barrows (1904, p. 79) reported that the Flicker was "one of the most abundant" species on Beaver and recorded full-grown young the second week in July; it was common and several specimens were collected on Beaver in 1937. One was recorded on Gull June 20, 1938. One was seen on North Fox July 2, 1939, and as many as four were seen in a day on South Fox in June 1939. Two were seen July 2-4, 1940, on North Manitou. Flickers were not seen regularly on any of the smaller islands except Trout, where one was noted June 25-27, 1938, feeding on anthills, which were exceptionally abundant there.

Pileated Woodpecker
Hylatomus pileatus subsp.

Beaver (obs.); Gull (sgn.); N. Manitou (sgn.).

N. A. Wood recorded the species on Beaver June 15, 1922, May 7 and 13, 1929; it was seen there frequently in June and July 1937. The distinctive drilling marks of the Pileated were noted on Gull (1938) and on North Manitou (1940).

Red-headed Woodpecker
Melanerpes erythrocephalus erythrocephalus (Linnaeus)

Beaver (spn.); Gull (spn.); S. Manitou (spn.).

Reported by N. A. Wood on Beaver June 21-25, 1925, and May 11, 1929; in 1932 V. H. Cahalane collected two males (May 16, 19); in 1937 a pair was noted at St. James and a pair collected nine miles southwest of there. An adult female was collected on Gull June 17, 1938. In 1940 five or more individuals were seen and an adult female collected (June 9) on South Manitou.

Yellow-bellied Sapsucker
Sphyrapicus varius varius (Linnaeus)

Beaver (spn.).

N. A. Wood noted the species on Beaver June 16, 1922, and May 2, 7, and 9, 1929. James H. Wood collected a specimen there May 14, 1932. Hinshaw collected a pair five and a half miles southwest of St. James on July 8, 1937.

Eastern Hairy Woodpecker
Dendrocopos villosus villosus (Linnaeus)

Beaver (spn., nst.); N. Manitou (spn., nst.); S. Fox (spn., nst.); S. Manitou (spn.); Trout (obs.).

Barrows (1904, p. 79) found this species "rather common" on Beaver and recorded full-grown young following parents on July 10; it was frequent there in 1937, and several specimens were collected. It was also frequent on both Manitou islands in 1940; a nest with half-grown young was found June 23, 1940, on North Manitou. A breeding pair was taken (June 22, 24) on South Fox in 1939. One individual was seen on Trout June 24, 1938.

Northern Downy Woodpecker
Dendrocopos pubescens medianus (Swainson)

Beaver (spn.); N. Fox (spn.); N. Manitou (spn.); S. Manitou (obs.).

More common than the Hairy Woodpecker on Beaver in 1937; three specimens collected, including an immature female, on July 22. One adult was collected on North Fox June 30, and two others were seen, June 29 and 30, in 1939. The species is apparently more common than the Hairy Woodpecker on both Manitou islands; two were collected on North Manitou June 22, 23, 1940.

Eastern Kingbird
Tyrannus tyrannus (Linnaeus)

Beaver (spn.); Gull (spn., nst.); Hat (spn., nst.); N. Fox (nst.); N. Manitou (spn., nst.); S. Fox (spn., nst.); S. Manitou (spn., nst.); Squaw (spn., nst.); Trout (spn.); Whiskey (obs.).

Abundant on Beaver in 1904 (Barrows, 1904, p. 79) and in 1937; N. A. Wood saw one there as early as May 15 (1929). At least six were seen on Gull in 1938; a female taken June 17 was laying. O. S. Pettingill, Jr., reported a pair with a nest on Hat July 1, 1940, and a pair there July 1, 1943; a nest was found there July 10, 1938. Common and nesting on both Fox islands in 1939 and on both Manitou islands in 1940. At least four were seen and a breeding female collected on Squaw July 5, 1938. A breeding male was collected on Trout June 26, 1938. One was seen daily on Whiskey June 28 to July 1, 1938.

Arkansas Kingbird
Tyrannus verticalis Say

N. Manitou (spn.).

Staebler collected an adult female on North Manitou June 20, 1940. It did not appear to be a breeding bird. This is one of only two specimens taken in the State.

Northern Crested Flycatcher
Myiarchus crinitus boreus Bangs

Beaver (spn.); Gull (spn.); N. Fox (obs.); N. Manitou (spn.); S. Fox (spn.); S. Manitou (obs.); Trout (spn.).

Uncommon on Beaver in 1937; V. H. Cahalane collected single specimens May 23 and 24, 1932. Several seen on Gull in 1938; two collected June 18. Seen in small numbers on both Fox islands in 1939; one collected on South Fox June 21, 1939. Common on both Manitou islands in 1940; one collected on North Manitou June 15, 1940. One was taken on Trout June 26, 1938.

Eastern Phoebe
Sayornis phoebe (Latham)

Beaver (obs.); S. Fox (spn., nst.); Trout (obs.).

Uncommon on Beaver in 1937. A pair was found nesting in a deserted barn and a specimen was collected (June 22) on South Fox in 1939. One was seen at the abandoned house on Trout June 24, 1938.

Yellow-bellied Flycatcher
Empidonax flaviventris (W. M. and S. F. Baird)

Beaver (spn.).

One collected by James H. Wood May 28, 1932.

Alder Flycatcher
Empidonax traillii subsp.

Beaver (rpt.).

Barrows (1904, p. 79) reported "a single specimen found in the alders along the edge of Font Lake July 10 [1904]."

Least Flycatcher
Empidonax minimus (W. M. and S. F. Baird)

Beaver (spn.); N. Manitou (spn.); S. Manitou (spn.).

N. A. Wood reported this species on Beaver June 23 and 24, 1925; V. H. Cahalane collected a specimen there May 28, 1932. Fairly common on North Manitou in 1940, less common on South Manitou.

Eastern Wood Pewee
Contopus virens (Linnaeus)

Beaver (spn.); Gull (obs.); N. Fox (spn.); N. Manitou (spn.); S. Fox (spn.); S. Manitou (spn.).

This species was recorded as common, and specimens in breeding condition were collected, on all of the above islands except Gull, where the species was noted only twice, on June 20 and 21, 1938.

Olive-sided Flycatcher
Nuttallornis borealis (Swainson)

Beaver (spn.).

V. H. Cahalane collected a male on Beaver May 23, 1932.

Prairie Horned Lark
Eremophila alpestris praticola (Henshaw)

Beaver (spn., nst.).

Seen frequently on Beaver in 1937; two in juvenal plumage were taken north of Sandy Bay July 22, 1937.

Tree Swallow
Iridoprocne bicolor (Vieillot)

Beaver (spn.); Gull (spn., nst.); Hat (spn.); N. Fox (spn.); N. Manitou (spn., nst.); S. Fox (spn.); S. Manitou (spn., nst.); Squaw (obs.); Trout (spn.); Whiskey (obs.).

Rather common, especially about the shores, on all of the large islands and on Hat. The species was apparently breeding on all of the islands listed above, though nests were actually found only on the islands indicated. Pairs were noted on the small islands in 1938 as follows: Gull, several; Squaw, two or more; Trout, one; Whiskey, two or more.

Bank Swallow
Riparia riparia riparia (Linnaeus)

Beaver (spn., nst.); N. Manitou (obs.); S. Fox (spn., nst.); S. Manitou (spn.).

Fairly common and nesting near St. James, Beaver Island, in 1937; C. C. Ludwig banded a total of 46 nestlings there in 1938 and 1939. Fairly common on North and South Manitou islands in 1940. In 1939 there was a colony of about 10 pairs in a bank on the east shore of South Fox.

Rough-winged Swallow
Stelgidopteryx ruficollis serripennis (Audubon)

S. Fox (spn.).

Several were seen in 1939 in company with the Bank Swallows on South Fox; a male collected there June 26 was in breeding condition.

Barn Swallow
Hirundo rustica erythrogaster Boddaert

Beaver (spn., nst.); N. Manitou (spn., nst.); Pismire (obs.); S. Fox (spn., nst.); S. Manitou (spn., nst.); Squaw (nst.); Whiskey (obs.).

The Barn Swallow was abundant and nesting at St. James, Beaver Island, according to Barrows (1904, p. 80), in 1904; this was also true in 1937 and 1938. In 1929 N. A. Wood reported the species at St. James by May 6. Common and nesting on both Manitou islands in 1940. One was seen at Pismire July 11, 1938, by Hatt. On June 23, 1937, Hatt (1938) found several nests with eggs (one of the nests constructed without mud) on South Fox; in 1939 one or two pairs were found nesting there in each of the larger clearings. Five occupied nests were found on Squaw Island July 2, 1938. Barn Swallows were observed July 1, 1938, on Whiskey Island although the only man-made shelter here was a small hut in thick arbor vitae. This structure contained no nests.

Cliff Swallow
Petrochelidon pyrrhonota subsp.

Beaver (nst.).

N. A. Wood found an occupied nest at St. James, Beaver Island, on June 22, 1925.

Purple Martin
Progne subis subis (Linnaeus)

Beaver (nst.); Gull (obs.); Hat (obs.); N. Manitou (nst.); S. Fox (nst.); S. Manitou (spn., nst.).

In 1937 the Purple Martin was common and nesting in bird houses or about buildings on Beaver (though not found there by Barrows in 1904), on both Manitou islands in 1940, and on South Fox in 1939. One was seen on Gull June 21, two June 22, 1938, and one on Hat July 8, 1938.

Northern Blue Jay
Cyanocitta cristata bromia Oberholser

Beaver (spn.); N. Fox (obs.); N. Manitou (obs.); S. Fox (spn.); S. Manitou (spn.).

The Blue Jay was common on Beaver in 1937 (young on the wing collected July 14 and 15). It was seen in considerable numbers on both Fox islands in 1939, when flocks containing up to 25 individuals were moving about South Fox as late as June 23; specimens taken there June 18 and 21 did not show enlarged gonads. In 1940 the species was much less common on the Manitou islands than on the Fox islands.

Eastern Crow
Corvus brachyrhynchos brachyrhynchos Brehm

Beaver (spn., nst.); Gull (nst.); Hat (nst.); Hog (obs.); N. Fox (nst.); N. Manitou (nst.); Pismire (nst.); S. Fox (spn., nst.); S. Manitou (nst.); Squaw (nst.); Trout (nst.); Whiskey (nst.).

The species was abundant on Beaver in 1937 (fledglings collected June 19 and 30). It was common on Gull in 1938, when a nest with a single young bird was found only eight feet from the ground in a white birch, although the island contains many acres of large trees in which nests could be placed at the usual elevations; the nestling was banded June 16 and was ready to leave the nest June 22; on the following January 20, it was found dead at Kalamazoo, Michigan. Several pairs of crows are regularly found by visitors to Hat; in 1937, C. C. Ludwig banded two nestlings there. Lincoln (1924a, p. 40) reported that in 1923 W. S. McCrea had a professional crow hunter exterminate the crows on Hat because of their raids on the gulls. Hatt recorded the species on the south end of Hog Island, July 11, 1938. Crows were common and nesting on the Fox islands in 1939 and on the Manitou islands in 1940. A nest with two young, found on Pismire July 11, 1938, was situated in low brush and touched the ground; a similar nest was reported there in 1939 by F. E. Ludwig. C. C. Ludwig banded nestlings on Pismire in 1936. Several pairs were feeding fledglings on Squaw in 1938. There were several pairs on Trout in 1938; a nest 18 feet from the ground in an arbor vitae contained three young about a week old on June 23. One or more pairs were feeding fledglings on Whiskey Island in 1938.

Black-capped Chickadee
Parus atricapillus atricapillus Linnaeus

Beaver (spn., nst.); Gull (spn.); N. Fox (spn., nst.); N. Manitou (obs.); S. Manitou (obs.); Squaw (obs.); Trout (obs.); Whiskey (obs.).

Abundant and breeding on Beaver in 1937. Several seen on Gull in 1938. In 1939 on North Fox a few were seen and a brood of young just out of the nest was noted (July 1). Seen in small numbers on North and South Manitou in 1940. At least one pair was found on Squaw, on Trout, and on Whiskey, in 1938.

White-breasted Nuthatch
Sitta carolinensis cookei Oberholser

Beaver (rpt.); N. Manitou (spn.); S. Manitou (obs.).

Noted by N. A. Wood on Beaver May 7, 1929. The male of a pair found on North Manitou was collected July 3, 1940. Hatt observed one in mature forest on South Manitou, August 30, 1944.

Red-breasted Nuthatch
Sitta canadensis Linnaeus

Beaver (spn.); Gull (obs.); Whiskey (obs.).

Recorded as common in one area on Beaver in 1904 (Barrows, 1904, p. 81); specimens taken on Beaver May 8, 1929; May 15, 17, and 23, 1932. One seen on Gull June 17, and one on Whiskey June 28, 1938.

Brown Creeper
Certhia familiaris americana Bonaparte

Beaver (spn.).

Barrows (1904, p. 81) recorded a Brown Creeper on Beaver the second week of July 1904. N. A. Wood noted the species several times May 2-9, and James H. Wood collected a specimen May 2, in 1929.

Eastern House Wren
Troglodytes aëdon aëdon Vieillot

N. Fox (obs.); N. Manitou (obs.); S. Fox (spn., nst.); S. Manitou (spn.).

In 1939 at least five singing males were heard on North Fox; House Wrens were found around all of the deserted buildings and in a few other places on South Fox. They were surprisingly scarce on the Manitou islands in 1940, but that was probably not an average season; they were unusually scarce that year in Cheboygan County on the nearby mainland (A. E. Staebler and Max M. Peet). Four specimens taken on South Fox and one on South Manitou are definitely of the dark, eastern subspecies; it is assumed that the birds observed on nearby North Fox and North Manitou were of the same race.

Western House Wren
Troglodytes aëdon parkmanii Audubon

Beaver (spn.); Gull (spn.); Squaw (spn., nst.); Trout (spn.); Whiskey (obs.).

Barrows (1904, p. 81), presumably referring mainly to Beaver Island, reported the House Wren "omnipresent, and as likely to be found in the depths of the swamp, or among the wooded sand dunes, as about the village." In 1937 it was common on Beaver. In 1938 there were at least six pairs on Gull (specimens in breeding condition collected), four or more pairs on Squaw (fledgling collected July 5), three or more singing males on Trout, and at least one male (probably *parkmanii*) on Whiskey.

Eastern Winter Wren
Troglodytes troglodytes hiemalis Vieillot

Beaver (obs.); Squaw (obs.); Whiskey (spn.).

Barrows (1904, p. 81) saw this species only "once or twice" on Beaver but heard its song "from every tamarack swamp visited." In 1937 a few were seen at Mt. Pisgah (five miles south of St. James). One was seen on Squaw by Morrill July 3, 1938. At least three singing males were heard on Whiskey in 1938, and a male in breeding condition collected June 28.

Short-billed Marsh Wren
Cistothorus platensis stellaris (Naumann)

Beaver (spn.); N. Fox (spn.); N. Manitou (spn.); S. Manitou (spn.).

A small colony was found on Beaver in 1937. The single specimen (an adult female) taken on North Fox (June 30, 1939) was not in breeding condition. In 1940 there was a colony on North and one on South Manitou. The wrens were apparently breeding, but no nests were actually found.

Catbird
Dumetella carolinensis (Linnaeus)

Beaver (spn.); N. Manitou (spn.); S. Manitou (spn.).

Fairly common at several points on Beaver in 1937. Three were seen on North Manitou and three on South Manitou in 1940; specimens collected were in breeding condition.

Brown Thrasher
Toxostoma rufum rufum (Linnaeus)

Beaver (spn., nst.); Gull (spn.); N. Manitou (spn.); S. Fox (spn.); S. Manitou (spn.).

Fairly common and breeding on Beaver in 1937. At least three were seen on Gull, and a breeding male was collected (June 16) in 1938. Fairly common and apparently breeding on both Manitou islands in 1940. A female in breeding condition, collected on South Fox, June 27, 1939, is the only record for that island.

Eastern Robin
Turdus migratorius migratorius Linnaeus

Beaver (spn., nst.); Bellow (nst.); Gull (obs.); N. Manitou (spn.); S. Fox (nst.); S. Manitou (spn.); Squaw (spn.).

Barrows (1904, p. 81) recorded the Robin on Beaver as "not uncommon in suitable places, yet by no means abundant," but in 1937 it was very common. C. C. Ludwig banded four nestlings on Bellow in 1939. One Robin was seen on Gull June 21, 1938. In 1939 several pairs were nesting around the lighthouse buildings on South Fox, and a few pairs were seen in the wooded parts of the island. The species was common on both Manitou islands in 1940. Two were recorded on Squaw in 1938.

Hermit Thrush
Hylocichla guttata subsp.

Beaver (rpt.).

Barrows (1904, p. 81) reported this as "the common woodland thrush of the islands," but it has not been recorded since on any island except Beaver. N. A. Wood's notes list the following dates of observation on Beaver: June 15, 1922; June 22, 1925; May 5, 8-11, 13, 1929. The Hermit Thrush was common there in June and July 1937. Apparently no specimens have been taken on the islands.

Olive-backed Thrush
Hylocichla ustulata subsp.

Beaver (rpt.).

Barrows' (1904, p. 81) report of a single bird near St. James (the second week of July, 1904) cannot be accepted as a positive record; obviously he was not familiar with the song of this species. N. A. Wood listed one seen, May 22, 1925, on Beaver. No specimens have been recorded from the islands.

Gray-cheeked Thrush
Hylocichla minima minima (Lafresnaye)

Beaver (spn.).

V. H. Cahalane collected a female May 16, 1932.

Willow Thrush
Hylocichla fuscescens salicicola Ridgway
Figure 36

Beaver (spn.); Gull (spn.); Hat (spn., nst.); N. Fox (spn., nst.); N. Manitou (spn.); S. Fox (spn., nst.); S. Manitou (spn.); Squaw (obs.); Trout (spn.); Whiskey (obs.).

The Willow Thrush was common on Beaver in 1937 and common on Gull in 1938; specimens taken were in breeding condition. A female was incubating four eggs on Hat Island July 10, 1938. The species was common on both Fox islands in 1939; a nest with four large young was found on North Fox July 1; on South Fox a nest with four fresh eggs was collected on June 17, and the set of four was completed the same day in another nest. The Willow Thrush was common and apparently breeding on both Manitou islands in 1940 and on Squaw and Trout in 1938. Several were seen on Whiskey Island June 27-July 1, 1938.

Eastern Bluebird
Sialia sialis sialis (Linnaeus)

Beaver (spn., nst.); Gull (spn.); N. Manitou (spn.); S. Fox (spn.); S. Manitou (spn.).

Abundant and nesting on Beaver in 1937. Three females (June 16-21) found on Gull in 1938. Fairly common on both Manitou islands in 1940 and on South Fox in 1939; some specimens taken on these islands were in breeding condition.

Eastern Golden-crowned Kinglet
Regulus satrapa satrapa Lichtenstein

Beaver (spn.); N. Manitou (spn.);

W. B. Tyrrell collected a female on Beaver May 7, 1929. A female was collected and at least three other individuals seen June 19, 1940, at the lake on North Manitou.

Eastern Ruby-crowned Kinglet
Regulus calendula calendula (Linnaeus)

Beaver (spn.).

N. A. Wood recorded this kinglet May 2, 6, 7, 9, 10, and 13, 1929; James H. Wood collected a female May 3, 1929.

Cedar Waxwing
Bombycilla cedrorum Vieillot

Beaver (spn., nst.); Gull (spn.); Hat (spn.); N. Fox (spn.); N. Manitou (spn.); S. Fox (spn.); S. Manitou (spn.); Squaw (obs.); Trout (spn., nst.); Whiskey (obs.).

Abundant and nesting on Beaver in 1938. Three to four seen on Gull June 18-21, 1938; a female taken June 21 was nearly ready to lay. A male taken on Hat July 9, 1938, was in breeding condition. The species was common on the Fox islands in 1939 and abundant on the Manitou islands in 1940. Five or more were seen on Squaw June 29-July 6, 1938. There were three or more pairs on Trout in 1938; a nest in an arbor vitae was three-quarters completed on June 27. At least four waxwings were seen on Whiskey June 28-July 2, 1938.

Starling
Sturnus vulgaris vulgaris Linnaeus

Beaver (spn., nst.); Gull (obs.); Hat (nst.); N. Fox (obs.); N. Manitou (nst.); Pismire (obs.); S. Fox (nst.); S. Manitou (spn., nst.); Squaw (spn., nst.); Whiskey (obs.).

Common and nesting on Beaver in 1937. At least five were seen on Gull June 16-21, 1938. O. S. Pettingill, Jr., found three occupied nesting holes on Hat July 1, 1940. A flock of about 25 was seen on North Fox July 2, 1939. Common on both Manitou islands in 1940, nesting mainly around the farm buildings and in fence posts. Hatt saw approximately 15 at Pismire on July 11, 1938. Several pairs were nesting about the lighthouse on South Fox in 1939. Two nests with young (June 29, July 2) were found on Squaw, and a flock of 11 full-grown young (July 6) was noted in 1938. At least five Starlings were seen on Whiskey June 27-July 1, 1938.

Red-eyed Vireo
Vireo olivaceus (Linnaeus)

Beaver (spn.); Gull (spn.); Hat (spn.); N. Fox (obs.); N. Manitou (spn.); S. Fox (spn.); S. Manitou (spn.); Squaw (spn.); Trout (obs.); Whiskey (obs.).

Common on Beaver Island (1937), the Fox (1939) and the Manitou (1940) islands. In 1938 several singing males were found on each of the following islands: Gull, Hat, Squaw, Trout, and Whiskey. Specimens taken were in breeding condition, and the species undoubtedly nests on all of the islands listed above.

Philadelphia Vireo
Vireo philadelphicus (Cassin)

Beaver (spn.).

V. H. Cahalane collected a male May 24, 1932.

Black and White Warbler
Mniotilta varia (Linnaeus)

Beaver (spn.); N. Manitou (spn.).

Common on Beaver in 1937; in 1904 Barrows (1904, p. 80) found it "one of the abundant and characteristic warblers, seemingly much more plentiful than on the mainland." W. B. Tyrrell collected a male on Beaver May 7, 1929. A number were seen and others heard on June 17, 1940, in an arbor vitae swamp at the north end of Lake Manitou, North Manitou Island; a male was collected there June 18.

Nashville Warbler
Vermivora ruficapilla ruficapilla (Wilson)

Beaver (spn.); N. Manitou (obs.); S. Manitou (spn.); Trout (spn.).

A few seen in 1937 on Beaver 4 miles south and 12 miles southwest of St. James. The species was rather common and apparently breeding in the swampy parts of both Manitou islands in 1940; one male was collected on South Manitou June 11. Males in breeding condition were collected on Trout June 22 and 24, 1938.

Eastern Yellow Warbler
Dendroica petechia aestiva (Gmelin)

Beaver (spn.); Gull (spn.); Squaw (spn.); Trout (spn.); Whiskey (spn.).

A pair was noted at St. James and several individuals were seen north of Sandy Bay, Beaver Island, in 1937; one collected July 20 is a juvenile. Barrows' (1904, p. 81) report of this species as "abundant" may have referred to the smaller islands he visited rather than to Beaver Island. A male in breeding condition was collected on Gull June 16, 1938. In 1938 the species was common, and breeding males were collected, on Squaw, Trout, and Whiskey islands.

Magnolia Warbler
Dendroica magnolia (Wilson)

Beaver (rpt.); Squaw (obs.); Trout (spn.).

Barrows (1904, p. 81) saw a few on Beaver in 1904. A male was seen on Squaw July 5, and an incubating female collected on Trout June 26, 1938.

Black-throated Blue Warbler
Dendroica caerulescens caerulescens (Gmelin)

Beaver (spn.); N. Fox (spn.); N. Manitou (obs.); S. Fox (obs.).

A male was collected two miles west of St. James, Beaver Island, June 27, 1937. The species was common and apparently breeding on both Fox islands in 1939; males were collected on North Fox July 1 and 2. One individual was seen and several heard June 21, 1940, on North Manitou.

Myrtle Warbler
Dendroica coronata coronata (Linnaeus)

Beaver (spn., nst.).

James H. Wood collected a male on Beaver May 2, 1929. Barrows (1904, p. 81) noted two males at widely separated points on the island and heard others in the second week of July 1904, but found the species "far from plentiful." It was abundant, however, in 1937. A specimen in juvenal plumage was collected July 12, 1937, (north of Sandy Bay).

Black-throated Green Warbler
Dendroica virens virens (Gmelin)

Beaver (spn.); Gull (spn.); Hog (obs.); N. Fox (spn.); N. Manitou (spn.); S. Fox (obs.); S. Manitou (spn.); Squaw (spn.); Trout (spn.); Whiskey (obs.).

Common and apparently nesting on all of the islands listed above. Specimens in breeding condition were collected on most of the islands, and singing males were noted on the others.

Blackburnian Warbler
Dendroica fusca (Müller)

Beaver (spn.); Gull (spn.); S. Manitou (obs.); Trout (spn.).

V. H. Cahalane collected single males on Beaver Island May 24 and 28, 1932; in 1937 the species was found at Sandy Bay, Bonner's Bluff, and Iron Ore Bay. A breeding male was collected on Gull June 21, 1938, and an incubating female collected on Trout June 24, 1938. A male was observed on South Manitou August 30, 1944.

Chestnut-sided Warbler
Dendroica pensylvanica (Linnaeus)

Beaver (spn.); N. Manitou (spn.); S. Fox (spn.); S. Manitou (obs.); Trout (obs.).

This warbler was noted at several points and specimens were taken on Beaver in 1937. Several were seen and three specimens collected on North Manitou June 15-16, 1940. The species was rather common on South Fox in 1939 (male collected June 17). An individual was seen on South Manitou June 10, 1940, and Morrill noted an adult male on Trout June 23, 1938.

Black-poll Warbler
Dendroica striata (Forster)

Beaver (spn.).

V. H. Cahalane collected a female May 28, 1932.

Western Palm Warbler
Dendroica palmarum palmarum (Gmelin)

Beaver (spn.).

W. B. Tyrrell collected two specimens May 7, 1929, and James H. Wood collected one May 24, 1932. N. A. Wood noted the species May 10 and 11, 1929.

Oven-bird
Seiurus aurocapillus aurocapillus (Linnaeus)

Beaver (spn., nst.); Gull (obs.); N. Fox (obs.); N. Manitou (spn., nst.); S. Fox (spn.); S. Manitou (spn.); Squaw (obs.); Whiskey (obs.).

Abundant and nesting on Beaver in 1937. Several singing males were noted on Gull June 17-21, 1938. Noted on North Fox June 29-30, 1939; rather common on South Fox (one collected June 17) in 1939. Fairly common on both Manitou islands in 1940 (a recently fledged young bird collected on North Manitou July 3). At least three singing males were noted on Squaw (July 3-5) and one or more on Whiskey (June 29-July 1) in 1938.

Mourning Warbler
Oporornis philadelphia (Wilson)

Beaver (spn.); Gull (spn.); Hat (spn.); Squaw (spn.).

In 1937 this species was noted at several places on Beaver, and a breeding male was collected seven miles south of St. James on June

15. In 1938 a breeding male was collected on Gull June 20 and one on Squaw July 3. An adult female was taken on Hat July 9, 1938.

Northern Yellow-throat
Geothlypis trichas brachidactyla (Swainson)

Beaver (spn.); Hat (rpt.); N. Manitou (spn.); S. Manitou (spn.); Trout (spn.).

The Yellow-throat was common and apparently breeding on Beaver in 1937. On Hat, O. S. Pettingill, Jr., recorded four males heard singing July 1, 1940, and one July 1, 1943. In 1940 a male was collected on South Manitou June 9, and at least 15 Yellow-throats (female collected July 4) were seen on North Manitou. A breeding male was taken on Trout June 23, 1938.

Wilson's Warbler
Wilsonia pusilla pusilla (Wilson)

Beaver (spn.).

V. H. Cahalane collected a male May 22, 1932.

American Redstart
Setophaga ruticilla (Linnaeus)

Beaver (spn.); Gull (spn., nst.); Hat (spn., nst.); Hog (obs.); N. Fox (spn., nst.); N. Manitou (spn.); S. Fox (spn.); S. Manitou (spn.); Squaw (obs.); Trout (spn.); Whiskey (spn.).

The Redstart was abundant and apparently nesting on Beaver in 1937 and was common on Gull in 1938 (nest with four eggs found June 17). There were at least three pairs on Hat in 1938 (two newly fledged young collected July 9). The species was noted by Hatt on Hog Island July 11, 1938. It was one of the most abundant birds on both Fox islands in 1939 and was common on both Manitou islands in 1940. (A ratio of about two adult males to three immature males was noted on South Manitou, whereas the ratio on North Manitou was more than three adult males to one immature.) The species was common on Squaw, Trout, and Whiskey islands in 1938.

English Sparrow
Passer domesticus subsp.

Beaver (obs.); N. Manitou (obs.); S. Manitou (obs.).

Abundant at St. James and about farm buildings on Beaver (1937). Common about farm buildings on the Manitou islands (1940).

Bobolink
Dolichonyx oryzivorus (Linnaeus)

Beaver (spn.); Gull (spn.); N. Manitou (spn.); S. Fox (spn., nst.); S. Manitou (spn.).

The Bobolink was common in the more luxuriant hay fields on Beaver in 1937 and on the Manitou islands in 1940. A non-breeding female, collected on Gull June 17, 1938, was the only Bobolink seen on that island. Bobolinks were seen frequently in 1939 in the large clearing on South Fox; a female taken there June 18 was laying.

Eastern Meadowlark
Sturnella magna magna (Linnaeus)

Beaver (spn., nst.); S. Fox (obs.); S. Manitou (spn.).

The Eastern Meadowlark was common on Beaver in 1937 (nest with five eggs found by Morrill June 28). A pair was seen in the large clearing on South Fox June 19-26, 1939. The species was common in the large fields on South Manitou in 1940 (a male collected June 10).

Western Meadowlark
Sturnella neglecta Audubon

Beaver (obs.).

Hinshaw observed a singing male July 3, 1937, a half mile south of Font Lake.

Eastern Red-wing
Agelaius phoeniceus phoeniceus (Linnaeus)

Beaver (spn.); Gull (spn., nst.); Hat (spn., nst.); N. Manitou (spn., nst.); Pismire (obs.); S. Manitou (spn.); Squaw (spn., nst.); Trout (spn., nst.); Whiskey (spn., nst.).

The Red-wing was common on Beaver in 1937. There were at least two pairs on Gull in 1938 (a nest with four eggs found June 16). Four or more pairs were noted on Hat in 1938 (an incubating female collected July 8). About 20 pairs were nesting in a swamp on the west side of North Manitou in 1940; by July 4 many of the young were able to fly. On July 11, 1938, Hatt saw about eight Red-wings on Pismire. Between June 8 and 13, 1940, five or more Red-wings were seen in the clearing on the east side of South Manitou or about the small inland lake. There were several pairs on Squaw in 1938, and the young had left some nests by July 3. Four or more pairs were found on Trout in 1938 (an incubating female collected June 26).

There is no marsh habitat of the sort usually required by nesting Red-wings on Gull, Hat, Trout, or Whiskey islands, but the birds had adjusted to this and were nesting in a variety of places in the area between the water and the forest edge.

Red-wings of these islands tend to differ from those of the mainland of southern Michigan, which are typical *A. p. phoeniceus*. They are rather long-winged (one male's wing actually measures 131 mm.) but do not have the heavy bill characteristic of *arctolegus*. Females are slightly more heavily marked with black than most females from the mainland. (A total of 5 adult males and 8 adult females from the Manitou islands, 16 adult males and 13 adult females from the Beaver group, were examined.)

Baltimore Oriole
Icterus galbula (Linnaeus)

Beaver (nst.); S. Fox (obs.); S. Manitou (obs.).

A pair was found nesting at St. James, Beaver Island, in June 1937. A male was seen at the Plank farm, South Fox, on June 26, 1939. Several were in the orchards on South Manitou in June 1940.

Rusty Blackbird
Euphagus carolinus (Müller)

Beaver (rpt.).

N. A. Wood saw one Rusty Blackbird on Beaver May 6, 1929.

Bronzed Grackle
Quiscalus versicolor Vieillot

Beaver (spn.); S. Manitou (spn.).

Bronzed Grackles were common at St. James, Beaver Island, in 1937. Four were seen and specimens collected about the main settlement on South Manitou June 10, 1940.

Eastern Cowbird
Molothrus ater ater (Boddaert)

Beaver (spn., "nst."); N. Manitou (spn.); S. Fox (spn.); S. Manitou (obs.).

The Cowbird was abundant on Beaver in 1904 (Barrows, 1904, p. 79) and 1937; fully fledged juveniles were collected there July

14 and 15, 1937. The species was seen on both Manitou islands in 1940 but was the more numerous on North Manitou, where adult females were collected June 16 and 20. Several Cowbirds were seen in the clearings on South Fox in 1939 (two females collected June 24). The complete absence of Cowbirds from all of the smaller islands studied is a remarkable fact and may have a considerable effect on the breeding success of warblers and other small birds on those islands.

Scarlet Tanager
Piranga olivacea (Gmelin)

Beaver (spn.); N. Manitou (spn.); S. Fox (spn.); S. Manitou (spn.).

The species was present in small numbers on Beaver in 1937, and V. H. Cahalane collected two males there May 26, 1932. It was fairly common on both Manitou islands in 1940. One male was collected June 18 and another seen on June 24 on South Fox in 1939.

Cardinal
Richmondena cardinalis subsp.

S. Manitou (obs.).

Case saw an adult male near a farm on South Manitou June 13, 1940.

Rose-breasted Grosbeak
Pheucticus ludovicianus (Linnaeus)

Beaver (spn., nst.); Gull (obs.); N. Manitou (spn.); S. Manitou (spn.).

This grosbeak was common on Beaver in 1937 (fully fledged young taken July 11); N. A. Wood saw one there May 13, 1929. A male was seen on Gull June 18, 1938. The species was common on both Manitou islands in 1940.

Indigo Bunting
Passerina cyanea (Linnaeus)

Beaver (spn., nst.); Gull (spn., nst.); N. Manitou (spn.); S. Fox (spn.); S. Manitou (spn.).

The species was common on Beaver in 1937 (a fledgling collected July 17). On Gull, Barrows (1904, p. 80) reported a singing male the second week of July in 1904, and Van Tyne saw a male (June 16) and collected an incubating female (June 21) in 1938. A few were found in the largest clearing on North Manitou in 1940. The species was abundant on South Manitou in 1940 and common in the clearings on South Fox in 1939.

Evening Grosbeak
Hesperiphona vespertina subsp.

Beaver (obs.).

James H. Wood saw a small flock on Beaver May 10, 1928.

Eastern Purple Finch
Carpodacus purpureus purpureus (Gmelin)

Beaver (spn., nst.?); N. Manitou (obs.); S. Fox (spn.).

This finch was abundant on Beaver in 1937; a juvenile collected July 15, 1937, had probably been raised there. Case saw an adult male near the main settlement on North Manitou June 15, 1940. Several Purple Finches were seen and three specimens were collected about the deserted buildings in the small clearings on South Fox June 17-27, 1939.

Northern Pine Siskin
Spinus pinus pinus (Wilson)

Gull (spn.); N. Manitou (obs.); S. Manitou (spn.).

A male in breeding condition was collected on Gull June 18, 1938. One was seen on North Manitou July 1, 1940. Several were seen on South Manitou June 8-12, and a male was collected there June 9, 1940.

Eastern Goldfinch
Spinus tristis tristis (Linnaeus)

Beaver (spn.); Gull (spn.); N. Fox (obs.); N. Manitou (spn.); S. Fox (spn.); S. Manitou (spn.); Squaw (obs.).

This goldfinch was common on Beaver in 1937. A female was collected on Gull June 18, 1938. Only two goldfinches were noted (singly, June 29 and July 2—flying overhead) at North Fox in 1939, but a number were seen in the clearings on South Fox June 18-27. The species was fairly common on both Manitou islands in 1940. A flock of about eight was seen on Squaw July 4, 1938.

Red Crossbill
Loxia curvirostra minor (Brehm)

Beaver (spn.).

James H. Wood collected a male and a female May 6 and a male May 8, 1929.

White-winged Crossbill
Loxia leucoptera leucoptera Gmelin

Beaver (rpt.); Hat (spn.).

Barrows (1904, p. 80) saw a flock of six or seven White-winged Crossbills at St. James July 13, 1904. On July 1, 1940, O. S. Pettingill, Jr., collected a male from among small flocks, totalling some 50 individuals, that arrived on Hat Island from the west and, after a short pause, departed in an easterly direction.

Red-eyed Towhee
Pipilo erythrophthalmus erythrophthalmus (Linnaeus)

Beaver (spn.); Marion (obs.); N. Fox (spn.); N. Manitou (obs.); S. Fox (spn.); S. Manitou (obs.).

The Red-eyed Towhee was common on Beaver in 1937. A few were seen on Marion Island July 23-28, 1923; they were living deep in the big hardwood forest that covered most of the island (Van Tyne, 1925, p. 623). A few were noted and breeding specimens collected on the Fox islands in 1939. Several were seen on the Manitou islands in 1940.

Churchill Savannah Sparrow
Passerculus sandwichensis oblitus Peters and Griscom

Beaver (spn.).

The Savannah Sparrow was common in the northern part of the island in 1937; specimens taken (July 4-12) were in breeding condition.

Eastern Grasshopper Sparrow
Ammodramus savannarum pratensis (Vieillot)

Beaver (spn.); N. Manitou (spn.); S. Fox (obs.); S. Manitou (spn.).

A few were seen and specimens in breeding condition collected in the northern part of Beaver July 4-20, 1937. A few were seen, and seemed to be nesting, in the largest clearing of South Fox June 25-27, 1939. The species was common in the large fields of both

Eastern Vesper Sparrow
Pooecetes gramineus gramineus (Gmelin)

Beaver (spn.); N. Fox (spn., nst.); N. Manitou (spn., nst.); S. Fox (spn.); S. Manitou (spn.).

The Vesper Sparrow was abundant on Beaver in 1937. It was common and apparently nesting about the shore lines of both Fox islands and in the larger clearings of South Fox in 1939. Fledglings were seen on North Fox on June 30. A few individuals were found in the largest fields of both Manitou islands in 1940; a nest with four eggs that were nearly ready to hatch was found on North Manitou June 15, 1940.

Slate-colored Junco
Junco hyemalis subsp.

Beaver (rpt.).

N. A. Wood saw a number (up to 10 in a day) May 3-15, 1929.

Eastern Chipping Sparrow
Spizella passerina passerina (Bechstein)

Beaver (spn., nst.); Gull (spn.); N. Manitou (spn.); S. Fox (spn.); S. Manitou (spn.).

The Chipping Sparrow was abundant on Beaver in 1904 (Barrows, 1904, p. 80) and in 1937, when adult specimens in breeding condition were taken (June 10-15) and a juvenile was collected (at Barney Lake, July 17). A breeding male was taken on Gull June 22, 1938. The species was fairly common in the larger clearings of South Fox in 1939. It was the most common sparrow and perhaps the most common bird on both Manitou islands in 1940.

Clay-colored Sparrow
Spizella pallida (Swainson)

S. Fox (spn.); Whiskey (spn.).

Several were heard singing and two males in breeding condition were collected in the largest clearing on South Fox June 26, 1939. On June 29, 1938, a singing male in breeding condition was collected on Whiskey Island. These are the first summer records of this species

Eastern Field Sparrow
Spizella pusilla pusilla (Wilson)

S. Fox (spn., nst.).

The Field Sparrow was quite common in the two larger clearings on South Fox in 1939; an incubating female was collected June 23.

White-crowned Sparrow
Zonotrichia leucophrys subsp.

Beaver (rpt.).

N. A. Wood reported this species May 8, 11, and 13, 1929.

White-throated Sparrow
Zonotrichia albicollis (Gmelin)

Beaver (spn.).

N. A. Wood reported the species May 6, 8, 9, 13, and 14, and W. B. Tyrrell collected a specimen May 7, in 1929. In 1937 several were seen in the vicinity of Sandy Bay, and four specimens in breeding condition were collected (June 24, July 22).

Swamp Sparrow
Melospiza georgiana georgiana (Latham)

Beaver (rpt.); N. Manitou (spn.).

N. A. Wood reported this species on Beaver June 15, 1922. An adult male was collected in a swamp on the west side of North Manitou June 19, 1940; it was not in breeding condition.

Mississippi Song Sparrow
Melospiza melodia euphonia Wetmore

Beaver (spn.); Gull (spn.); Hat (spn., nst.); N. Fox (spn., nst.); N. Manitou (spn.); S. Fox (spn.); S. Manitou (spn.); Squaw (spn., nst.); Trout (spn., nst.); Whiskey (obs.).

The Song Sparrow was abundant on Beaver in 1904 (Barrows, 1904, p. 80) and in 1937. The species occurred on all of the small islands (Gull, Hat, Squaw, Trout, and Whiskey) that were visited in 1938 but was common only on Hat. The species was restricted to the west shores of the Fox islands (1939) but was common there. Only 10 or 12 were seen on the Manitou islands in 1940. Specimens taken on all of the islands were in breeding condition, but laying females or young birds were taken only on the islands listed above for which nesting has been indicated. A total of 39 specimens was collected on the islands.

Snow Bunting
Plectrophenax nivalis subsp.

Beaver (rpt.).

N. A. Wood saw one Snow Bunting on Beaver May 4, 1929.

7. The Mammals

FEW SPECIES of mammals have reached and established themselves on the islands without the help of man. The evidence indicates that but a quarter of the species represented on the nearby mainland can be included in our list of indigenous island mammals.

Most of those mammals which appear not to have reached the islands may be grouped in one or another of several categories based on an explanation of absence. For other species the record is not satisfactory, or the reasons for their (at least apparent) absence are not understood.

Recent arrivals on the mainland shores:

These animals, prairie or second-growth inhabitants, have reached the mainland opposite the islands so recently that they have not had adequate opportunity to cross, or sufficient population pressure to induce them to cross, the barriers of water or ice.

    Coyote   Prairie Deermouse (1 exception)
    Ground Squirrel   White-footed Mouse*
                Cottontail (2 exceptions)

Winter Sleepers:

These animals are largely inactive during the winter season, when crossing to the islands would be easiest, and none of them are species that inhabit driftwood in which they might unwittingly be transported.

    Bear   Woodchuck
    Skunk   Woodland Jumping Mouse
    Raccoon   Meadow Jumping Mouse
                Porcupine

Large animals inadequately recorded:

These animals may once have been on several of the islands though no record of their presence remains.

    Marten   Wolf
    Fisher   Cougar
    Wolverine   Canada Lynx
    Gray Fox   Moose

---

*Peromyscus leucopus noveboracensis

Beyond these listed animals there is a considerable assortment of species inhabiting the eastern and northern shores of Lake Michigan which are not known on the islands. For several, there is a distinct possibility that their (seeming) absence from the islands is due only to the brevity of the collecting time or inadequacy of collecting techniques. Such may be considered particularly possible in the case of four species of bats, five species of shrews, two species of weasel, the Bobcat, and, already listed as sleepers, two jumping mice. Other animals excluded from the list of indigenous island mammals are:

Star-nosed Mole	**Southern Flying Squirrel**
Prairie Mole	Lemming Vole
Badger	Red-backed Vole
Least Chipmunk	Meadow Vole
Red Squirrel	Pine Vole
(one record)	Muskrat
Gray Squirrel	Wharf Rat
Fox Squirrel	House Mouse
Northern Flying Squirrel	Deer

Of these, two species commensal with man, the Wharf Rat and House Mouse, appear to have made colonies that failed to survive, owing perhaps to the dwindling human occupation of the islands. Their temporary establishment may be as confidently attributed to human introduction as was that of the Deer and Raccoon of North Manitou, the Skunks of North Fox, and others.

The Deer, now present only where introduced, may easily have been an inhabitant of the larger islands and a visitor to the others before the time of firearms.

Of the remaining animals on the above list there appears to be no exclusion based on inadequacy of island habitats on the larger islands, and we must examine the extent of the water and ice barriers for reasons for their absence. This seems to be particularly difficult to understand in the case of such noted swimmers as the Muskrat and the Red Squirrel. That the Eastern Chipmunk, *Tamias*, has bridged the waters several times, and the Least Chipmunk, *Eutamias*, has not, is not understood, though it may be pointed out that the more distant Wisconsin-Upper Peninsula shore is the eastern limit of *Eutamias*, whereas *Tamias* is abundant on both this shore and the eastern shore. Chipmunks have not attained the Apostle Islands of Lake Superior (Jackson, 1920), though shrews, Meadow and Red-backed Voles are present there. Lake currents would favor introductions by drift from the eastern shore.

Absence of certain mammals from certain islands does not, of course, necessarily imply an inability to reach the islands, or extermination by man. On many there is no suitable cover for a particular species or the size of the islands is not great enough to permit establishment of a permanent colony. Absence of suitable habitat, for example, would explain the absence of the Muskrat from Gull, Trout, Whiskey, Squaw, Hat, Shoe, Pismire, the Foxes, and Marion, but not from the Manitous, Beaver, and High before introductions. Nor will absence of suitable habitat explain the disappearance of a thriving Muskrat colony from South Manitou Island.

Eastern Chipmunks are established on at least five of the islands. Of these, the Manitous, Beaver, and South Fox have all supported flourishing agricultural and lumbering communities, and the possibility of introduction by boat is not to be excluded. On North Fox, however, there has never been well-established human occupation and the possibility of introduction by this means appears negligible. Nor is there knowledge that the Indians would ever introduce such an animal as a chipmunk in their canoes. It is considered that chipmunks are on the islands by virtue of their having reached them on driftwood; that the larger islands, because they are better targets for floating drift and have more extensive favorable ecologic conditions, are those on which chipmunks are established.

For other mammals known or believed to occur on the islands there appears likelihood of access by drift in a few instances: shrew, weasel, Red Squirrel (problematical), and Woodland Deermouse.

The two bats recorded on the islands obviously crossed by flight.

Animals known to have used the winter ice for crossings are the Red Fox, Hare, and Caribou. No island mammal but the chipmunk could be excluded as a traverser of the ice, although the distances seem too great for mice and shrews to travel over snow or ice without sustenance.

Man has purposely introduced the Raccoon, Skunk, Gray Squirrel, Fox Squirrel, Beaver, Muskrat, and Deer. With the exception of the Skunk, Beaver, and one of the Muskrat introductions, these species have become well established.

Man's commensal species, cat, Wharf Rat, House Mouse, and hog, have from time to time become part of the islands' wild faunas, but none of these is known to have long survived independent of human habitation.

Man has extirpated from the islands at least three of the species once reported there: Otter, Beaver, and Woodland Caribou.

Of the mammals that occur in both the Upper Peninsula and the Lower Peninsula and are represented by distinct subspecies on each side of the Lake, only three have island records. One of these, the Mink, is not known by any island specimen, and another, the Gray Squirrel, is believed to be introduced. Thus, among the mammals, only the chipmunk *Tamias* might give a clue to the source of island faunas. As this genus is thought to have reached its several islands recently by means of either flotsam or boats, it would not be expected that the island populations would show marked somatic differences, and the specimens in general bear this out. Hooper (1942b) stated that chipmunks of South Fox Island resemble the Upper Peninsula race; those on Beaver Island, the Lower Peninsula subspecies; and that specimens from the Manitou Islands are more like the Lower Peninsula stock than that of the Upper Peninsula. The absence of *Eutamias* from the islands is important evidence *against* the Upper Peninsula origin of the island faunas.

ANNOTATED LIST

Short-tailed Shrew
Blarina brevicauda kirtlandi Bole and Moulthrop

Marion (spn.).

Dice (1925a) found this shrew common on Marion Island, but we have no clear proof of its presence on any other island. Considerable trapping in favorable habitats and unavailing search for the characteristic tunnels in the forest leaf mold have convinced us that shrews occur rarely, if at all, on the other islands. That some species of shrew is present on North Manitou is, however, suggested by descriptions by North Manitou residents. One described an animal seen as "like a mole, but not a mole. It had a sharp nose and was much smaller than a mouse." In 1940 we found a few tunnels in the leaf mold of the beech-maple forest at the northeast corner of the island, which may have been shrew work.

Little Brown Bat
Myotis lucifugus lucifugus (Le Conte)
Trout (spn.).

An adult male was caught June 15, on Trout Island, by a bird net hung in the abandoned house in which we made camp. Other bats, which were probably of this species, were seen in flight above Whiskey and Beaver islands.

Red Bat
Lasiurus borealis borealis (Müller)
N. Manitou (obs.); S. Fox (spn.).

In 1916 Hatt saw a Red Bat hanging in a hollow stub, exposed to a moderate degree of sunlight and not over eight feet from the ground. Another North Manitou sight record of this species is from one of the residents. A mandible was recovered from a fox(?) scat on South Fox Island. There is no reason to doubt that this and all the species of bats known on the mainland occur on all of the islands.

Raccoon
Procyon lotor lotor (Linnaeus)
Beaver (unce.); N. Fox (unce.); N. Manitou (obs., intr.); S. Manitou (unce.); S. Fox (unce.).

The Raccoon, because it is not active in the winter nor habitually a swimmer, probably has not reached any of these islands without the help of man. On North Manitou it was introduced several years before 1937 and by that year was abundant. The presence on the island of many old hardwoods and two inland lakes with marshy shores proved favorable to the Raccoons, and their increase made them unpopular because of their supposed predation upon gallinaceous birds which were also introduced on the island. On one rainy afternoon Hatt encountered three of the animals. The first, seen about 2:00 p.m., was at the edge of a clearing near the west shore; the others, seen together about 3:30 p.m., were in the wet woods bordering the larger inland lake. All three took refuge in hollow trees. Tracks were encountered on the Lake Michigan beaches and in trails and woodlands elsewhere on the island.

Two informants stated that Raccoons were once introduced on South Manitou by Mr. Henry Haice but were now gone. We could find no evidence of their presence in 1940 or 1944.

There is one report of Raccoon on Beaver Island, but it has no support in our observations. A scat found on South Fox may possibly have been that of a Raccoon. One of our party saw tracks on North Fox which he attributed to Raccoons.

Weasels
Mustela frenata noveboracensis (Emmons) and other weasels
Marion (spn.); N. Manitou (rpt.).

Three species of weasels (*M. frenata noveboracensis, M. erminea cicognanii* and *M. rixosa allegheniensis*) occur on the mainland of the Lower Peninsula, and two of them are known to occur near the beaches directly opposite the Manitous, but there is no known specimen from any of the islands except Marion, on which Dice (1925a, p. 6) trapped a specimen of *M. f. noveboracensis*. Mr. Ed McKee reported specifically having seen a white weasel on North Manitou Island one winter, and another resident spoke of a few being there.

Mink
Mustela vison mink Peale and Beauvois
Marion (rpt.).

The report of a few Mink on Marion Island is quoted by Dice (1925a, p. 7).

Otter
Lutra canadensis canadensis (Schreber)
Beaver (rpt.).

Otter were reported scarce on the Beaver Islands by Strang (1855, p. 282). We have no recent record of them on these islands.

Skunk
Mephitis mephitis nigra (Peale and Beauvois)
N. Fox (rpt., intr.).

A prospectus of the North Fox Island Fur Farm, received about 1922, states: "We already have 500 to 600 skunks on the island and they are doing fine. As everyone knows, the skunk is the most hardy and most prolific animal of the animal kingdom." A letter from an official of the company, written subsequently, was however more modest, for he stated that "a few" were introduced in 1920.

We sought some remnant of this colony in 1938, but without success. On the sand dune of the island there were some pits similar to those made by Skunks in search of beetle larvae, but the maker's tracks were obliterated. Scats secured, identified by an independent observer as "probably Skunk," contained remains of berries, beetles, bird, chipmunk, and the mandible of a young Hare, well chewed.

Red Fox
Vulpes fulva (Desmarest)

Beaver (sgn., rpt.); Gull (sgn.); N. Fox (sgn., rpt.); N. Manitou (spn.); S. Fox (sgn., rpt.); S. Manitou (sgn., rpt.); Squaw (rpt.); Whiskey (sgn.).

The Red Fox is an active winter wanderer that is not infrequently seen on the ice of Lake Michigan, and there is good reason to believe that it has many times visited every island in the lakes. Some of the islands are too small to support foxes for any length of time, and on the smaller, a fox marooned with few Hares and few mice might soon starve or be forced to swim to another island. Dr. F. E. Ludwig has reported to us that in 1939 there were no successful gull nests on Hat Island and that at the time of his visit, though many nests had been built, only a few old birds were on the island. Broken eggs were found under bushes, and it was postulated that a fox had been marooned on the island and had turned to the nests for food. The larger islands probably have a few foxes at all times.

One of the most persistent stories of the island region is that on North Manitou foxes are abundant but that on South Manitou they do not stay because the farmers are too active with their guns. This story has been repeated to us by many people and for many years and may have a slight basis in fact. North Manitou is considerably larger, less settled, furnished with more cover and more chipmunks and should have more foxes. That foxes are common there in some years is incontestable, but on South Manitou, also, we found their tracks and have this proof of their occurrence. There was another story to the effect that about 1936 three foxes crossed to South Manitou from North Manitou, that two of these returned, leaving only one (three-legged) fox on the island. Such tracks as we found on South Manitou were of four-legged foxes.

Foxes have been occasionally seen on the ice between North Manitou and the mainland by Tracy Grosvenor, mail boat pilot. We have records of successful fox hunts on this island, in 1921 and 1922, and the word of many persons that foxes are usually common here and unpopular, for attempts have been made to reduce their numbers. An adult female fox was shot by Hatt July 4, in a woods road on the west side, where she had been seen almost daily by others that summer. Her measurements were: total length, 1000 mm.; tail, 360; hind foot, 160; ear, 90. There was no indication that she had recently bred. Her stomach contained one deermouse, one chipmunk, and parts of two or more beetles.

If there is anything in a name, foxes must long have been on the Fox islands. We have a tuft of fur of the Red Fox, picked out of some brush near the beach on South Fox, but this could have blown in with the wind. The lightkeepers here knew there was some "large animal" on the island that came across on the ice about 1929, but they did not know whether it was fox, Coyote, dog, Bobcat, or something else. We found freshly made tracks in the soft algal drift on the north end of the island (Fig. 22) and preserved them, also sketched and measured them when fresh, but it cannot be said conclusively that these were Red Fox tracks. If they were, the soft under-footing made them atypical, or the animal was an extraordinarily large fox. Staebler reports fox tracks in the sand on South Fox in 1939 and also on North Fox. What would seem to be Red Fox scats, secured on South Fox, contained the following: arbor vitae leaves, grape seed, berries, crayfish carapace, beetle wings, fish vertebrae, feathers, mandible of a Red Bat, chipmunk bones, large skull and other fragments of an adult Hare. Some of these items suggest Raccoon rather than Red Fox. A single scat, probably of a fox, was secured on North Fox. It contained remnants of a bird, and beetle wings. A former light keeper of South Fox told us that he had known of foxes crossing on the ice from the mainland on one or two occasions. The best record is that of Mr. I. H. Bartlett who saw a Red Fox on South Fox Island in May 1945.

Of the Beaver Islands, Strang (1855, p. 282) stated: "Foxes, red, quite numerous. Foxes, black, scarce; silver grey, very rare." By the last the Gray Fox may have been meant. In 1938, Hatt found a rather large and conspicuous den in a sandy forested ridge in back of Point Lapar. The several Hare skulls on the talus suggested Red Fox, but the prominence of the sand pile was strange, as was the presence of five openings to the den. Residents stated that fox shooting is little done on Beaver island.

On Gull Island, fox tracks were frequently seen on the beaches in 1938, sometimes passing close to occupied gull nests without there being evidence of disturbance. Hares were abundant on the island as a good food supply.

A fox scat from Whiskey Island contained teeth of a Hare.

On Squaw Island fishermen reported that both fox and Hare tracks were common here in the winter of 1937-38 and that the foxes were heard barking in the early summer. These same men stated that both the foxes and Hares cross from one island to another every winter.

House Cat
Felis catus Linnaeus

S. Manitou (obs.).

House Cats were encountered as far as two miles from dwellings on South Manitou Island, and several residents spoke of them as established as a wild species there. One of those seen in the woods was short-tailed, as are many of the less feral cats of South Manitou.

Bobcat
Lynx rufus rufus (Schreber)

Beaver (unce.).

We have the word of a Beaver Island resident that he once saw the skin of a Bobcat that had been taken on Beaver Island.

Eastern Chipmunks
Tamias striatus griseus Mearns

S. Fox (spn.).

and
Tamias striatus peninsulae Hooper

Beaver (spn.); N. Fox (spn.); N. Manitou (spn.); S. Manitou (spn.).

Chipmunks are conspicuous in the forests of each of the larger islands on which collecting was done. Their absence from the smaller islands, even Marion, which lies close to the mainland, is equally noticeable. Their absence from these little islands may be a matter of chance, a small island being a smaller target for the driftwood which may ferry chipmunks, but it is equally likely, if the island populations are cyclic, that the smaller areas do not support an adequate residual population for breeding at the low point of a population cycle.

Jackson (1920, p. 63) concluded that absence of chipmunks from the Apostle Islands, Lake Superior, could be explained on the basis of their winter inactivity alone. Yet in Lake Michigan we have the bridging of far greater water gaps by these animals, and, at least on Beaver Island, the populations have been long established, for Strang reported them there in 1853. Swimming, and crossing of ice, being improbable means of access, and intentional introduction unlikely, only driftwood remains as a likely vehicle for them.

The apparent differences of chipmunks on these islands indicated by Hooper (1942b) are not inconsistent with the postulated accidental distribution by drift or boat. The occurrence of *griseus* on South Fox and *peninsulae* on the Manitous and Beaver is surprising but not impossible.

In the region of the upper Lakes Eastern Chipmunks are typically found in virgin forests or second-growth hardwood forests, though occurring also about dwellings and in brushy areas in or bordering the forests. On the islands this distribution also holds. They are seen everywhere among the hardwoods, occasionally at heights of 25 feet or more in the trees. Though we took them at the border of a marsh on Beaver Island, this was still in the forest. We have not taken them nor seen them in the driftwood of the Lake Michigan beaches, where they should be found if one is to postulate their distribution by driftwood.

The abundance of the chipmunks on islands where they occur at all is bound to impress one. Whether this apparently universal abundance is due to our having collected chiefly at places and times the animals were at peak of population; whether they are always abundant on these islands owing to the absence of predators or competition, or freedom from parasites, we cannot say. But the abundance is real, and not merely a delusion occasioned by animals active and fearless from lack of predator restraint.

On North Manitou in August 1931 we found them very abundant, and again so in June and July 1940. For example, 48 traps in 2 days held 7 chipmunks and no mice. Perhaps twice this many chipmunks entered the traps and were able to escape. On Beaver in late July 1938, 100 traps held 20 chipmunks and one mouse on the first day set, and similar ratios occurred other days on other lines set on this island.

Red Squirrel
Tamiasciurus hudsonicus loquax (Bangs)

N. Manitou (obs.); S. Manitou (unce.).

Although the Red Squirrel is abundant along the shores of Wisconsin and Michigan and is known to be a capable swimmer (Hatt, 1929, p. 35) and has been seen in the middle of Lake Champlain, where the lake is seven miles broad, the animal has been unsuccessful in establishing itself on any of the islands in upper Lake Michigan. Ecologically, all of these islands which bear forests appear well suited to the squirrel, but the water barriers, even in the instance of the one-mile stretch separating Marion Island from Mission Point, have proved effectual. The Red Squirrel is well established on Isle Royale, where it has become a distinct species, and it also is reported (Jackson, 1920, p. 62) in the Apostle Islands of Lake Superior where the narrowest water gap from mainland to an island is 1.5 miles. In this latter instance it was Jackson's inference that the Red Squirrels gained access to the island over the ice. Two informants on South Manitou Island were sure that Red Squirrels were on the island, and one of these men said that the squirrels were introduced. Three others, however, asserted vigorously that the Red Squirrel has never been on this island and that those who claimed it was present must have mistaken chipmunks for Red Squirrels. Though we spent much time in suitable habitats there we found no trace of these animals more definite than a few old jack pine cones which appeared to have been opened by a Red Squirrel.

On North Manitou all informants agreed that the Red Squirrel was not present, and all evidence which Hatt collected would substantiate this, but Case, on July 2, reported being scolded by a Red Squirrel that remained in full view at a distance of but 15 feet. Though Hatt searched the same area the following day, he could find no trace of Red Squirrels. The spot was in a hardwood stand in about the center of the east shore. Hatt's earlier (1924, p. 399) credence of a report of this animal on the Fox islands now seems certainly unjustified.

One must conclude that the Red Squirrel seen on North Manitou either was a recent arrival or one of very few present. If Red Squirrels have reached South Manitou they have not founded a population any more conspicuous than on North Manitou.

The possibility remains that the Red Squirrel, whose numbers are subject to periodic fluctuation, may be a species restricted in its island distribution by its inability to remain established when the population is at a low ebb.

Gray Squirrel
Sciurus carolinensis hypophaeus Merriam

Beaver (spn., intr.); High (rpt., intr.).

The Gray Squirrel is presumably an introduction on Beaver Island, since Strang (1855, p. 282) did not report it in the last century and it is not known to occur on the other islands except High Island where, according to Mr. Sherman Moore, it was introduced about 1910. The two squirrels which we took were on a red pine ridge about 500 yards behind Point Lapar.

Burt (1943, p. 6) considers Beaver Island specimens referable to the Upper Peninsula form, *hypophaeus,* rather than to *leucotis* of the Lower Peninsula. There appears to be no record or memory of the introduction.

Mr. Moore, who conducted lake surveys in this region during summers around 1915, is also authority for the statement that the High Island colonists of the House of David, constrained from killing by their religious beliefs, would live-trap the squirrels when the corn was ripe, pen them up and feed them and turn them loose after the harvest.

Fox Squirrel
Sciurus niger rufiventer (Geoffroy)

N. Manitou (obs., intr.); S. Manitou (sgn., intr.).

The Fox Squirrel, popular as a game species and not generally considered a nuisance, has been introduced on the Manitous and is now established on both. It was introduced on North Manitou about 1905, according to Mr. John Mileski, who had lived much of his life there. Other reports of its presence reached us in 1922. In 1940 both the squirrels and their nests were frequently seen by our party.

The South Manitou introduction dates from about 1920, according to Mr. Henry Haice, a resident at that time. The squirrel did not seem common in the summer of 1940. A few tracks were seen at the end of the island farthest from the settlement.

Fox Squirrels are known to have been present on the mainland of Leelanau County in 1875 (Etta Wilson, personal communication) and have probably always been there.

Beaver
Castor canadensis subsp.

Beaver (rpt.); N. Manitou (rpt., intr.).

Two adult Beaver were introduced into Tamarac Lake on North Manitou Island between 1921 and 1931, and here they built a lodge which was conspicuous until at least 1940, but the Beaver have since disappeared. It is commonly presumed that the Beaver may have been of one sex since no progeny was ever observed. The two may, however, simply have moved out, for in 1940 on the northwest shore of Lake Manitou, several miles from the point of introduction, Hatt saw cuttings, probably one to two years old, and heard one report that a Beaver was seen in Lake Michigan about 1939, near the east shore of the island.

Beaver Island doubtless has its name from the former presence of Beaver on the island. Maps as early as 1744 named the island *Ile du Castor*. A building said to have been once occupied by the American Fur Company still stands in the village of St. James. Strang noted (1855, p. 282) that Beaver were extinct in his time. It may be presumed that the Beavers originally occupied Beaver Island by swimming there. Small colonies might have occupied High Island and the Manitous since there are inland lakes on each, but the other islands would seem to have afforded no suitable permanent shelter.

Woodland Deermouse
Peromyscus maniculatus gracilis (Le Conte)
Figure 43

Beaver (spn.); Gull (spn.); Marion (spn.); N. Fox (spn.); N. Manitou (spn.); S. Fox (spn.); S. Manitou (spn.); Squaw (spn.); Trout (spn.); Whiskey (spn.).

The Woodland Deermouse, though almost entirely replaced on the mainland by *P. leucopus noveboracensis* (in the forests) and *P. m. bairdii* (in the cleared land in southern Michigan, and on beaches and dunes), remains abundant on many of the islands, on beaches and in woods. It is believed to be absent only from the smallest (Hat, Shoe, Pismire) islands. On some it is the only resident mammal, and it is the only native mouse known to occur on any of the islands on which our expeditions made collections. Though the island beaches would be favorable for *bairdii*, and most of the islands, being wooded, would be suitable for *noveboracensis*, it is probable that each of these has reached the mainland shores near the islands too recently to have made the passage.

The Woodland Deermice, which on the mainland are restricted to dense mixed forest (Dice, 1925b, p. 22; Hooper, 1942a, p. 193), occurred in all of the situations on the islands in which trapping was done, though they may not occur over the larger sand dunes or in some of the wetter areas. We obtained the mice on the islands on open sandy beach, the driftwood line of the upper beaches, in wet muddy beaches, in the reedy borders to beach pools, in varied heath lands, in fields, and in all forest types, from arbor vitae swamp and mature beech-maple forest to young second growth. Thus, without interspecific competition these mice flourish in virtually all terrestrial habitats, whereas on the mainland they would be supplanted in many of these sites by two other deermice, by the House Mouse, and by the Meadow Vole.

The island deermice are, however, not equally successful in all habitats, as indicated by trap-catch ratios on single islands. For example, on Gull Island the catch per 100 trap-nights was as follows: upper beach, 30; balsam forest, 18; heaths, 12.

Populations on different islands in any one season vary greatly in density. In 1938 the catch per 100 trap-nights on islands in the Beaver group was as follows: Trout, 2; Beaver, 4; Gull, 17; Whiskey, 22; Squaw, 23. In only one instance does what seems to us a satisfactory explanation of these differences appear, namely, that of similar and adjacent Trout and Whiskey islands. On the former, where mice and other ground-dwelling vertebrates were very rare, ants of several species were exceptionally abundant, so much so as to preëmpt many situations in which mice would occur. This matter is more fully discussed on p. 152. The findings reported by Elton (1942) of simultaneous fluctuations of lemming populations on isolated islands would lead one to presume that the differences in abundance reported above are not representative of cyclic differences, but rather of environmental differences not yet adequately analyzed. This particular group of islands seems to offer a very good place in which to study normal fluctuations of island populations of mice.

Fleas were removed from three of the Woodland Deermice collected on Trout Island. There were four species, each previously known from deermice in the eastern United States. As identified by Dr. Karl Jordan, Director of the Zoological Museum, Tring, England, these are:

Ctenophthalmus pseudargytes Baker
Peromyscopsylla hesperomys (Baker)
Epitedia wenmanni (Rothschild)
Orchopeas leucopus Baker

Our notes do not suggest that these mice were more than usually parasitized, and there is no reason to suppose that the local rarity of mice is to be attributed to a high incidence of parasitism. Of 12 mice examined July 16 on South Manitou Island, all had fleas (apparently of two or more species though they are not yet identified). One also had a dead tick behind an ear, and another was mangy, lacking a third of its hair.

The nests of these mice, as true of most rodents, are made of whatever suitable material is at hand. One nest under drift on a wet beach was entirely of green moss. Most of the many nests found under beach drift were of comminuted dry vegetable matter, a few of them lined with gull feathers. In one, breast feathers of a flicker were conspicuous. One striking nest (Fig. 43) was found under a bushel basket at the edge of a dry field. Half the basket was filled with the dry, lustrous white seed parachutes of the common milkweed, from which all of the seeds had been eaten. One nest cavity occurred in this bulky mass.

The partially carnivorous nature of the mice is indicated by the varied debris around their nests in beach drift. Bird bones, fish bones, crayfish armor, and snail shells were almost invariably found at feeding spots under drift close to the nest. At one nest, under an old door, about 10 feet from the water's edge on a protected shore, were found three, somewhat fresh, small fish and two crayfish, seemingly stored for later use.

Prairie Deermouse
Peromyscus maniculatus bairdii (Hoy and Kennicott)

Fisherman's (spn.).

This invader from the South was found by Dice (1925b, p. 24) on Fisherman's Island, Charlevoix County. The "island," however, is insular only in years of high water, and so this occurrence is without significance to problems of island distribution.

Meadow Vole
Microtus pennsylvanicus pennsylvanicus (Ord)

Marion (spn.).

Not the least interesting of the oddities of island distribution is the presence of this mouse on the beaches and in the forests of Marion Island (Dice, 1925a, p. 7). Here, out of their normal milieu, they were almost as abundant as the deermice.

Careful search for these mice in apparently favorable situations on the other islands failed to reveal their presence. Jackson (1920), however, found them on islands of the Apostle group where separation from the mainland was not less than 1.5 miles.

Muskrat
Ondatra zibethica zibethica (Linnaeus)

Beaver (rpt., intr.); S. Manitou (rpt., intr.).

Muskrats, which could probably reach any island in this group either by swimming or traveling over the ice, are absent even where they would be expected to thrive. Possibly the large lake trout form a cordon they cannot pass, or possibly Muskrats over a period spanning a population cycle require more of a reservoir of population than these islands could maintain, though mainland observations on restricted colonies seem not to support such a theory. Islands with suitable habitats for the Muskrat are South and North Manitou, Beaver, High, Garden, and Hog. Only on Beaver are they now established and this, according to report, by introduction. On this island the animals are said to occur in only some of the lakes. In Miller's Marsh, where conditions seemed ideal, Hatt found no Muskrat houses.

Muskrats were introduced on South Manitou several years ago, and two of the island's residents claim the honor of the introduction. One of these men stated that he put out two males and four females and that for a time the colony thrived to such an extent that he was able to trap 30. In times of high water the animals were said to move into the marsh at the head of the island lake. Eventually, however, the animals disappeared and certainly were not there in 1940 when our field work was done.

House Mouse
Mus musculus Linnaeus

N. Manitou (spn.).

The only definite island record of the House Mouse is a specimen which was trapped in 1931 on North Manitou. This was taken in a barn at the main settlement. It is quite possible, of course, that if more trapping had been done in dwellings many more records of this mouse would have been made.

Wharf Rat
Rattus norvegicus (Erxleben)

N. Manitou (rpt.); S. Fox (rpt.); S. Manitou (rpt.).

The Wharf Rat is common in towns and on farms on the mainland shores. Doubtless, during the days when larger boats came to some of the islands this rat was temporarily established.

Informants stated that rats were on South Manitou in the days of schooners but are now gone, and a similar statement was made concerning South Fox Island by a lightkeeper there. A life-long resident of North Manitou told us in 1931 that a few years earlier, house rats "overran" the island but that they were now all gone. An earlier credited report (Hatt, 1924, p. 397) of their occurrence on unfarmed North Fox is retracted.

Porcupine
Erethizon dorsatum dorsatum (Linnaeus)

N. and S. Fox (unce.).

Though one member of our expedition reported Porcupine tracks on each of the Fox islands it is considered by the editor that their presence there, unnoted by others, is so unlikely that the identification should not be accepted until supported.

Snowshoe Hare, "Lobfoot"
Lepus americanus phaeonotus Allen

Beaver (spn.); Gull (spn.); Hat (sgn.); High (spn.); N. Fox (spn.); N. Manitou (sgn.); S. Fox (spn.); S. Manitou (obs.); Squaw (sgn.); Trout (spn.); Whiskey (spn.).

The Snowshoe Hare, active in winter and widely ranging over the ice, has probably visited every island in Lake Michigan, for on all but the smallest, living Hares, bones, or Hare scats were found. It is firmly established on all of the larger islands, and doubtless is a major food source for the foxes. Whether its own cyclic decline eliminates island populations or whether the foxes alone are responsible is not known, but Hare bones occurred on some small islands on which no Hares existed at the time of our visits. Any island or every island may be presumed to get new Hare stock in any winter that the ice covers the intervening waters and mainland populations are high.

Hares do not escape epidemics on the islands. On South Fox an abandoned barn was found in which there were 14 dead Hares that had used the place for shelter or gone there frequently to gnaw the salty boards. Pope saw one live Hare on South Fox which Purple Martins were chasing through the grass near the lighthouse. The Hare appeared sick. Lightkeepers there said that the Hares died by the hundreds from ticks, about two years previously (1935), and recalled that during a period of over-abundance some years earlier, when the island was farmed, the women drove the Hares to the gunners. Staebler found many tracks of Hares in 1938.

In 1940, Hares were scarce on the Manitous, according to visual evidence and reports by residents. The Hares may have been at the peak of a population cycle on Gull Island in 1938, for we found them very abundant that summer, several being seen each evening on heath or beach. They were not so timid there as is usual on the mainland, and fed on the heath during the day. The island vegetation, particularly the arbor vitae, showed heavy browsing and barking by the Hares of the past winter. On Trout, Whiskey, Squaw, and Hat islands there was evidence of a recent Hare population, but no evidence of their presence that summer (1938). On Beaver Island, too, the population must have been low, for we saw no Hares in 1938, though six skulls were recovered from in front of a fox den. Strang's (1855, p. 282) reference to the presence on Beaver of "Hare, or rabbit. Two species, large and small," certainly includes this Hare, though the identity of the alternate species, if any, is dubious.

Domestic Rabbit
Oryctolagus cuniculus (Linnaeus)

S. Manitou (obs.).

Case saw some domestic rabbits living beneath an old store building at the ghost town on the bay of South Manitou. A boy on the island stated that they were pets which he liberated a few years earlier and that they had apparently not increased their numbers.

Cottontail
Sylvilagus floridanus mearnsi (Allen)

Beaver (unce.); Marion (spn.); S. Manitou (obs.).

The Cottontail in the upper part of Michigan's southern peninsula is a recent arrival, one of the several species which came in from the south with the clearing of the land. Jackson (1920, p. 63) observed that the Cottontail had reached the mainland shore opposite Lake Superior's Apostle Islands not more than a decade before the time of his observations and that it had not yet moved to the islands, despite the narrowness of the straits to be crossed.

The Cottontail has not been on the mainland east of the Lake Michigan islands long enough to have invaded many of the islands. Only on South Manitou was it observed, and one resident reported that it did not come over (on the ice) until about 1925. A Coast Guard officer, resident from 1916 to 1928, said that the Cottontails arrived during this period and became numerous. One informant stated that the Cottontail was more common than the Snowshoe Hare, but this may only seem to be the case, as the Cottontail is the less shy and more an occupant of cultivated lands. Hatt's earlier accepted reports (1924, p. 401) of the Cottontail on North Manitou and on the Fox islands are considered erroneous in the light of firsthand knowledge of these islands now available. Strang's (1855) reference to the presence of two kinds of rabbits on Beaver Island is almost certainly also wrong. Dice (1925b, p. 32) reports the Cottontails to have first reached the mainland of Charlevoix County about 1900, and they could scarcely have been on the islands a half century earlier. Dice (1925a, p. 8) also records this animal from Marion Island in Traverse Bay.

There is one unsubstantiated recent report of Cottontails on Beaver Island, which may be due to confusion with the Snowshoes not reported by the same observer.

Domestic Hog
Sus scrofa Linnaeus

S. Fox (rpt.).

Walter Hastings states that in 1905 when he visited South Fox there were feral hogs on the island. This was before the date of

134   ISLAND LIFE

extensive lumbering on that island. It is somewhat unlikely that any of the breeds of hog found in Michigan could survive many winters without human care.

White-tailed Deer
Odocoileus virginianus borealis Miller

Beaver (obs., intr.); N. Manitou (obs., intr.); S. Fox (rpt., intr.).

Deer have occurred on the mainland shores near the islands both in recent time and earlier, as evidenced by our finds of Deer bones in fossil forests on Sleeping Bear dune, Leelanau County. They were scarce in some periods and in Leelanau County were nearly or quite extinct from about 1910 to about 1930. Opposite the Beaver

TABLE 11
DEER MORTALITY ON NORTH MANITOU ISLAND

According to Mr. I. H. Bartlett of the Game Division, Michigan State Department of Conservation.

Year	FROM HUNTING				Total
	Adult		Immature		
	Bucks	Does	Bucks	Does	
1937	15	1		2	18
1938	25	12	2	2	41
1939	40	5			45
1940	55	29	8	3	95
1941	91	40	4	4	139
1942	91	70	11	4	176
1943	89	116	39	48	292
1944	155	104	20	23	302
1945	33	9	6	2	50
1946	113	23	2		138
Total	707	409	92	88	1296
	FROM STARVATION OR OTHER CAUSES				
1937			2	3	5
1939			3	2	5
1941	6	2			8
1942	8	4	7	6	25
1943	7	9	8	8	32
1944			10	10	20
1945	3	1			4
1946			11	11	22
1947	11	13	70	70	164
Total	35	29	111	110	285

Islands, however, both in the Lower and Upper Peninsulas, they have always been present in numbers. Probably the Deer have visited all the islands by coming across the ice, but on only two are they now established: Beaver and North Manitou, the two largest islands. On both, the present colonies date from introductions. They were not on Beaver Island, and probably not on any of the islands, in 1853, for Strang (1855, p. 282), writing that year on the natural history of the islands stated: "American deer are found as near as Green Bay [Wisconsin] and Manistee river [about 100 miles south of Beaver Island], *piloting civilization.*"

The North Manitou introduction was of five does and four bucks, placed there in 1925 by the Manitou Island Association. Two of the bucks were killed by dogs on the following day. One estimate of their population in 1931, was "about 75," which would seem to be the maximum possible.

In the spring of 1937 a few Deer, dead of starvation, were found, and in the fall of 1937 hunting was started under a commercial system. The kill thereafter, as recorded for the Michigan Department of Conservation is given in Table 11.

In 1940 an estimate of 1,000 head on the island was made by one resident, and certainly the Deer were in great abundance, for they were regularly seen. On a morning hunt through the woods, July 4, Hatt encountered 18 scattered Deer, one a fawn. Antler rubbing marks were frequently seen, particularly on the poplars. We found two dead Deer, one with a hunter's bullet in its skull, but there was no evidence of starvation of Deer in the preceding winter.

The Deer are fed each winter by the Association, which manages the herd for the sake of its yield. Between 1,500 and 3,200 bushels of oats have been fed each year since 1937. Feeding yards are established at two sites, and here grain is placed in elevated feeding boxes.

In late June of 1940 the Deer were feeding on Jack-in-the-pulpit, bracken, wood anemone, and other things. There was a strongly marked browse line on the arbor vitae, where the Deer had taken everything within winter reach. Some few trees had been killed.

Despite the proximity of the islands and the over-population on North Manitou, the Deer apparently never go over to South Manitou.

One Deer was reported found dead on the ice between North Manitou and the mainland.

Deer were introduced on South Fox Island about 1915, according to a report reaching Mr. I. H. Bartlett. These are said to have increased to about 40 head by 1925. Perhaps the herd was reduced by the occasional visitors to the island, for we saw no Deer at all, and Bartlett in a search in May 1945 could find no certain evidence of Deer in that year. Mr. Plank is believed to have been the man who introduced the Deer herd.

The Michigan Department of Conservation is authority for the statement that "prior to 1927, Deer had been exterminated on Beaver Island," which carries the presumption that there were Deer on the island at an earlier period. In 1927, 3 bucks and 10 does were released on the island by Mr. R. W. Bundy, and in 1928, 4 more does were released. These Deer are said to have come from a private herd near Frankenmuth. The Deer were not abundant on Beaver Island in 1938, though the animals were occasionally seen. The island was opened to Deer hunting the autumn of 1938. The recorded kill (Deer removed from the island) was as follows: 1938, 18 bucks; 1941, 78 bucks and does; 1942, 82 bucks; 1943, 61 bucks; 1944, 66 bucks; 1945, 65 bucks; 1946, 75 bucks.

Woodland Caribou
Rangifer caribou caribou (Gmelin)

Beaver Islands (rpt); High (rpt.).

Caribou records of any kind for the State of Michigan are rare. The species occurred in the Upper Peninsula in the last century, and a single specimen of antler has been recovered from a peat bog in Sanilac County, Lower Peninsula (Burt, 1942, p. 214). Two island records are of interest. The first is the report of Strang (1855, p. 282), who stated: "Caribou, or reindeer, range as far south as here, but visit the islands only on the ice and very rarely." Mr. Sherman Moore was on High Island when the Israelites dug up an antlered Caribou head from a peat bog. It was placed above the doorway of one of the dwellings. When we searched for the head in 1938 we found no trace of it.

8. Modification of Habits

A SPECIES once on an island may find conditions somewhat different from those in its usual mainland abode, yet not intolerable when other choice is unavailable; so from place to place among the islands we find numerous instances of the unexpected, and other cases which, though usual, are strictly insular in character. The nesting colonies of gulls and terns, all but unknown on the mainland shores, illustrate the latter. The islands afford the isolation which these birds require for nesting and raising their young, and we may thus consider their lives adjusted to island existence. But it is the opposite situation, in which species deviate from the norm in these islands, that is the subject of this chapter. To some extent these adjustments on the part of isolated colonies of animals, though astonishing, seem the key to their survival on the islands. Such is the breeding of the Spring Peeper in the marginal waters of Lake Michigan. Of other cases, such as the ground nesting of the Duck Hawk and, on Pismire Island, of the Great Blue Heron and Crow, when to human eyes better sites offered themselves on nearby Hog Island, there seems no proper explanation. Some of the cases are these:

The Spring Peepers on North Fox Island had no possible breeding places except the shallow water between shore boulders, in water continuous with, and not more than 10 feet from, the open water of Lake Michigan (Fig. 32), and there we found them calling. No eggs were found, but they may either have been overlooked or not yet laid. The Peeper heard on Gull Island was in a permanent beach pool well removed from the lake, and this did not seem very different from mainland breeding sites.

The toads of South Fox Island, as noted in greater detail in the annotated list, were apparently restricted in their breeding to the use of beach pools available only in years of suitable lake level, since we found no young toads on the island.

Though, as noted above, the Common Terns are adapted in their breeding habits to the isolation of the small remote islands and on these usually occur in great numbers, in one instance (on Whiskey Island) a single nest was found on the beach.

On Pismire Island a Crow's nest was found, among recumbent bushes, that touched the ground. No better nesting site was available on the island, but the wonder remains that the Crow nested on this tiny islet at all.

The Great Blue Heron nested on three of the islands: Squaw, Hat, and Pismire. Squaw has many high balsams, and the herons nested at heights of 30 to 50 feet. On Hat Island the nests were only 10 to 20 feet up (Fig. 35), for here the few trees that did grow higher were not good platform trees. On Pismire Island (Fig. 19), where there was but a single nest and but one tree, the nest was on the ground. Why the birds should have chosen these three islands for nest colonies and avoided others is certainly not obvious. From Squaw and Hat islands the parent birds were regularly seen winging across the open lake to other islands for feeding. They were not seen feeding around the islands on which they nested.

In one place on Gull Island, although suitable beach sites for nests were by no means all occupied, the Herring Gulls nested in a clearing from which the young birds would need to traverse a stretch of dense woods one hundred yards across to reach the beach and the sight of water. In other places on this island, at the margins of large nesting colonies, a few birds had made nests in damp areas with high piles of debris that assured a dry nest (Fig. 39). These nests, in several instances, had been used for more than a season since their bases were overgrown with cinquefoil.

A pair of Duck Hawks was found nesting directly on the ground on the side of a sand dune on South Fox Island (Figs. 37, 38). Redwings nested in trees and bushes along the shores of some islands where marsh habitat was lacking, as W. P. Nickell has also reported on Kelly's Island, Lake Erie.

A South Fox Island Barn Swallow nest, built in a chimney hole and quite without mud (Hatt, 1938), is an anomaly that cannot be associated with island restrictions since it was among many normal nests.

Crested Flycatchers inhabited evergreen, as well as hardwood, forests on Gull Island, and on Marion Island the Towhees lived deep in the big hardwood forest, a habitat quite unlike the open brush in which they are usually found. Lack (1942, p. 20) has reported a similar "habitat adaptation" among birds of the small islands about Great Britain.

The only known modifications of habit of island mammals are those of ecological distribution. Dice (1925a, p. 3) has already reported the Meadow Voles of Marion Island which overran the forests. On the small islands of the Beaver group it was striking to find the Woodland Deermice abundant in beach drift, a situation preëmpted by two other races of deermice on the mainland. On uninhabited Gull Island, where Hares were abundant in 1938, they seemed less fearful of humans than on the mainland, but they were far from fearless.

9. Factors of Distribution

IT REMAINS for us to review the evidences of time, mode, extent, and source of island invasions and also to determine why not all species of the mainland are found upon the islands.

Island occupancy may be controlled by several partially interdependent factors which we will list:

1. The age of an island and the period of presence of animal species on the mainland, which together provide opportunity for contact.
2. The proximity of any island to the mainland or to other islands nearer the mainland. This factor is modified by the depth of the channel (which, if shallow, may become a land bridge); the frequency and duration of ice bridging; the direction of prevailing winds in relation to the channel; the character of habitats on the mainland shore.
3. The variety, age, and permanence of the available island habitats.
4. The absolute size of an island and the extent of any one type of plant community on which an animal is dependent. These are of importance both in relation to the amplitude of fluctuations in the animal population cycles and to the size of the shore target for the invading animals.
5. The frequency and extent of variation in lake level. High water may periodically eliminate or inhibit population growth of shore faunas, low water make an island available to shore breeding species. Further, these lake fluctuations provide the conditions necessary for animal dispersal on flotsam.
6. The abundance of beach drift out of reach of all but exceptional storms.
7. The locomotor habits of any particular animal species.
8. The adaptability of a species to new conditions.
9. The life cycle and habits of any species in such matters as egg laying and winter inactivity.
10. The degree of interspecific competition after an island is attained.

FACTORS OF DISTRIBUTION 141

MEDIA OF DISPERSAL

Air, water, and ice are the media by which most vertebrates have reached the islands. Obviously the bats came by flight, the birds either by flight or swimming. It is probably not unreasonable to presume that all the amphibians (other than the Red-backed Salamander), the turtles, Water Snake, Garter, and Ribbon Snakes came by swimming, though the distances to be traversed and the hazards from enemies seem great. Beaver and Otter, reported in the last century on Beaver Island, must also have arrived by swimming. There is, however, no clear case for any other species coming through the water by its own efforts.

The temporary bridges of ice are of no importance to birds, amphibians, or reptiles but regularly are highways for some mammals. Others may not have used the ice because of their winter lethargy. Such are the Bear, Skunk, Raccoon, Woodchuck, Ground Squirrel, Porcupine, and jumping mice. Still others, because the ice surface requires great exposure, have probably not travelled far over it. Among these, with exceptions for Marion Island, may be mentioned the moles, shrews, Mink and weasels, tree squirrels (with one possible exception), flying squirrels, Least Chipmunk, Prairie Deermouse, White-footed Mouse, voles, and Wharf Rat.

The species which have reached the islands over the ice are few: Caribou, Red Fox, Hare and Cottontail for certain, possibly also the Woodland Deermouse, Red Squirrel in one instance, the shrews, and, on Marion Island, Meadow Voles and weasel.

The pre-Nipissing lowering in lake level would have joined many of the islands to the mainland or so reduced the degree of their insularity as to provide access to most of the islands for most of the land vertebrates. Unfortunately, nothing at all is known of the faunas of this area during that time and one must seek evidence for such dry-land distribution in the record of present distributions. Those animals which move freely by air, through the open lake, or over the winter ice, will of course give no clue. Neither may we seek it among those species which are known to be recent invaders from the south or west. It must come from species common to the larger islands for which other means of dispersal seem highly problematic, or, from the completeness of mainland representation. The question must receive its answer on the evidence of the origin of island populations of the Red-backed Salamander, Ring-neck, Red-bellied and Milk snakes, Eastern Chipmunk, and Woodland Deermouse. These animals can only have come to the islands by a land "bridge," by agency of man or his watercraft, or by the accident of transshipment on beach drift. The salamander is not known as a beach inhabitant, but possibly a log in which adults or eggs were present could be set adrift in a river, carried into the lake, and eventually stranded on an island. The Ring-neck Snake and Milk Snake, which do live in beach drift, could be transported as either eggs or adults. The Red-bellied Snake (which is ovoviviparous), like the chipmunk and mouse, could come across only in an active stage. If the island species came by land bridge, the long period of their isolation would tend to produce differentiation. If the invasions were accidental the likelihood of an entire island population having arisen from a single gravid female is fairly high, and opportunity for perpetuation of a deviant from normal is thus greater. It does not seem to us that the observed differences in the chipmunks, Red-backed Salamander, Milk Snake, and Water Snake, while other species remain typical, weigh more strongly in favor of one mode of distribution than of another. It is indicated in the land bridge hypothesis that isolation has been complete over a period of time insufficient to permit complete differentiation or that the tempo of evolution has varied from species to species. In the case of accidental introductions, either the same conclusion applies or the portion of the fauna that has remained stable has been receiving a constant infiltration of "new blood" from the mainland. It is surprising, however, that so aquatic a form as the Water Snake shows differentiation if the islands are constantly receiving additions to the fauna from the mainland.

One other source of evidence remains, and that is the character of the distribution pattern. A land bridge should provide access to the islands for all forms alike. On the larger islands, with a diversity of cover, one would expect an almost complete mainland fauna (assuming, of course, that today's fauna is largely the same as that existing at the time of the post-Nipissing lowering of lake level). The big islands do not, however, have any reasonably high percentage of the mainland faunas. Thus, after corrections to eliminate obvious chance records and introductions, of 44 mammals present on adjacent shores of Michigan, Beaver Island has but 9, North Manitou 7, and South Manitou 6. Corresponding counts for the reptiles are 17 for the mainland, 7 for Beaver, 4 each for the Manitous. The amphibian counts for the same areas are 16, 9, 7, and 3. Thus, though the possibility of some species being distributed on the islands by land bridge is not ruled out, the evidence for it is far from conclusive. Either the fauna now present on the mainland had not sufficient time following glacial retreat to invade northern Michigan and thus utilize the island "peninsulas"; or ecological conditions on the islands, on the "bridge," or on both, were such as to set up an effective barrier to the dispersal of many species. With so little knowledge of the habits of the fauna, and even less knowledge of palaeogeographic conditions, we can do no more than present our evidence in support of each theory and await more ample data before arriving at any definite conclusion.

The case for the accidental dispersal of those few species abundant enough to make us reasonably sure our records are fairly complete and for which other modes of distribution are not known, is fairly strong, as has been indicated several places above. To summarize, the evidence lies in—

1. Such spotty distribution as that of the Red-backed Salamander, Jefferson's Salamander, Wood Frog, Milk Snake, and Red-bellied Snake.

2. The absence of many mainland species for which suitable habitat is abundantly available on the islands, indicating a somewhat hit-and-miss composition.

3. The components of the fauna which are not known to have arrived by other means are generally those which would lend themselves to accidental dispersal by logs or as stowaways on boats.

The source of supposedly accidental introductions seems to be largely the Lower Peninsula rather than the Upper Peninsula or the Wisconsin shore. Two species present on the islands, the Ribbon Snake and Milk Snake, are unknown from the latter regions. The Western House Wren is found on all of the Beaver group, but the eastern form is found on the Fox and Manitou islands. The Least Chipmunk (*Eutamias*) of the Upper Peninsula has not invaded the islands. The chipmunks which are on the islands (*Tamias*) are referable to the Lower Peninsula subspecies, with the exception of those on South Fox Island. These chipmunks of South Fox, the Caribou (which formerly crossed on the ice to High and probably to Beaver Island), the Western House Wren on the Beaver group, and the Painted Turtle on Beaver Island (which has the plastral pattern of the northern form though the same carapace type as the Lower Peninsula turtle) are the sole indications of northern or western elements in the island fauna. Further evidence of an eastern origin for the fauna of Beaver Island is to be found on High Island. This island, lying several miles to the west of Beaver (though comparatively small in size) is in a favorable position to receive any derelicts from the west or north. Yet despite the abundance of suitable habitats, neither the Ring-neck Snake nor the Red-backed Salamander, both exceedingly abundant on Beaver Island, was found by Stuart and Grobman even though they searched intensively.

It may be pointed out, for such bearing as it may have, that the prevailing winds in upper Lake Michigan are from the southwest and west, as attested both by weather records and the topography of the islands, but that the water gaps are narrower to the east. Driftwood has been abundant on the lake for only about a century, a period approximately corresponding to that of frequent contacts of sailing and steam vessels with the islands. Thus, in this short recent period, opportunities for small animals to reach the islands have been greatest, but there was a vastly greater period when fewer vehicles for their transport were available.

Currents in Lake Michigan, as indicated by the travels of drifting bottles, are shown by Harrington (1895) to consist of a general southward current along the west shores and a northerly current along the eastern edge. This drift, supplemented by the wave action and ice action, accounts for the moving of blue slag pebbles from an old smelter site at Leland, Michigan, for at least two miles northward in a period of about fifty years. There is a broad, indefinite stream setting from the western to the eastern longitudinal currents. In the vicinity of the Beaver Islands there is a swirling current which could well carry driftwood from mainland points along the east shore to the islands. These currents flow from 4 to 90 miles per day, so that it is not necessary to presume long exposure on the water for any animal set adrift.

LAG IN OCCUPATION

Though many vertebrate animals have invaded the adjacent mainland in past centuries without yet having established populations on the islands, a few species have come into the area only in the past century, and their success in surmounting the water gaps can to some extent be measured. Thus, Van Tyne points out that the Starling did not reach the Charlevoix County mainland until 1927, yet was established by 1938 on all islands with head-high vegetation. The English Sparrow, longer on the mainland, has come across to Beaver Island and the Manitous, where, however, it is confined to the areas of human habitation. The Cottontail, which probably first came to Leelanau County in the early twentieth century, is found on Marion and South Manitou islands, but on no other*. The Prairie Deermouse, which has but recently invaded the northern part of the Lower Peninsula, has attained only semi-insular Fisherman's Island. The White-footed Mouse and the Coyote have, strangely, not yet been found on any of the islands considered.

THE INFLUENCE OF MAN

Aboriginal man is not known to have influenced the population of island animals, but European man has indeed stepped in to extirpate some species, to introduce or re-establish others, to modify the cover to the detriment of some species and the benefit of others, and to build and then desert dwellings which have been a temporary boon to many of the animals.

Of exterminations there are not many records. The fur trade and the development of the frontier eliminated the Beaver and the Caribou and in all probability other large animals of which we have no certain island records—such as the Elk and Deer, the Cougar, Lynx, Wolf, Gray Fox, and Bear. The Passenger Pigeon, which Strang recorded, is gone, as is the Osprey.

Introductions of bird species have been confined, so far as we know, to gallinaceous birds (Ruffed Grouse, Sharp-tailed Grouse, Ring-necked Pheasant, Hungarian Partridge), none of which has survived. Some mammal introductions have thrived, notably Gray and Fox Squirrels, Raccoon, and Deer. Muskrats in one instance flourished for a time, then disappeared; in another instance, became well established. The fate of the one Skunk colony is yet open to question. Two Beavers released on one island, seem not to have been a pair and did not establish a colony.

The only animals possibly feral on the islands appear to be house cats and domestic rabbits on South Manitou. Hogs were once wild on another island but are not known to have bred there. Colonies

---

*A dubious sight record for Beaver Island may prove an exception.

of House Mice and Old World rats seem never to have become firmly established.

It is acknowledged that chipmunks and deermice may have reached the islands through human agency, but there is no proof of it. European Starlings and English Sparrows, though introduced in North America, reached the islands of their own accord.

In the cutting of the forests and the making of farms man vastly increased the variety of cover available to wildlife and thereby, no doubt, provided conditions which permitted increase in the number of bird species and in the population of others. Birds of the field and second-growth forest would have been all but unknown on the islands in the eighteenth century, but now, on the more open islands, constitute a considerable part of the population.

Through the building of houses, farm buildings, etc., conditions have been much improved for Barn Swallows, House Wrens, Chimney Swifts, and Phoebes, and where Martin houses are provided these birds are notably common. Only on minute Shoe and Pismire islands were evidences of human dwellings completely lacking. On the Manitous, South Fox, Beaver, High, Trout, Squaw, Garden, and Hog islands are deserted buildings of some magnitude.

Not only may man be credited with the establishment of dwellings, fields, meadows, and second-growth forest, but a major habitat on all the islands, the zone of driftwood, is 90 per cent of his making. Search of the drift reveals no logs that do not bear the mark of saw or axe, and there is an astonishing assortment of debris in the drift — bottles and unbroken light bulbs, parts of boats (one even from Tampico!), and the numerous objects set adrift by boats in passage as well as by wrecks.

DIVERSITY OF PLANT COMMUNITIES LEADS TO DIVERSITY OF FAUNAS

Shelford (1937, p. 303) has defined a "Law of Toleration," stating that a single factor, effective on an activity taking place within the narrowest limits, such as breeding, may be critical in determining distribution, except for the visits of migratory species. Liebig (Hesse, Allee, and Schmidt, 1937, p. 21) in his "Law of the Minimum" recognized the same factor as operative among plants. Though elsewhere in this report it is shown that island animals have frequently occupied cover types which they do not use on the mainland, it remains

FACTORS OF DISTRIBUTION

TABLE 12
CORRELATION OF FAUNAL VARIETY WITH ECOLOGICAL DIVERSITY

Those islands whose faunas are inadequately studied are not included, nor are those which are closest to the mainland. The enumeration of plant communities employs the system of Dice (1932), omitting the rock succession communities and the aerial. Species known to have been introduced on the islands by man are excluded. Species now extirpated from the adjacent mainland are not included except when island records are known. The bird list is based in part on presumed breeding status. The figures exclude the Caspian Tern and Ring-billed Gull. Bats also are omitted, since island records for them are incomplete. Certain dubious reports are ignored.

Area	Communities	Land Vertebrates	Mammals	Breeding Birds	Reptiles	Amphibians
Adjacent Mainland	33	203	44	126	17	16
1. Beaver Island	30	120	9	95	7	9
2. North Manitou	25	88	7	70	4	7
3. South Manitou	27	77	6	64	4	3
4. South Fox	16	68	5	59	2	2
5. North Fox	10	38	4	27	4	3
6. Gull	10	37	3	33	0	1
7. Whiskey	5	27	2	20	4	1
8. Trout	6	36	3	28	1	4
9. Squaw	10	42	3	34	3	2
10. Hat	4	19	1	18	0	0
11. Shoe	1	2	0	2	0	0
12. Pismire	3	8	0	8	0	0

TABLE 13
CORRELATION OF FAUNAL VARIETY (BIRDS AND BATS OMITTED) WITH ECOLOGICAL DIVERSITY

	Plant Communities	Animal Species	Index $\frac{\text{Species}}{\text{Communities}}$
Mainland	33	77	2.33
1. Beaver Island	30	25	.83
2. North Manitou	25	18	.72
3. South Manitou	27	13	.48
4. South Fox	16	9	.56
5. North Fox	10	11	1.10
6. Gull	10	4	.40
7. Whiskey	5	7	1.40
8. Trout	6	8	1.33
9. Squaw	10	8	.80
10. Hat	4	1	.25
11. Shoe	1	0	.00
12. Pismire	3	0	.00

a general truth that the *islands with the greatest diversity of cover also have the most varied faunas;* the absence of a single cover type is in many instances clearly correlated with the absence of species normally associated with such a habitat. We have taken Dice's (1932) classification of the major terrestrial ecological communities of the Alleghenian Biotic Province in Michigan, and applying these as well as may be to the islands, we have drawn up the accompanying table (No. 12) which bears witness to the general truth just stated.

THE ROLE OF ABSOLUTE AREA

Among the birds, it has been pointed out, there are several instances in which a species has been reported on Beaver Island and on only one or two of the small islands. Here, it seems to us that the reason for the absence of such species from other islands may be that, though the species at one time or another reach all of the islands, on the smaller ones there are frequent temporary losses of colonies.

The absence of gallinaceous birds from the islands, and the comparative failure of their several plantings there, may be due, as Leopold (1931, p. 155) has suggested, to the requirements of a large area for minimum population reserve at the low point of the population cycles. The same factor probably militates against the maintenance of Hare populations on smaller islands. Lack (1942, p. 15) has pointed out that the small number of a given species that can exist on a small island makes the species very susceptible to accidental extirpation, after which there may be long delay before recolonization. This may account for certain gaps noted in faunas of several of the small islands.

Though 15 species of birds occur only on Beaver Island, no species of bird is confined to one or more small islands (herons and terns, however, *nest* only on the small islands, possibly because of greater freedom from predation).

As for the mammals, it may be presumed that the absence of stable island colonies of large species is in large part a direct result of their requirements of large areas for the maintenance of a minimum breeding stock, for adequate food production, and for escape from man and other enemies.

FACTORS OF DISTRIBUTION

That the correspondence of faunal variety is generally with ecological diversity rather than with absolute area is further indicated by Table 14. Here it may be seen that North Fox and Gull islands, though differing greatly in size, have the same number of communities and almost equal representation of land vertebrates. In this order, Whiskey, Trout, and Squaw are progressively smaller but, in inverse order, more varied in flora. Again, the animal list increases with the number of plant communities in spite of reduction in size of the island. Pismire, with more diverse flora than Shoe Island but about the same size, has more species of birds occupying it. That the correlation is not a simple and direct one is shown in Table 13 in which theoretically the ratios of animal species to plant communities should always give a similar index.

TABLE 14*

CORRELATION OF FAUNAL VARIETY WITH ECOLOGICAL DIVERSITY IN RELATION TO AREA

Area	Acres	Plant Communities	Land Vertebrates
Mainland		33	203
1. Beaver Island	37,400	30	120
2. North Manitou Island	13,000	25	88
3. South Manitou Island	5,000	27	77
4. South Fox Island	3,400	16	68
5. North Fox Island	895	10	38
6. Gull Island	270	10	37
7. Whiskey Island	130	5	27
8. Trout Island	115	6	36
9. Squaw Island	75	10	42
10. Hat Island	16	4	19
11. Shoe Island	3	1	4
12. Pismire Island	2.5	3	8

POPULATION CYCLES AND ISLAND OCCUPATION

Though without repeated capture and release of animals on the same island for several seasons, no proof can be offered of disharmonious population cycles on different islands, some of our field evidence would suggest that such occur. The figures presented in the account of the deermice, for example, show that in one season the catch of these animals for 100 trap-nights ranged from 1.9 on Trout Island to 23.2 on Squaw Island. In one instance (Trout Island)

---

*Data selected as for Table 12, except that in Table 14 all gulls and terns are included.

there seemed another likely explanation for the low population, namely, the presence of too many ants, and on the second lowest in population (Beaver Island) the catch was probably not truly representative because chipmunks and cattle sprang a high percentage of the traps. On the other islands, in which the range was from 16.9 to 23.2, the samples are believed to have been representative and the island habitats roughly equal in suitability.

The Snowshoe Hare population on South Fox Island appears to have reached epidemic proportions in 1935 and to have been reduced to a low point in 1937. In 1938, the Hares on Gull Island were common enough to lead one to believe that they were near a peak of abundance there. On other islands visited that year they were inconspicuous and presumably few.

There was also a large difference in relative abundance of snakes on various islands, for which ecological factors may not have been wholly responsible. The difference between the animal populations of Trout and Whiskey islands, discussed on page 152, may be cited as a possible example of disharmonic cycles.

As has been indicated in the previous chapter and elsewhere, a complete correlation between habitat diversity and vertebrate populations does not exist. This is perhaps due to the ecological adaptation of the species, since on the islands species occupy habitats in which they are not found on the mainland. Further reasons for lack of close correlation are the inability of many species to reach the islands and the lack of absolute area of the smaller islands sufficient to maintain an adequate reservoir of individuals to assure perpetuation of the species.

LAKE LEVEL FLUCTUATION AND ITS EFFECT

The height of lake level is an important factor in populations of all shore dwelling animals. For those dependent on shore pools for breeding sites, as are several amphibians on the smaller islands, a shift in lake level may create or destroy the only breeding areas. Instances of this are given in the accounts of the Toad, Spring Peeper, and Jefferson's Salamander. The only birds affected are the gulls and terns. These thrive at times of low lake level when gravel bars are of greatest size and beaches wide. During high lake level some islands used as nest sites are completely under water and other areas awash in storms. Beaches may be covered, as on Squaw

Island in 1939, where nesting colonies of gulls and terns were well established in 1938, but, by report of Dr. F. E. Ludwig (personal communication), there were none in 1939 when there was a four-inch rise in lake level. It is, of course, characteristic (Ludwig, 1943, p. 243) of gull colonies to shift from island to island.

The amplitude of fluctuation in mean water level in upper Lake Michigan, as indicated by United States Lake Survey records from Mackinac, during June to October, 1935 to 1946, is 2.82 feet. This is quite adequate to change almost completely the condition of beach habitats on the islands studied.

The zoogeographical significance of the changes in lake level lies not only in the resultant extension or restriction of beach habitats and the creation or destruction of beach pools, but in the provision of a mechanism for the removal of beach drift and its fauna from one island to another.

PREDATORS AND PESTS

In some instances it seems that predators account for the absence of food animals from the islands, and that food animals thrive where predators are absent. The chief predatory species on the islands appears to be the fox. It was stated earlier that on Gull Island fox tracks were commonly seen lacing between nests of the Herring Gull without evidence of disturbance. On this island there were Hares and mice, though no chipmunks, as main food stocks for the foxes. It has also been noted that one year the gull colony on Hat Island was not successful in nesting, apparently because of the presence of a fox. Hat Island has no regular population of Hares, chipmunks, or mice, and it is assumed that here the carnivore that destroyed nests did so by force of necessity. It seems obvious, too, to one who has witnessed the destruction of nestling gulls subsequent to any disturbance in the colony, that the usual isolation of these colonies is necessary for their survival.

The at least apparent absence of Water Snakes in Lake Manitou, North Manitou Island, was regarded by Pope as possibly owing to an abundance of Bullfrogs, which might tend to eliminate the young snakes.

The presence of large colonies of nesting gulls may result in the reduction of other shore populations, and the lack of driftwood-inhabiting snakes and toads on Gull Island and Hat Island suggests this, but the isolation of the former and the small size of the latter may be more logical explanations, especially since snakes, toads, and mice occur on the beaches of Squaw Island, where gulls nest in numbers.

The concentration of birds of prey on islands during migrations has been suggested by Leopold (1931, p. 155) as a possible cause of limitation of island faunas of game birds, but we have no indication that such a factor operates on the islands here considered.

That invertebrate animals may take part in determining vertebrate populations in this area is suggested by the contrast between Trout and Whiskey islands. These two islands, but 4.25 miles apart, and almost alike in conditions of size, cover, etc., and both studied within the same 10 days, contrast strongly in the differences between their faunas, which are:

TROUT ISLAND	WHISKEY ISLAND
Ants of several species exceptionally abundant, large colonies occupying almost all the beach drift and great mounds in and near the forest.	Ants, though present, occupying a small portion of the beach drift. No large ant mounds discovered.
Mosquitoes moderately common.	Mosquitoes so abundant that working without a head net or screened tent was impractical.
Dog flies moderately common.	Dog flies so abundant that we resorted to bathing on a reef a half mile offshore.
Only one snake found	25 snakes of 4 species secured in first half hour on the island, and about 20 Water Snakes each day.
1.9 deermice caught per 100 trap nights.	22.1 deermice per 100 trap nights, or about 12 times as many as on Trout Island.
Birds, scarce.	Birds, abundant: 25 species listed in first 10 hours.
2 species of *Hyla* recorded.	No *Hyla* recorded.
Few gulls; a few unoccupied nests.	Gulls more numerous, nesting.
Old Hare sign only.	Fresh Hare sign.

The markedly lesser numbers of ground inhabiting vertebrates on Trout Island appears to us related to the excessive abundance of ants.

FACTORS OF DISTRIBUTION

ABILITY TO INVADE AND OCCUPY

"Species senescence" has been proposed as an explanation of the failure of a species to invade new territory around it. An examination of the lists of those species of vertebrate animals which, though long present on the mainland, have, for no obvious reason, failed to populate the islands, leads one to search for "senescent species." Particularly suspected are those birds which can, and as individuals sometimes do, reach the islands but have not become established as summer residents and, in addition, those birds known on Beaver Island and a few of its satellites, though unknown on the Manitou and Fox islands. These birds are listed in Table 6 and 8 (pp. 71 and 72). In a few species, notably water birds and birds of prey, absence of suitable habitat or of food supply may be presumed. For others, the southern islands may be just outside the normal breeding range, though a few species, especially flycatchers and thrushes, are probably incapable of colonization beyond the mainland.

A rough index of the ability of major vertebrate groups to invade the islands is given in Table 15. As one would presume, the birds easily lead not only in actual numbers of species but in terms of the

TABLE 15
RELATIVE ABILITIES OF THE SEVERAL LAND VERTEBRATES TO INVADE ISLANDS

$$\% = \frac{\text{Island species}}{\text{Mainland species}}$$

	All Islands		Beaver Island		North Fox Island	
	Number	%	Number	%	Number	%
Amphibians	10	62	9	56	3	19
Snakes	6	60	5	50	4	40
Turtles	2	66	2	66	0	0
Birds	110	87	95	72	27	21
Mammals	17	39	9	20	4	9

percentage of species found on the mainland. If the birds' 87 per cent representation of mainland fauna indicates about a 13 per cent inadequacy of island habitats (a margin must be allowed because of limited time of collecting), the figures suggest that amphibians and reptiles are about 20 per cent less able to establish themselves than are the birds. The mammals are least able to occupy the islands despite their presence the year around and, for most of them, their winter activity. One explanation for the low percentage is that the mainland supports a relatively great number of large mammals and carnivores which the islands could not long sustain.

THE EVALUATION OF DATA

Many things tend to affect the adequacy of the data on which our conclusions rest, but we believe that proper allowance has been made for them. Chance is undoubtedly the greatest modifying factor, operating through the limitation of length and season of the collecting period, the weather, the year, and other matters sometimes beyond the investigator's control.

In 1904 Barrows commented on the total absence of seven species of birds he failed to find in six days of collecting on Beaver Island, but since then these species have been regularly observed there. Had we visited Squaw Island only in 1939, we would not have recorded nesting colonies of gulls and terns, which in 1938 were extensive there. In 1940 we had noted the absence of Leopard Frogs on South Manitou, but in 1944 a re-examination of the same area revealed them as common. The Spring Peepers of Gull and North Fox islands would not have been discovered had the animals not been singing; and, in numerous instances, both the amphibian and bird records changed character with the advent of sunny weather. Collecting techniques, too, must weigh heavily, for had we not diligently sought out and raked through old sawdust piles we would have missed some herpetological records. The reader will have noted numerous records of the presence of a species on an island based on a single observation or on chance finds of identifiable bones.

These many uncertainties do affect the handling of our data and rule out quite largely the use of statistical methods, but we believe that the well established populations, which are the more significant ones, were found and recognized and that we have good basis for our several theses.

In the immediate future the animal populations of the islands will probably increase in diversity. The human populations have long been decreasing, with the cultural development of the mainland. Timber resources are temporarily low. Farms often cannot be profitably operated, because of the reduction of lake transportation.

Lighthouses and Coast Guard stations are fewer, other safeguards to navigation reducing the need for them. Commercial fishermen operate best from mainland bases, religious colonies no longer exist in the area, the Indians are fewer and less dependent on natural resources of the forest. As a result of all these factors, deserted dwellings, and clearings grown to brush, provide a maximum of shelter. Though media of dispersal are now less common on the lake, there are animals progressively invading the nearby mainland shores which in time may find their own way to the islands or be introduced by man.

Appendix

List of the Vertebrate Faunas arranged by Islands.

These abbreviations are employed:
  intr. = introduced by man
  nst. = breeding record by one of our parties
  obs. = sight record by one of our parties
  rpt. = acceptable report by others
  sgn. = scats, tracks, or other clear sign of presence
  spn. = specimen obtained or examined by us
  unce. = uncertain record
  voi. = voice heard

Beaver Island

Amphibia
Triturus v. viridescens (spn.)
Plethodon c. cinereus (spn.)
Bufo terrestris americanus (spn.)
Hyla v. versicolor (voi.)
Hyla c. crucifer (spn.)
Rana sylvatica cantabrigensis (spn.)
Rana catesbiana (spn.)
Rana clamitans (spn.)
Rana p. pipiens (spn.)

Reptilia
Chelydra s. serpentina (spn.)
Chrysemys picta marginata (spn.)
Diadophis punctatus edwardsii (spn.)
Natrix s. sipedon (spn.)
Thamnophis s. sauritus (spn.)
Thamnophis s. sirtalis (spn.)
Lampropeltis t. triangulum (spn.)

Aves
Gavia immer elasson (spn.)
Colymbus grisegena holböllii (spn.)
Colymbus auritus (spn.)
Phalacrocorax auritus (rpt.)
Ardea h. herodias (obs.)
Botaurus l. lentiginosus (spn.)
Ixobrychus exilis (obs.)
Anas platyrhynchos (obs.)
Anas rubripes (spn., nst.)
Anas acuta (obs.)
Anas discors (spn.)
Aix sponsa (spn.)
Aythya americana (obs.)
Aythya collaris (spn.)
Aythya valisineria (obs.)
Aythya affinis (spn.)
Glaucionetta clangula (obs.)
Clangula hyemalis (spn.)
Mergus merganser americanus (nst.)
Mergus serrator (obs.)
Accipiter gentilis atricapillus (spn., nst.)
Accipiter striatus velox (spn.)
Accipiter cooperii (obs.)
Buteo jamaicensis (obs.)
Buteo lineatus (obs.)
Haliaeetus leucocephalus washingtoniensis (nst.)
Circus cyaneus (obs.)
Pandion haliaëtus (unce.)
Falco s. sparverius (spn.)
Phasianus colchicus (sgn.)
Rallus l. limicola (spn.)
Porzana carolina (rpt.)
Charadrius melodus circumcinctus (rpt.)
Charadrius v. vociferus (spn., nst.)
Philohela minor (obs.)
Capella gallinago delicata (spn.)
Actitis macularia (spn.)
Tringa s. solitaria (spn.)
Totanus melanoleucus (spn.)
Totanus flavipes (spn.)
Erolia minutilla (spn.)
Larus argentatus smithsonianus (spn.)
Larus delawarensis (obs.)
Sterna h. hirundo (spn.)
Hydroprogne caspia (spn.)

Aves (Beaver Island) *continued*

Zenaidura macroura (obs.)
Coccyzus erythropthalmus (spn., nst.)
Caprimulgus v. vociferus (obs.)
Chordeiles m. minor (spn.)
Chaetura pelagica (spn.)
Archilochus colubris (obs.)
Megaceryle alcyon (obs., nst. rpt.)
Colaptes auratus luteus (spn., nst.)
Hylatomus pileatus (obs.)
Melanerpes e. erythrocephalus (spn.)
Sphyrapicus v. varius (spn.)
Dendrocopos v. villosus (spn., nst.)
Dendrocopos pubescens medianus (spn.)
Tyrannus tyrannus (spn.)
Myiarchus crinitus boreus (spn.)
Sayornis phoebe (obs.)
Empidonax flaviventris (spn.)
Empidonax traillii (rpt.)
Empidonax minimus (spn.)
Contopus virens (spn.)
Nuttallornis borealis (spn.)
Eremophila alpestris praticola (spn., nst.)
Iridoprocne bicolor (spn.)
Riparia r. riparia (spn., nst.)
Hirundo rustica erythrogaster (spn., nst.)
Petrochelidon pyrrhonota (nst.)
Progne s. subis (nst.)
Cyanocitta cristata bromia (spn.)
Corvus b. brachyrhynchos (spn., nst.)
Parus a. atricapillus (spn., nst.)
Sitta carolinensis cookei (rpt.)
Sitta canadensis (spn.)
Certhia familiaris americana (spn.)
Troglodytes aëdon parkmanii (spn.)
Troglodytes troglodytes hiemalis (obs.)
Cistothorus platensis stellaris (spn.)
Dumetella carolinensis (spn.)
Toxostoma r. rufum (spn.)
Turdus m. migratorius (spn., nst.)
Hylocichla guttata (rpt.)
Hylocichla ustulata (rpt.)
Hylocichla m. minima (spn.)
Hylocichla fuscescens salicicola (spn.)
Sialia s. sialis (spn., nst.)
Regulus s. satrapa (spn.)
Regulus c. calendula (spn.)
Bombycilla cedrorum (spn., nst.)
Sturnus v. vulgaris (spn., nst.)
Vireo olivaceus (spn.)
Vireo philadelphicus (spn.)
Mniotilta varia (spn.)
Vermivora r. ruficapilla (spn.)
Dendroica petechia aestiva (spn.)
Dendroica magnolia (rpt.)
Dendroica c. caerulescens (spn.)
Dendroica c. coronata (spn., nst.)
Dendroica v. virens (spn.)
Dendroica fusca (spn.)
Dendroica pensylvanica (spn.)
Dendroica striata (spn.)
Dendroica p. palmarum (spn.)
Seiurus a. aurocapillus (spn., nst.)
Oporornis philadelphia (spn.)
Geothlypis trichas brachidactyla (spn.)
Wilsonia p. pusilla (spn.)
Setophaga ruticilla (spn.)
Passer domesticus (obs.)
Dolichonyx oryzivorus (spn.)
Sturnella m. magna (spn., nst.)
Sturnella neglecta (obs.)
Agelaius p. phoeniceus (spn.)
Icterus galbula (nst.)
Euphagus carolinus (rpt.)
Quiscalus versicolor (spn.)
Molothrus a. ater (spn., "nst.")
Piranga olivacea (spn.)
Pheucticus ludovicianus (spn., nst.)
Passerina cyanea (spn., nst.)
Hesperiphona vespertina (obs.)
Carpodacus p. purpureus (spn., nst.?)
Spinus t. tristis (spn.)
Loxia curvirostra minor (spn.)
Loxia l. leucoptera (rpt.)
Pipilo e. erythrophthalmus (spn.)
Passerculus sandwichensis oblitus (spn.)
Ammodramus savannarum pratensis (spn.)
Pooecetes g. gramineus (spn.)
Junco hyemalis (rpt.)
Spizella p. passerina (spn., nst.)
Zonotrichia leucophrys (rpt.)
Zonotrichia albicollis (spn.)
Melospiza g. georgiana (rpt.)
Melospiza melodia euphonia (spn.)
Plectrophenax nivalis (rpt.)

Mammalia

Procyon l. lotor (unce.)
Lutra c. canadensis (rpt.)
Vulpes fulva (sgn., rpt.)
Lynx r. rufus (unce.)
Tamias striatus peninsulae (spn.)
Sciurus carolinensis hypophaeus (spn., intr.)
Castor canadensis (rpt.)
Peromyscus maniculatus gracilis (spn.)
Ondatra z. zibethica (rpt., intr.)
Sylvilagus floridanus mearnsii (unce.)
Lepus americanus phaeonotus (spn.)
Odocoileus virginianus borealis (obs., intr.)
Rangifer c. caribou (rpt.)

APPENDIX

Bellow Island

Aves
　Larus argentatus smithsonianus (spn., nst.)　　Turdus m. migratorius (nst.)

Fisherman's Island

Aves
　Gavia immer elasson (obs.)　　　　　　Larus argentatus smithsonianus (nst.)
　Anas platyrhynchos (obs.)　　　　　　　Larus delawarensis (rpt.)
　Anas rubripes (obs.)　　　　　　　　　Hydroprogne caspia (obs.)

Mammalia
　　　　　　Peromyscus maniculatus bairdii (spn.)

Garden Island
(No collecting done)

Aves
　Actitis macularia (rpt.)　　　　　　　　Sterna h. hirundo (nst. rpt.)

Gull Island

Amphibia
　　　　　　Hyla c. crucifer (voi.)

Aves
　Gavia immer elasson (obs.)　　　　　　Progne s. subis (obs.)
　Ardea h. herodias (obs.)　　　　　　　Corvus b. brachyrhynchos (nst.)
　Anas platyrhynchos (obs.)　　　　　　　Parus a. atricapillus (spn.)
　Anas rubripes (obs.)　　　　　　　　　Sitta canadensis (obs.)
　Anas discors (obs.)　　　　　　　　　　Troglodytes aëdon parkmanii (spn.)
　Glaucionetta clangula (obs.)　　　　　　Toxostoma r. rufum (spn.)
　Mergus merganser americanus (obs.)　　Turdus m. migratorius (obs.)
　Mergus serrator (obs.)　　　　　　　　Hylocichla fuscescens salicicola (spn.)
　Haliaeetus leucocephalus washington-　　Sialia s. sialis (spn.)
　　iensis (spn., nst.)　　　　　　　　　　Bombycilla cedrorum (spn.)
　Circus cyaneus (obs.)　　　　　　　　　Sturnus v. vulgaris (obs.)
　Charadrius v. vociferus (spn.)　　　　　Vireo olivaceus (spn.)
　Actitis macularia (spn., nst.)　　　　　　Dendroica petechia aestiva (spn.)
　Ereunetes pusillus (spn.)　　　　　　　Dendroica v. virens (spn.)
　Larus argentatus smithsonianus (spn., nst.)　Dendroica fusca (spn.)
　Hydroprogne caspia (obs.)　　　　　　　Seiurus a. aurocapillus (obs.)
　Coccyzus erythropthalmus (spn.)　　　　Oporornis philadelphia (spn.)
　Chaetura pelagica (obs.)　　　　　　　Setophaga ruticilla (spn., nst.)
　Colaptes auratus luteus (obs.)　　　　　Dolichonyx oryzivorus (spn.)
　Hylatomus pileatus (sgn.)　　　　　　　Agelaius p. phoeniceus (spn., nst.)
　Melanerpes e. erythrocephalus (spn.)　　Pheucticus ludovicianus (obs.)
　Tyrannus tyrannus (spn., nst.)　　　　　Passerina cyanea (spn., nst.)
　Myiarchus crinitus boreus (spn.)　　　　Spinus p. pinus (spn.)
　Contopus virens (obs.)　　　　　　　　Spinus t. tristis (spn.)
　Iridoprocne bicolor (spn., nst.)　　　　　Spizella p. passerina (spn.)
　　　　　　Melospiza melodia euphonia (spn.)

Mammalia
　Vulpes fulva (sgn.)　　　　　　　　　Peromyscus maniculatus gracilis (spn.)
　　　　　　Lepus americanus phaeonotus (spn.)

Hat Island

Aves
- Gavia immer elasson (obs.)
- Ardea h. herodias (nst.)
- Botaurus l. lentiginosus (obs.)
- Anas rubripes (obs.)
- Mergus merganser americanus (obs.)
- Mergus serrator (nst.)
- Haliaeetus leucocephalus washingtoniensis (obs.)
- Actitis macularia (spn., nst.)
- Larus argentatus smithsonianus (spn., nst.)
- Larus delawarensis (spn., nst.)
- Sterna h. hirundo (nst. rpt.)
- Hydroprogne caspia (spn., nst.)
- Tyrannus tyrannus (spn., nst.)
- Iridoprocne bicolor (spn.)
- Progne s. subis (obs.)
- Corvus b. brachyrhynchos (nst.)
- Hylocichla fuscescens salicicola (spn., nst.)
- Bombycilla cedrorum (spn.)
- Sturnus v. vulgaris (nst.)
- Vireo olivaceus (spn.)
- Oporornis philadelphia (spn.)
- Geothlypis trichas brachidactyla (rpt.)
- Setophaga ruticilla (spn., nst.)
- Agelaius p. phoeniceus (spn., nst.)
- Loxia l. leucoptera (spn.)
- Melospiza melodia euphonia (spn., nst.)

Mammalia
- Lepus americanus phaeonotus (sgn.)

High Island
(No adequate collecting done)

Amphibia
- Bufo terrestris americanus (spn.)

Reptilia
- Chrysemys picta marginata (rpt.)
- Thamnophis s. sirtalis (spn.)
- Lampropeltis t. triangulum (spn.)

Aves
- Sterna h. hirundo (spn., nst.)
- Hydroprogne caspia (spn., nst.)

Mammalia
- Sciurus carolinensis hypophaeus (rpt., intr.)
- Rangifer c. caribou (rpt.)
- Lepus americanus phaeonotus (spn.)

Hog Island
(No collecting done)

Aves
- Ardea h. herodias (rpt.)
- Corvus b. brachyrhynchos (obs.)
- Dendroica v. virens (obs.)
- Setophaga ruticilla (obs.)

Marion Island

Aves
- Mergus serrator (nst.)
- Haliaeetus leucocephalus washingtoniensis (nst.)
- Actitis macularia (nst.)
- Megaceryle alcyon (nst.)
- Pipilo e. erythrophthalmus (obs.)

Mammalia
- Blarina brevicauda kirtlandi (spn.)
- Mustela frenata noveboracensis (spn.)
- Mustela vison mink (rpt.)
- Peromyscus maniculatus gracilis (spn.)
- Microtus p. pennsylvanicus (spn.)
- Sylvilagus floridanus mearnsii (spn.)

North Fox Island

Amphibia
- Plethodon c. cinereus (spn.)
- Bufo terrestris americanus (spn.)
- Hyla c. crucifer (spn.)

APPENDIX

Reptilia (North Fox Island) *continued*
   Diadophis punctatus edwardsii (spn.)
   Natrix s. sipedon (spn.)
   Thamnophis s. sirtalis (spn.)
   Lampropeltis t. triangulum (spn.)

Aves
   Gavia immer elasson (nst.)
   Mergus merganser americanus (spn., nst.)
   Accipiter gentilis atricapillus (obs.)
   Haliaeetus leucocephalus washingtoniensis (obs.)
   Charadrius v. vociferus (spn.)
   Actitis macularia (obs.)
   Larus argentatus smithsonianus (obs.)
   Hydroprogne caspia (obs.)
   Archilochus colubris (obs.)
   Colaptes auratus luteus (obs.)
   Dendrocopos pubescens medianus (spn.)
   Tyrannus tyrannus (nst.)
   Myiarchus crinitus boreus (obs.)
   Contopus virens (spn.)
   Iridoprocne bicolor (spn.)
   Cyanocitta cristata bromia (obs.)
   Corvus b. brachyrhynchos (nst.)
   Parus a. atricapillus (spn., nst.)
   Troglodytes a. aëdon (obs.)
   Cistothorus platensis stellaris (spn.)
   Hylocichla fuscescens salicicola (spn., nst.)
   Bombycilla cedrorum (spn.)
   Sturnus v. vulgaris (obs.)
   Vireo olivaceus (obs.)
   Dendroica c. caerulescens (spn.)
   Dendroica v. virens (spn.)
   Seiurus a. aurocapillus (obs.)
   Setophaga ruticilla (spn., nst.)
   Spinus t. tristis (obs.)
   Pipilo e. erythrophthalmus (spn.)
   Pooecetes g. gramineus (spn., nst.)
   Melospiza melodia euphonia (spn., nst.)

Mammalia
   Procyon l. lotor (unce.)
   Mephitis mephitis nigra (rpt., intr.)
   Vulpes fulva (sgn., rpt.)
   Tamias striatus peninsulae (spn.)
   Peromyscus maniculatus gracilis (spn.)
   Erethizon d. dorsatum (unce.)
   Lepus americanus phaeonotus (spn.)

North Manitou Island

Amphibia
   Plethodon c. cinereus (spn.)
   Bufo terrestris americanus (spn.)
   Hyla c. crucifer (voi.)
   Rana sylvatica cantabrigensis (spn.)
   Rana catesbiana (spn.)
   Rana clamitans (spn.)

Reptilia
   Chelydra s. serpentina (obs.)
   Diadophis punctatus edwardsii (spn.)
   Thamnophis s. sauritus (spn.)
   Thamnophis s. sirtalis (spn.)

Aves
   Gavia immer elasson (obs.)
   Ardea h. herodias (obs.)
   Anas rubripes (obs.)
   Anas discors (spn.)
   Glaucionetta albeola (obs.)
   Mergus merganser americanus (spn.)
   Mergus serrator (obs.)
   Accipiter striatus velox (obs.)
   Accipiter cooperii (obs.)
   Buteo jamaicensis (obs.)
   Haliaeetus leucocephalus washingtoniensis (nst.)
   Rallus l. limicola (spn., nst.)
   Charadrius melodus circumcinctus (spn.)
   Charadrius v. vociferus (spn., nst.)
   Philohela minor (obs.)
   Actitis macularia (spn.)
   Larus argentatus smithsonianus (obs.)
   Hydroprogne caspia (obs.)
   Zenaidura macroura (obs.)
   Coccyzus americanus (obs.)
   Coccyzus erythropthalmus (spn.)
   Bubo virginianus (obs.)
   Chaetura pelagica (spn.)
   Archilochus colubris (spn.)
   Colaptes auratus luteus (spn.)
   Hylatomus pileatus (sgn.)
   Dendrocopos v. villosus (spn., nst.)
   Dendrocopos pubescens medianus (spn.)
   Tyrannus tyrannus (spn., nst.)
   Tyrannus verticalis (spn.)
   Myiarchus crinitus boreus (spn.)
   Empidonax minimus (spn.)
   Contopus virens (spn.)

Aves (North Manitou Island) *continued*

Iridoprocne bicolor (spn., nst.)
Riparia r. riparia (obs.)
Hirundo rustica erythrogaster (spn., nst.)
Progne s. subis (nst.)
Cyanocitta cristata bromia (obs.)
Corvus b. brachyrhynchos (nst.)
Parus a. atricapillus (obs.)
Sitta carolinensis cookei (spn.)
Troglodytes a. aëdon (obs.)
Cistothorus platensis stellaris (spn.)
Dumetella carolinensis (spn.)
Toxostoma r. rufum (spn.)
Turdus m. migratorius (spn.)
Hylocichla fuscescens salicicola (spn.)
Sialia s. sialis (spn.)
Regulus s. satrapa (spn.)
Bombycilla cedrorum (spn.)
Sturnus v. vulgaris (nst.)
Vireo olivaceus (spn.)
Mniotilta varia (spn.)
Vermivora r. ruficapilla (obs.)
Dendroica c. caerulescens (obs.)
Dendroica v. virens (spn.)
Dendroica pensylvanica (spn.)
Seiurus a. aurocapillus (spn., nst.)
Geothlypis trichas brachidactyla (spn.)
Setophaga ruticilla (spn.)
Passer domesticus (obs.)
Dolichonyx oryzivorus (spn.)
Agelaius p. phoeniceus (spn., nst.)
Molothrus a. ater (spn.)
Piranga olivacea (spn.)
Pheucticus ludovicianus (spn.)
Passerina cyanea (spn.)
Carpodacus p. purpureus (obs.)
Spinus p. pinus (obs.)
Spinus t. tristis (spn.)
Pipilo e. erythrophthalmus (obs.)
Ammodramus savannarum pratensis (spn.)
Pooecetes g. gramineus (spn., nst.)
Spizella p. passerina (spn.)
Melospiza g. georgiana (spn.)
Melospiza melodia euphonia (spn.)

Mammalia

Lasiurus b. borealis (obs.)
Procyon l. lotor (obs., intr.)
Mustela (rpt.)
Vulpes fulva (spn.)
Tamias striatus peninsulae (spn.)
Tamiasciurus hudsonicus loquax (obs.)
Sciurus niger rufiventer (obs., intr.)
Castor canadensis (rpt., intr.)
Peromyscus maniculatus gracilis (spn.)
Mus musculus (spn.)
Rattus norvegicus (rpt.)
Lepus americanus phaeonotus (sgn.)
Odocoileus virginianus borealis (obs., intr.)

Pismire Island

Aves

Ardea h. herodias (spn., nst.)
Anas rubripes (obs.)
Mergus serrator (spn., nst.)
Larus argentatus smithsonianus (nst.)
Larus delawarensis (nst.)
Sterna h. hirundo (nst.)
Hydroprogne caspia (nst.)
Hirundo rustica erythrogaster (obs.)
Corvus b. brachyrhynchos (nst.)
Sturnus v. vulgaris (obs.)
Agelaius p. phoeniceus (obs.)

Shoe Island

Aves

Larus argentatus smithsonianus (nst.)
Larus delawarensis (nst.)
Sterna h. hirundo (spn., nst.)
Hydroprogne caspia (spn., nst.)

South Fox Island

Amphibia

Plethodon c. cinereus (spn.)
Bufo terrestris americanus (spn.)

Reptilia

Diadophis punctatus edwardsii (spn.)
Thamnophis s. sirtalis (spn.)

APPENDIX

Aves (South Fox Island) *continued*
- Gavia immer elasson (obs.)
- Ardea h. herodias (obs.)
- Mergus merganser americanus (obs.)
- Mergus serrator (spn., nst.)
- Accipiter gentilis atricapillus (obs.)
- Buteo jamaicensis (obs.)
- Haliaeetus leucocephalus washingtoniensis (nst.)
- Falco peregrinus anatum (spn., nst.)
- Charadrius melodus circumcinctus (spn.)
- Charadrius v. vociferus (spn.)
- Philohela minor (obs.)
- Actitis macularia (spn.)
- Larus argentatus smithsonianus (obs.)
- Hydroprogne caspia (obs.)
- Zenaidura macroura (obs.)
- Coccyzus americanus (obs.)
- Coccyzus erythropthalmus (obs.)
- Caprimulgus v. vociferus (spn.)
- Chordeiles m. minor (voi.)
- Chaetura pelagica (spn.)
- Archilochus colubris (spn.)
- Colaptes auratus luteus (spn.)
- Dendrocopos v. villosus (spn., nst.)
- Tyrannus tyrannus (spn., nst.)
- Myiarchus crinitus boreus (spn.)
- Sayornis phoebe (spn., nst.)
- Contopus virens (spn.)
- Iridoprocne bicolor (spn.)
- Riparia r. riparia (spn., nst.)
- Stelgidopteryx ruficollis serripennis (spn.)
- Hirundo rustica erythrogaster (spn., nst.)
- Progne s. subis (nst.)
- Cyanocitta cristata bromia (spn.)
- Corvus b. brachyrhynchos (spn., nst.)
- Troglodytes a. aëdon (spn., nst.)
- Toxostoma r. rufum (spn.)
- Turdus m. migratorius (nst.)
- Hylocichla fuscescens salicicola (spn., nst.)
- Sialia s. sialis (spn.)
- Bombycilla cedrorum (spn.)
- Sturnus v. vulgaris (nst.)
- Vireo olivaceus (spn.)
- Dendroica c. caerulescens (obs.)
- Dendroica v. virens (obs.)
- Dendroica pensylvanica (spn.)
- Seiurus a. aurocapillus (spn.)
- Setophaga ruticilla (spn.)
- Dolichonyx oryzivorus (spn., nst.)
- Sturnella m. magna (obs.)
- Icterus galbula (obs.)
- Molothrus a. ater (spn.)
- Piranga olivacea (spn.)
- Passerina cyanea (spn.)
- Carpodacus p. purpureus (spn.)
- Spinus t. tristis (spn.)
- Pipilo e. erythrophthalmus (spn.)
- Ammodramus savannarum pratensis (obs.)
- Pooecetes g. gramineus (spn.)
- Spizella p. passerina (spn.)
- Spizella pallida (spn.)
- Spizella p. pusilla (spn., nst.)
- Melospiza melodia euphonia (spn.)

Mammalia
- Lasiurus b. borealis (spn.)
- Procyon l. lotor (unce.)
- Vulpes fulva (sgn., rpt.)
- Tamias striatus griseus (spn.)
- Peromyscus maniculatus gracilis (spn.)
- Rattus norvegicus (rpt.)
- Erethizon d. dorsatum (unce.)
- Lepus americanus phaeonotus (spn.)
- Sus scrofa (rpt.)
- Odocoileus virginianus borealis (rpt., intr.)

South Manitou Island

Amphibia
- Plethodon c. cinereus (spn.)
- Bufo terrestris americanus (spn.)
- Rana p. pipiens (spn.)

Reptilia
- Chelydra s. serpentina (rpt.)
- Chrysemys picta marginata (spn.)
- Diadophis punctatus edwardsii (spn.)
- Thamnophis s. sirtalis (spn.)

Aves
- Gavia immer elasson (obs.)
- Phalacrocorax auritus (obs.)
- Ardea h. herodias (obs.)
- Mergus merganser americanus (spn., nst.)
- Mergus serrator (obs.)
- Cathartes aura (obs.)
- Accipiter cooperii (obs.)
- Buteo jamaicensis (nst.)
- Buteo p. platypterus (spn.)
- Haliaeetus leucocephalus washingtoniensis (obs.)
- Porzana carolina (spn.)
- Charadrius melodus circumcinctus (obs.)
- Charadrius v. vociferus (spn.)

Aves (South Manitou Island) *continued*

Philohela minor (obs.)
Actitis macularia (spn., nst.)
Tringa s. solitaria (spn.)
Totanus flavipes (obs.)
Larus argentatus smithsonianus (nst.)
Larus delawarensis (obs.)
Hydroprogne caspia (obs.)
Coccyzus erythropthalmus (spn.)
Caprimulgus v. vociferus (voi.)
Chordeiles m. minor (voi.)
Chaetura pelagica (spn.)
Archilochus colubris (spn.)
Megaceryle alcyon (obs.)
Melanerpes e. erythrocephalus (spn.)
Dendrocopos v. villosus (spn.)
Dendrocopos pubescens medianus (obs.)
Tyrannus tyrannus (spn., nst.)
Myiarchus crinitus boreus (obs.)
Empidonax minimus (spn.)
Contopus virens (spn.)
Iridoprocne bicolor (spn., nst.)
Riparia r. riparia (spn.)
Hirundo rustica erythrogaster (spn., nst.)
Progne s. subis (spn., nst.)
Cyanocitta cristata bromia (spn.)
Corvus b. brachyrhynchos (nst.)
Parus a. atricapillus (obs.)
Sitta carolinensis (obs.)
Troglodytes a. aëdon (spn.)
Cistothorus platensis stellaris (spn.)
Dumetella carolinensis (spn.)

Toxostoma r. rufum (spn.)
Turdus m. migratorius (spn.)
Hylocichla fuscescens salicicola (spn.)
Sialia s. sialis (spn.)
Bombycilla cedrorum (spn.)
Sturnus v. vulgaris (spn., nst.)
Vireo olivaceus (spn.)
Vermivora r. ruficapilla (spn.)
Dendroica v. virens (spn.)
Dendroica fusca (obs.)
Dendroica pensylvanica (obs.)
Seiurus a. aurocapillus (spn.)
Geothlypis trichas brachidactyla (spn.)
Setophaga ruticilla (spn.)
Passer domesticus (obs.)
Dolichonyx oryzivorus (spn.)
Sturnella m. magna (spn.)
Agelaius p. phoeniceus (spn.)
Icterus galbula (obs.)
Quiscalus versicolor (spn.)
Molothrus a. ater (obs.)
Piranga olivacea (spn.)
Richmondena cardinalis (obs.)
Pheucticus ludovicianus (spn.)
Passerina cyanea (spn.)
Spinus p. pinus (spn.)
Spinus t. tristis (spn.)
Pipilo e. erythrophthalmus (obs.)
Ammodramus savannarum pratensis (spn.)
Pooecetes g. gramineus (spn.)
Spizella p. passerina (spn.)

Melospiza melodia euphonia (spn.)

Mammalia

Procyon l. lotor (unce.)
Vulpes fulva (sgn., rpt.)
Felis catus (obs.)
Tamias striatus peninsulae (spn.)
Tamiasciurus hudsonicus loquax (unce.)
Sciurus niger rufiventer (sgn., intr.)

Peromyscus maniculatus gracilis (spn.)
Ondatra z. zibethica (rpt., intr.)
Rattus norvegicus (rpt.)
Lepus americanus phaeonotus (obs.)
Oryctolagus cuniculus (obs.)
Sylvilagus floridanus mearnsii (obs.)

Squaw Island

Amphibia

Plethodon c. cinereus (spn.)

Bufo terrestris americanus (spn.)

Reptilia

Natrix s. sipedon (spn.)

Storeria occipitomaculata (spn.)

Thamnophis s. sirtalis (spn.)

Aves

Gavia immer elasson (obs.)
Ardea h. herodias (nst.)
Anas rubripes (spn., nst.)
Anas acuta (spn., nst.)
Anas discors (obs.)

Mergus merganser americanus (obs.)
Mergus serrator (obs.)
Haliaeetus leucocephalus washingtoniensis (obs.)
Circus cyaneus (obs.)

APPENDIX

Aves (Squaw Island) *continued*

Porzana carolina (spn., nst.)
Charadrius v. vociferus (nst.)
Philohela minor (obs.)
Actitis macularia (spn., nst.)
Totanus flavipes (spn.)
Larus argentatus smithsonianus (nst.)
Larus delawarensis (spn., nst.)
Sterna h. hirundo (spn., nst.)
Hydroprogne caspia (obs.)
Coccyzus erythropthalmus (obs.)
Chaetura pelagica (obs.)
Tyrannus tyrannus (spn., nst.)
Iridoprocne bicolor (obs.)
Hirundo rustica erythrogaster (nst.)
Corvus b. brachyrhynchos (nst.)
Parus a. atricapillus (obs.)
Troglodytes aëdon parkmanii (spn., nst.)
Troglodytes troglodytes hiemalis (obs.)
Turdus m. migratorius (spn.)
Hylocichla fuscescens salicicola (obs.)
Bombycilla cedrorum (obs.)
Sturnus v. vulgaris (spn., nst.)
Vireo olivaceus (spn.)
Dendroica petechia aestiva (spn.)
Dendroica magnolia (obs.)
Dendroica v. virens (spn.)
Seiurus a. aurocapillus (obs.)
Oporornis philadelphia (spn.)
Setophaga ruticilla (obs.)
Agelaius p. phoeniceus (spn., nst.)
Spinus t. tristis (obs.)
Melospiza melodia euphonia (spn., nst.)

Mammalia

Vulpes fulva (rpt.)
Lepus americanus phaeonotus (sgn.)
Peromyscus maniculatus gracilis (spn.)

Trout Island

Amphibia

Ambystoma jeffersonianum (spn.)
Bufo terrestris americanus (spn.)
Hyla v. versicolor (voi.)
Hyla c. crucifer (spn.)

Reptilia

Thamnophis s. sirtalis (spn.)

Aves

Gavia immer elasson (obs.)
Ardea h. herodias (obs.)
Anas acuta (obs.)
Mergus merganser americanus (spn.)
Mergus serrator (obs.)
Charadrius v. vociferus (obs.)
Actitis macularia (spn.)
Larus argentatus smithsonianus (nst.)
Larus delawarensis (obs.)
Sterna h. hirundo (spn.)
Hydroprogne caspia (obs.)
Coccyzus erythropthalmus (obs.)
Archilochus colubris (obs.)
Colaptes auratus luteus (obs.)
Dendrocopos v. villosus (obs.)
Tyrannus tyrannus (spn.)
Myiarchus crinitus boreus (spn.)
Sayornis phoebe (obs.)
Iridoprocne bicolor (spn.)
Corvus b. brachyrhynchos (nst.)
Parus a. atricapillus (obs.)
Troglodytes aëdon parkmanii (spn.)
Hylocichla fuscescens salicicola (spn.)
Bombycilla cedrorum (spn., nst.)
Vireo olivaceus (obs.)
Vermivora r. ruficapilla (spn.)
Dendroica petechia aestiva (spn.)
Dendroica magnolia (spn.)
Dendroica v. virens (spn.)
Dendroica fusca (spn.)
Dendroica pensylvanica (obs.)
Geothlypis trichas brachidactyla (spn.)
Setophaga ruticilla (spn.)
Agelaius p. phoeniceus (spn., nst.)
Melospiza melodia euphonia (spn., nst.)

Mammalia

Myotis l. lucifugus (spn.)
Lepus americanus phaeonotus (spn.)
Peromyscus maniculatus gracilis (spn.)

Whiskey Island

Amphibia
    Bufo terrestris americanus (spn.)

Reptilia
Natrix s. sipedon (spn.)
Storeria occipitomaculata (spn.)
Thamnophis s. sirtalis (spn.)
Lampropeltis t. triangulum (spn.)

Aves
Gavia immer elasson (obs.)
Ardea h. herodias (obs.)
Anas rubripes (obs.)
Anas acuta (obs.)
Anas discors (obs.)
Mergus merganser americanus (obs.)
Mergus serrator (obs.)
Charadrius v. vociferus (obs.)
Actitis macularia (spn., nst.)
Larus argentatus smithsonianus (nst.)
Larus delawarensis (spn.)
Sterna h. hirundo (nst.)
Hydroprogne caspia (spn.)
Coccyzus erythropthalmus (spn.)
Tyrannus tyrannus (obs.)
Iridoprocne bicolor (obs.)
Hirundo rustica erythrogaster (obs.)
Corvus b. brachyrhynchos (nst.)
Parus a. atricapillus (obs.)
Sitta canadensis (obs.)
Troglodytes aëdon parkmanii (obs.)
Troglodytes troglodytes hiemalis (spn.)
Hylocichla fuscescens salicicola (obs.)
Bombycilla cedrorum (obs.)
Sturnus v. vulgaris (obs.)
Vireo olivaceus (obs.)
Dendroica petechia aestiva (spn.)
Dendroica v. virens (obs.)
Seiurus a. aurocapillus (obs.)
Setophaga ruticilla (spn.)
Agelaius p. phoeniceus (spn., nst.)
Spizella pallida (spn.)
Melospiza melodia euphonia (obs.)

Mammalia
Vulpes fulva (sgn.)
Lepus americanus phaeonotus (spn.)
Peromyscus maniculatus gracilis (spn.)

Bibliography

Major historic references, although uncited, are included in this bibliography.

ADAMS, CHARLES C.
  1909. An Ecological Survey of Isle Royale, Lake Superior. Lansing, xv + 468 pp.

ANON.
  1902. A Short History of the Beaver Islands. Mich. Pioneer and Historical Colls., Vol. 32, pp. 176-179.

BAIRD, ROBERT L.
  1931. A Bald Eagle Swims. Wilson Bull., Vol. 43, pp. 308-309.

BARROWS, WALTER B.
  1904. Birds of the Beaver Islands, Michigan. Bull. Mich. Ornith. Club, Vol. 5, pp. 63-66; 78-81.
  1912. Michigan Bird Life. Spec. Bull., Mich. Agric. Coll., xiv + 822 pp.

BLANCHARD, FRANK N.
  1921. A Revision of the King Snakes: Genus *Lampropeltis*. U. S. Nat. Mus. Bull. 114, vi + 260 pp.
  1927. Eggs and Young of the Eastern Ring-neck Snake, *Diadophis punctatus edwardsii*. Papers Mich. Acad. Sci., Arts and Letters, Vol. 7 (1926), pp. 279-292, pls. 13-19.
  1928a. Amphibians and Reptiles of the Douglas Lake Region in Northern Michigan. Copeia, No. 167, pp. 42-51.
  1928b. Topics from the Life History and Habits of the Red-backed Salamander in Southern Michigan. Amer. Nat., Vol. 62, pp. 156-164.
  1930. Further Studies on the Eggs and Young of the Eastern Ring-neck Snake, *Diadophis punctatus edwardsii*. Bull. Antivenin Inst. Amer., Vol. 4, No. 1, pp. 4-10.
  1937a. Data on the Natural History of the Red-bellied Snake, *Storeria occipito-maculata* (Storer), in Northern Michigan. Copeia, 1937, No. 3, pp. 151-162.
  1937b. Eggs and Natural Nests of the Eastern Ringneck Snake, *Diadophis punctatus edwardsii*. Papers Mich. Acad. Sci., Arts and Letters, Vol. 22 (1936), pp. 521-532, pls. 53-57.

BURGER, J. WENDELL
  1935. *Plethodon cinereus* (Green) in Eastern Pennsylvania and New Jersey. Amer. Nat., Vol. 69, pp. 578-586.

BURT, WILLIAM H.
  1942. A Caribou Antler from the Lower Peninsula of Michigan. Jour. Mammalogy, Vol. 23, p. 214.
  1943. Changes in the Nomenclature of Michigan Mammals. Occ. Papers Mus. Zool. Univ. Mich., No. 481, 9 pp.

BUTLER, AMOS W.
  1898. The Birds of Indiana. 22nd Ann. Rept. Dept. Geology and Natural Resources of Indiana (1897), pp. 515-1197.

CONANT, ROGER, and CLAY, WILLIAM M.
  1937. A New Subspecies of Water Snake from Islands in Lake Erie. Occ. Papers Mus. Zool. Univ. Mich., No. 346, 9 pp., 3 pls.

COULTER, SAMUEL MONDS
  1904. An Ecological Comparison of Some Typical Swamp Areas. Missouri Bot. Gard., 15th Ann. Rept., pp. 38-71, pls. 1-24.

DARLINGTON, HENRY T.
  1940. Some Vegetational Aspects of Beaver Island, Lake Michigan. Papers Mich. Acad. Sci., Arts and Letters, Vol. 25 (1939), pp. 31-37, 3 pls.

DARWIN, CHARLES R.
  1859. On the Origin of Species by Means of Natural Selection. London, and subsequent editions.

DARWIN, CHARLES R., and WALLACE, ALFRED RUSSEL
  1858. On the Tendency of Species to Form Varieties. Jour. Linn. Soc., Vol. 3, p. 45.

DICE, LEE R.
  1925a. The Mammals of Marion Island, Grand Traverse County, Michigan. Occ. Papers Mus. Zool. Univ. Mich., No. 160, 8 pp., 1 pl.
  1925b. A Survey of the Mammals of Charlevoix County, Michigan, and Vicinity. Occ. Papers Mus. Zool. Univ. Mich., No. 159, 33 pp., 3 pls.
  1932. A Preliminary Classification of the Major Terrestrial Ecologic Communities of Michigan, Exclusive of Isle Royale. Papers Mich. Acad. Sci., Arts and Letters, Vol. 16 (1931), pp. 217-239.

EATON, RICHARD JEFFERSON
  1934. The Migratory Movements of Certain Colonies of Herring Gulls in Eastern North America, Part III. Bird-Banding, Vol. 5, pp. 70-84.

EHLERS, GEORGE M.
  1945. Stratigraphy of the Surface Formations of the Mackinac Straits Region. Mich. Dept. Conserv., Geol. Surv., Pub. 44, Geol. Ser. 37, pp. 21-120.

ELTON, CHARLES
  1942. Voles, Mice and Lemmings; Problems in Population Dynamics. Oxford, The Clarendon Press, 496 pp.

[FORD, EDWARD R.]
  1931. Colony Banding in the Great Lakes. Inland Bird Banding News, Vol. 3, No. 3, pp. 7-11.

FULLER, GEORGE D.
  1918. Some Perched Dunes of Northern Lake Michigan and their Vegetation. Trans. Ill. State Acad. of Science, Vol. 11, pp. 111-122.

GOODRICH, CALVIN
  1941. *Lymnaea contracta* Currier. Nautilus, Vol. 54, pp. 121-122.

GROSS, ALFRED O.
  1940. The Migration of Kent Island Herring Gulls. Bird-Banding, Vol. 11, pp. 129-155.

HARRINGTON, MARK W.
  1895. Currents of the Great Lakes as Deducted from the Movements of Bottle Papers During the Seasons of 1892, 1893 and 1894. U. S. D. A., Weather Bureau, Bull. B, 14 pp., 6 charts.

HATT, ROBERT T.
  1924. The Land Vertebrate Communities of Western Leelanau County, Michigan, with an Annotated List of the Mammals of the County. Papers Mich. Acad. Sci., Arts and Letters, Vol. 3 (1923), pp. 369-402, pls. 24-26.
  1929. The Red Squirrel. Roosevelt Wildlife Annals, Vol. 23, No. 1, 146 pp.
  1938. Barn Swallow's Nest without mud. Auk, Vol. 55, pp. 536-537.
HESSE, RICHARD, ALLEE, W. C., and SCHMIDT, KARL P.
  1937. Ecological Animal Geography. New York, J. Wiley & Son, xiv + 597 pp.
HOOPER, EMMET T.
  1942a. An Effect on the *Peromyscus maniculatus* Rassenkreis of Land Utilization in Michigan. Jour. Mammalogy, Vol. 23, pp. 193-196.
  1942b. Geographic Variation in the Eastern Chipmunk, *Tamias striatus*, in Michigan. Occ. Papers Mus. Zool. Univ. Mich., No. 461, 5 pp.
JACKSON, H. H. T.
  1920. An Apparent Effect of Winter Inactivity upon Distribution of Mammals. Jour. Mammalogy, Vol. 1, pp. 58-64.
JOHNSON, IDA AMANDA
  1919. The Michigan Fur Trade. Michigan Hist. Comm. Univ. Ser. 5, 201 pp.
KARPINSKI, LOUIS C.
  1931. Bibliography of the Printed Maps of Michigan, 1804-1880. Lansing, Mich. Hist. Comm., 539 pp.
LACK, DAVID
  1942. Ecological Features of the Bird Faunas of British Small Islands. Jour. Animal Ecol., Vol. 11, pp. 9-36.
LANDES, KENNETH K., EHLERS, GEORGE M., and STANLEY, GEORGE M.
  1945. Geology of the Mackinac Straits Region and Sub-surface Geology of Northern Southern Peninsula. Mich. Dept. Conserv., Geol. Surv., Publ. 44, Geol. Ser. 37, 204 pp. and map.
LAWLER, WILLIAM F.
  1938. Michigan Islands. Mich. Hist. Mag., Vol. 22, No. 3, pp. 281-310.
LEACH, M. L.
  1902. History of the Grand Traverse Region. Mich. Pioneer and Historical Colls., Vol. 32, pp. 14-175.
LEOPOLD, ALDO
  1931. Report on a Game Survey of the North Central States. Madison, Wis., Sporting Arms and Ammunition Manufacturers' Institute, 299 pp.
LEVERETT, FRANK, and TAYLOR, FRANK B.
  1915. The Pleistocene of Indiana and Michigan and the History of the Great Lakes. U. S. G. S., Mem. 53, 529 pp.
LINCOLN, FREDERICK C.
  1924a. Banding Gulls in Lake Michigan. Wilson Bull., Vol. 36, pp. 38-41.
  1924b. Returns from Banded Birds, 1920 to 1923. U. S. D. A. Bull. No. 1268, 55 pp.
  1926. Banding Gulls and Terns in Lake Michigan; 1924 and 1925. Wilson Bull., Vol. 38, pp. 240-244.

LUDWIG, FREDERICK E.
  1942. Migration of Caspian Terns Banded in the Great Lakes Area. Bird-Banding, Vol. 13, pp. 1-9.
  1943. Ring-billed Gulls of the Great Lakes. Wilson Bull., Vol. 55, pp. 234-244.

LYON, WILLIAM I.
  1927. Bird Banding in 1927 on Lakes Michigan and Huron. Wilson Bull., Vol. 39, pp. 178-184.

MANSFIELD, H. B.
  1899. History of the Great Lakes. Chicago, J. H. Beers Co. Vol. 1, 928 pp.

NICKELL, WALTER P.
  1943. Some 1943 Notes on the Birds of Camp Sherwood. Jack-Pine Warbler, Vol. 21, pp. 78-82, pl. 9.

PAGE, H. R., AND COMPANY
  1884. The Traverse Region. Chicago, H. R. Page and Co. 369 pp.

QUAIFE, MILO M.
  1930. The Kingdom of St. James. New Haven, Yale Univ. Press, 284 pp.
  1944. Lake Michigan. Indianapolis, Bobbs-Merrill Co., 384 pp.

REYNOLDS, A. E.
  1937. Additional Observations on the Salamanders of Putnam County and Vincinity. Proc. Ind. Acad. Sci., Vol. 46, pp. 225-229.

RIEGEL, O. W.
  1935. Crown of Glory. New Haven, Yale Univ. Press, 276 pp.

SHELFORD, VICTOR E.
  1937. Animal Communities in Temperate America. Chicago, Univ. Chicago Press, xiv + 368 pp.

SPRAGUE, ELVIN L., AND SMITH, MRS. GEORGE N.
  1903. Sprague's History of Grand Traverse and Leelanau Counties Michigan. B. F. Brown. 806 pp.

STANLEY, GEORGE M.
  1936. Lower Algonquin Beaches of Penetanguishene Peninsula. Bull. G. S. A., Vol. 47, pp. 1933-1960, 4 pls., 5 figs.
  1937. Lower Algonquin Beaches of Cape Rich, Georgian Bay. Bull. G. S. A., Vol. 48, pp. 1665-1686, 6 pls., 5 figs.
  1945. Pleistocene Geology of the Mackinac Straits Region. Mich. Dept. Conserv., Geol. Surv., Publ. 44, Geol. Ser. 37, pp. 7-18.

STRANG, JAMES J.
  1855. Some Remarks on the Natural History of Beaver Islands, Michigan. 9th Ann. Rept. Smiths. Inst. (1854), pp. 282-288.

STRONG, R. M.
  1923. Further Observations on the Habits and Behavior of the Herring Gull. Auk, Vol. 40, pp. 609-621, pl. 36.

VAN TYNE, JOSSELYN
  1925. Notes on the Birds of Charlevoix County and Vicinity. Papers Mich. Acad. Sci., Arts and Letters, Vol. 4-1 (1924), pp. 611-627.

WAIT, S. E., AND ANDERSON, W. S.
  1918. Old Settlers. Traverse City. 86 pp.

WALKER, BRYANT
  1896. Report upon the Mollusca Collected in the Vicinity of Charlevoix, Michigan, in the Summer of 1894. Bull. Mich. Fish Comm., No. 6, App. 5, pp. 96-99.

WALLACE, ALFRED RUSSEL
  1880. Island Life: or, the Phenomena and Causes of Insular Faunas and Floras, Including a Revision and Attempted Solution of the Problem of Geological Climates. London, Macmillan and Co., xvii + 526 pp.

WARD, HENRY B.
  1896. A Biological Examination of Lake Michigan in the Traverse Bay Region. Bull. Mich. Fish Comm., No. 6, 99 pp., 5 pls. Appendices: 1. Aquatic Plants, by H. D. Thompson; 2. Protozoa, by C. A. Kofoid; 3. Rotifera, by H. S. Jennings; 4. Turbellaria, by W. McM. Woodworth; 5. Mollusca, by Bryant Walker. [Part 5 is the same as Walker, 1896, above.]

WOOD, NORMAN A.
  1911. The Results of the Mershon Expedition to the Charity Islands, Lake Huron. Birds. Wilson Bull., Vol. 23, pp. 78-112.
  1931. Rare Birds from Keweenaw County, Michigan. Auk, Vol. 48, pp. 616-618.
  1943. Many Holboell's Grebes Caught in Fishermen's Nets at James Bay [= St. James, Beaver Island]. Jack-Pine Warbler, Vol. 21, p. 88.

Index

This index is basically an index to the species and areas treated in the study. It has been simplified in varied ways. Larger geographical entities (the Great Lakes, state names, county names, Upper and Lower Peninsulas of Michigan) as well as casual references to areas outside the island region, are omitted. Larger taxonomic entities (amphibians, reptiles, snakes, turtles, birds) are not indexed, nor are any plant names. The occurrence of zoological names in the appendix are not indexed because the same information, namely the record of island occurrences, is available under the main treatment of each species. Similarly, island names, where recording occurrence of individual species are not indexed since that information is summarized in the appendix. The names of members of the Institute-University expeditions, where merely used to identify distribution records, are omitted. There is no index to general topics (*e.g.*: fur trade, ice transport, night-hunting, nesting, beaches, driftwood) for it is believed that the Table of Contents and chapter sub-heads provide adequate reference to them.

An asterisk denotes a main reference.

A

Accipiter cooperii, see Cooper's Hawk
   gentilis atricapillus, see Eastern Goshawk
   striatus velox, see Sharp-shinned Hawk
Actitis macularia, see Spotted Sandpiper
Adams, C. C., 1
Agelaius p. phoeniceus, see Eastern Red-wing
Aix sponsa, see Wood Duck
Alces a. americana, see Moose
Algoma beaches, 14, 18, 41
Algonquin, Lake and features, 12-14, 40, 41
Ambystoma jeffersonianum, see Jefferson's Salamander
American Fur Company, 24, 27, 34, 127
Ammodramus savannarum pratensis, see Eastern Grasshopper Sparrow
Anas acuta, see Pintail
   discors, see Blue-winged Teal
   platyrhynchos, see Mallard
   rubripes, see Black Duck
Andrews, A. W., 60
Angell, W. R., iv
ants, 44, 52, 61, 91, 152, Fig. 31
Apostle Islands, 2, 116, 123, 125, 130, 133
Archilochus colubris, see Ruby-throated Hummingbird
Ardea h. herodias, see Great Blue Heron
Aythya affinis, see Lesser Scaup
   americana, see Redhead
   collaris, see Ring-necked Duck
   valisineria, see Canvas-back

B

Badger, 116
Baird, R. L., 83
Bald, F C., iv

Barrows, W. B., 6, 70, 71, 76, 77, 81, 83-85, 88, 89, 91-94, 96, 98-100, 103, 104, 108, 109, 111-113, 154
Bartlett, I. H., 122, 134, 136
Bartramia longicauda, see Upland Plover
Bassett Island, *31, 39
Bat, Little Brown, *119
   Red, *119, 122
bats, 116, 117, *119, 141, 147
Bear, 115, 141, 145
Beaver, 34, 63, 117, 118, *127, 141, 145
Beaver Archipelago (Group, Islands, etc.), 4, 6-10, 13, 23-27, 29, *31, 33, 38, 50, 55, 69, 70, 75, 76, 87, 88, 108, 122, 128, 139, 143, 144
Beaver Island, 1, 2, 4, 6-10, 12, 23-30, *31, *33-34, 37, 38, 40, 54-56, 69-75, 117, 118, 141-150, 153, 154, *157, Figs. 1, 10, 11
Bellow Island, 30, *34, 35, 51, 69, *159
birds, gallinaceous, 119, 145, 148
Bittern, American, 72, *77
   Least, 72, *78
Blackbird, Rusty, 70, *108
Blanchard, F. C., 8
Blanchard, F. N., 8, 58, 65, 68, 69
Blarina brevicauda kirtlandi, see Short-tailed Shrew
Bluebird, Eastern, 73, *101
Bobcat, 116, 122, *123
Bobolink, 73, 74, *107
Bombycilla cedrorum, see Cedar Waxwing
Bonasa umbellus togata, see Ruffed Grouse
Botaurus l. lentiginosus, see American Bittern
Bubo virginianus, see Horned Owl

INDEX

Buffle-head, °80
Bufo terrestris americanus, see American Toad
Bullfrog, °62, 63, 151
Bundy, R. W., 136
Bunting, Indigo, 73, °109-110
  Snow, °114
Burger, J. W., 58
Burt, W. H., 126, 136
Buteo jamaicensis, see Red-tailed Hawk
  lineatus, see Red-shouldered Hawk
  p. platypterus, see Broad-winged Hawk
Butler, A., 6, 87

C

Cahalane, V. H., 8, 84, 87, 92-95, 100, 103-106, 109
Calhoun, J. B., 91
Canis l. latrans, see Coyote
  lupus lycaon, see Wolf
Canvas-back, °79
Capella gallinago delicata, see Wilson's Snipe
Caprimulgus v. vociferus, see Eastern Whip-poor-will
Cardinal, 74, °109
Caribou, Woodland, 117, 118, °136, 141, 143, 145
Carpodacus p. purpureus, see Eastern Purple Finch
Case, L. D., Sr., v, xi, 4, 5, 69
Cass, C. L., 6, 81, 87-89
Castor canadensis, see Beaver
Cat, House, 118, °123, 145
Catbird, 73, °99
Cathartes aura, see Turkey Vulture
Certhia familiaris americana, see Brown Creeper
Cervus c. canadensis, see Elk
Chaetura pelagica, see Chimney Swift
Charadrius melodus circumcinctus, see Piping Plover
  v. vociferus, see Killdeer
Charity Islands, 1
Chelydra s. serpentina, see Snapping Turtle
Chickadee, Black-capped, °97
Chicken, Prairie, 71
Chipmunk, Eastern, 116-118, 121, 122, °123-124, 142, 143, 146, 150, 151
  Least, 116, 118, 141, 143
chipmunks, 116, °123, 146, 151
Chlidonias nigra surinamensis, see Black Tern
Chordeiles m. minor, see Eastern Nighthawk
Chrysemys picta, see Painted Turtle
Circus cyaneus, see Marsh Hawk
Cistothorus platensis stellaris, see Short-billed Marsh Wren
Citellus t. tridecemlineatus, see Ground Squirrel

Clangula hyemalis, see Old-squaw
Clay, W. M., 66, 67
Clethrionomys g. gapperi, see Red-backed Vole
Coccyzus americanus, see Yellow-billed Cuckoo
  erythropthalmus, see Black-billed Cuckoo
Colaptes auratus luteus, see Northern Flicker
Colymbus auritus, see Horned Grebe
  grisegena holböllii, see Holboell's Grebe
Conant, R., 66, 67
Condylura cristata, see Star-nosed Mole
Contopus virens, see Eastern Wood Pewee
Coot, 71
Cormorant, Double-crested, °77
Corvus b. brachyrhynchos, see Eastern Crow
Cottontail, 115, °133, 141, 145
Cougar, 115, 145
Coulter, S. M., 6, 43
Cowbird, Eastern, 73, °108-109
Coyote, 115, 122, 145
Crane Island, °34, 52
Creeper, Brown, 73, °98
Crossbill, Red, °111
  White-winged, °111
Crow, Eastern, 44, 71, 75, °97, 137, 138
Crowe, W. R., 9
Cuckoo, Black-billed, 75, °90
  Yellow-billed, 75, °89
Cyanocitta cristata bromia, see Northern Blue Jay

D

Darlington, H. T., 7, 33
Deer, White-tailed, 43, 48, 51, 116, 117, °134-136, 145
deermice, 41, 146
Deermouse, Prairie, 115, 127, 128, °129-130, 141, 145
  Woodland, 117, 122, °127-129, 130, 139, 141, 142, 149, 151, 152, Fig. 43
Dendrocopos pubescens medianus, see Northern Downy Woodpecker
  v. villosus, see Eastern Hairy Woodpecker
Dendroica c. caerulescens, see Black-throated Blue Warbler
  castanea, see Bay-breasted Warbler
  c. coronata, see Myrtle Warbler
  fusca, see Blackburnian Warbler
  magnolia, see Magnolia Warbler
  p. palmarum, see Western Palm Warbler
  pensylvanica, see Chestnut-sided Warbler
  petechia aestiva, see Yellow Warbler
  p. pinus, see Pine Warbler
  striata, see Black-poll Warbler
  tigrina, see Cape May Warbler
  v. virens, see Black-throated Green Warbler

174   ISLAND LIFE

Diadophis punctatus edwardsii, see Ring-
    neck Snake
Dice, L. R., 7, 39, 128-130, 133, 139, 147,
    148
dog, 122, 135
Dolichonyx oryzivorus, see Bobolink
Dove, Mourning, 72, °89
Duck, Black, 44, °78
    Lesser Scaup, °79
    Mallard, °78
    Ring-necked, °79
    Wood, 72, °79
Dumetella carolinensis, see Catbird

E

Eagle, Northern Bald, °82-83
Eaton, R. J., 87
Ectopistes migratorius, see Passenger Pigeon
Ehlers, G. M., 9-11, 38, 51
Elk, 145
Elton, C. R., 128
Empidonax flaviventris, see Yellow-bellied
    Flycatcher
  minimus, see Least Flycatcher
  traillii, see Alder Flycatcher
Eremophila alpestris praticola, see Prairie
    Horned Lark
Erethizon d. dorsatum, see Porcupine
Ereunetes pusillus, see Semipalmated Sand-
    piper
Erolia minutilla, see Least Sandpiper
Euphagus carolinus, see Rusty Blackbird
Eutamias minimus jacksoni, see Least Chip-
    munk

F

Falco peregrinus anatum, see Duck Hawk
  s. sparverius, see Eastern Sparrow Hawk
Felis catus, see House Cat
  concolor couguar, see Cougar
Finch, Eastern Purple, 73, °110
Fisher, 115
Fisherman's Island, 2, 7, 30, °34, 69, 145,
    °159
Flicker, Northern, °91
Flycatcher, Alder, 71, 72, °94
    Least, 70, 72, °94
    Northern Crested, 72, 75, °93-94, 138
    Olive-sided, 70, 71, °95
    Yellow-bellied, 70, °94
flycatchers, 153
Ford Island, see Marion Island
Fox, Gray, 115, 122, 145
    Red, 117, °121-123, 132, 141, 151
Frei, F. E., 91
French pioneers, 23-26, 34
Frog, Bull, °62, 63, 151
    Green, °62-63, 68
    Leopard, °63, 154, Fig. 33

Tree, 54, °61, 152
    Wood, 54, °62, 143
Fulica a. americana, see Coot
Fuller, G. D., 7, 37

G

Gaige, H. T., iv
Gallinula chloropus cachinnans, see Florida
    Gallinule
Gallinule, Florida, 71
Garden Island, 7-9, 11, 23, 30, 31, °34-35,
    38, 43, 50, 69, 72, 77, 86, 130, 146,
    °159
Gavia immer elasson, see Lesser Loon
Geothlypis trichas brachidactyla, see Yellow-
    throat
Glaucionetta albeola, see Buffle-head
  clangula, see Golden-eye
Glaucomys sabrinus macrotis, see Northern
    Flying Squirrel
  v. volans, see Southern Flying Squirrel
Golden-eye, °79
Goldfinch, Eastern, 73, °110
Goodrich, C., 9
Goshawk, Eastern, 72, °81
Grackle, Bronzed, 73, °108
Grape Island, 2, 31, °35
Gravel Island, see Shoe Island
Grebe, Holboell's, 7, °76
    Horned, °76
    Pied-billed, 71
Grobman, A. B., iv, xi, 4
Grosbeak, Evening, °110
    Rose-breasted, 73, °109
Gross, A. O., 87
Grosvenor, T., iv, 121
Grouse, Ruffed, 71, 145
    Sharp-tailed, 145
Gull, Herring, 6, 34, 36, 37, 44, 50, 82, 83,
    °87, 88, 138, 151, Frontis., Figs. 39-
    42
    Ring-billed, 6, 44, 50, °87-88, 147
Gull Island (Leelanau County), see Bellow
    Island
    (Charlevoix County), 4, 6, 7, 30, 31, °35-
    36, 40, 54, 57, 59, 72-74, 75, 88,
    117, 137-139, 147, 149-151, 154,
    °159, Frontis., Figs. 12, 13, 39-42
gulls, 6-8, 9, 44, 51, 52, 59, 82, 121, 122,
    137, 150-152, 154
Gulo luscus, see Wolverine

H

Haice, H., 119, 126
Haliaeetus leucocephalus washingtoniensis,
    see Northern Bald Eagle
Harbor Island, °36, 39
Hare, Snowshoe, 36, 117, 121-123, °131-
    132, 133, 139, 141, 148, 150-152

INDEX

Harrington, M. W., 144
Hartweg, N., iv, 64
Hastings, W., 8, 133
Hat Island, 4, 6-9, 30, 31, °36-37, 38, 44, 59, 73, 74, 117, 127, 138, 147, 149, 151, °160, Figs. 14, 35
Hatt, R. T., iii-v, xi, 2, 4, 5, 7, 8, 52, 96, 125, 138
Hawk, Broad-winged, °82
   Cooper's, °81
   Duck, 75, °83, 137, 138, Figs. 37, 38
   Eastern Sparrow, 72, °83
   Marsh, 71, 74, °83
   Red-shouldered, 72, °82
   Red-tailed, 72, °82
   Sharp-shinned, 72, °81
Heron, Great Blue, 8, 36, 44, 51, 75, °77, 137, 138, 148
Hesperiphona vespertina, see Evening Grosbeak
High Island, 4, 6, 7, 9, 12, 23-25, 30, 31, 35, °37, 38, 40, 49, 51, 54, 55, 69, 72, 117, 127, 130, 143, 144, 146, °160
High Island Gravel Bar, °38, 88
Hinshaw, T. D., v, xi, 4, 9
Hirundo rustica erythrogaster, see Barn Swallow
Hog, Domestic, 47, 118, °133-134, 145
Hog Island, 4, 8, 30, 31, 35, 36, °38, 43, 44, 51, 69, 72, 130, 137, 146, °160
Hooper, E. T., 118, 124, 128
horse, 41, 47
Horton, M. M., 9
House of David, 37, 126
Hummingbird, Ruby-throated, 72, °91
Hydroprogne caspia, see Caspian Tern
Hyer, E. H., 8
Hyla c. crucifer, see Spring Peeper
   v. versicolor, see Tree Frog
Hylatomus pileatus, see Pileated Woodpecker
Hylocichla fuscescens salicicola, see Willow Thrush
   guttata, see Hermit Thrush
   m. minima, see Gray-cheeked Thrush
   mustelina, see Wood Thrush
   ustulata, see Olive-backed Thrush

I

Icterus galbula, see Baltimore Oriole
Ile aux Galets, 10, 24, 28, 36, °38
Indians (see also Ottawas, Ojibways), 23, 24, 26, 28, 33, 35, 37, 53, 117, 145, 155
Iridoprocne bicolor, see Tree Swallow
Isle Royale, 1, 113, 125
Ixobrychus exilis, see Least Bittern

J

Jackson, H. H. T., 2, 116, 123, 125, 130, 133
Jay, Northern Blue, 72, 75, °96
Jewell, W., xi, 2, 4, 5
Jordan, K., 129
Junco hyemalis, see Slate-colored Junco
Junco, Slate-colored, 71, °112

K

Karpinski, L. C., 25
Kelly's Island, 138
Killdeer, °85
Kingbird, Arkansas, 74, °93
   Eastern, 71, °93
Kingfisher, 72, °91
Kinglet, Eastern Golden-crowned, °101
   Eastern Ruby-crowned, °101

L

Lack, D., 70, 75, 139, 148
Lagler, K. F., 10
Lampropeltis t. triangulum, see Milk Snake
Landes, K. K., 10, 38, 51
Lark, Prairie Horned, 72, °95
Larus argentatus smithsonianus, see Herring Gull
   delawarensis, see Ring-billed Gull
Lasiurus b. borealis, see Red Bat
Law, Liebig's, 146
Law of the Minimum, 146
Law of Toleration, 146
Lawlor, W. F., 23
Leach, M. L., 34
Leopold, A., 71, 148, 152
Lepus americanus phaeonotus, see Snowshoe Hare
Lincoln, F. C., 8, 85, 88, 89, 97
Loon, Lesser, °76
Loxia curvirostra minor, see Red Crossbill
   l. leucoptera, see White-winged Crossbill
Ludwig, C. C., 9, 77, 88, 95, 97, 100
Ludwig, F. E., 9, 51, 87-89, 97, 121, 151
Lutra c. canadensis, see Otter
Lynx, Canada, 115, 145
Lynx c. canadensis, see Canada Lynx
   r. rufus, see Bobcat
Lyon, W. I., 8, 77, 88, 89

M

McCrea, W. S., 7, 8, 97
McKechnie, C. R., iv
McKee, E., iv, 120
Mackinac, Straits of, 10, 13, 69
Mackinac Island, 23, 24, 27, 28, 31, 151
   Valley, 13
Mackinaw Company, 27

176 ISLAND LIFE

Mallard, °78
Manitou Island Association, iv, 43, 135
Marion Island, 7, 30, 31, 34, 36, °39-40, 69, 75, 123, 125, 138, 139, 141, 145, °160
Marmota monax, see Woodchuck
Marten, 115
Martes a. americana, see Marten
  pennanti, see Fisher
Martin, Purple, 48, 72, 74, °96, 132, 146
Meadowlark, Eastern, 73, °107
  Western, 74, °107
Megaceryle alcyon, see Kingfisher
Melanerpes e. erythrocephalus, see Red-headed Woodpecker
Melospiza g. georgiana, see Eastern Swamp Sparrow
  melodia euphonia, see Mississippi Song Sparrow
Mephitis mephitis nigra, see Skunk
Merganser, American, °80, 81
  Red-breasted, °80-81
Mergus merganser americanus, see American Merganser
  serrator, see Red-breasted Merganser
mice, jumping, 116, 141
Microtus p. pennsylvanicus, see Meadow Vole
Mileski, J., 126
Mink, 118, °120, 141
Mitchell, J., 27
Mniotilta varia, see Black and White Warbler
Mole, Prairie, 116
  Star-nosed, 116
moles, 118, 141
Molothrus a. ater, see Cowbird
Moore, S., iv, 7, 21, 126, 136
Moose, 115
Mormons, 1, 6, 23-25, 28, 29, 34, 37, 47
Morrill, R. E., xi, 4, 5, 9, Fig. 3
Mouse, House, 116, 118, 128, °131, 146
  Meadow Jumping, 115
  White-footed, 115, 127, 128, 141, 145
  Woodland Jumping, 115
Mus musculus, see House Mouse
Muskrat, 116, 117, °130, 145
Mustela erminea cicognanii, see Weasel
  frenata noveboracensis, see Weasel
  rixosa alleghiensis, see Weasel
  vison mink, see Mink
Myiarchus crinitus boreus, see Northern Crested Flycatcher
Myotis l. lucifugus, see Little Brown Bat

N

Napaeozapus insignis frutectanus, see Woodland Jumping Mouse
Natrix sipedon, see Water Snake
Nelson, T., 69

Newt, °57
Nickell, W. P., 69, 138
Nighthawk, Eastern, 72, °90
Nipissing, Lake and features, 13, 14, 41, 47, 52, 56, 141, 142
North Fox Island, iii, 2, 4, 10, °11-21, 30, °40-42, 45, 54, 55, 69, 72-75, 116, 117, 122, 125, 131, 137, 143, 147, 149, 153, 154, °160-161, Figs. 2, 5, 16-18, 32
North Manitou Island, 1, 2, 4, 6-8, 10, 12, 13, 23-28, 30, 40, °42-43, 45, 66, 69, 72-75, 88, 116-118, 130, 133, 142, 145-147, 149, 151, °161-162
Nuthatch, Red-breasted, 73, °98
  White-breasted, 72, °98
Nuttallornis borealis, see Olive-sided Flycatcher

O

Odocoileus virginianus borealis, see White-tailed Deer
Ojibways, 23, 27, 33
Old-squaw, °80
Ondatra z. zibethica, see Muskrat
Opheodrys vernalis, see Green Snake
Oporornis philadelphia, see Mourning Warbler
Oriole, Baltimore, 73, °108
Orton, G., iv
Oryctolagus cuniculus, see Domestic Rabbit
Osprey, 76, °83, 145
Ottawas, 23, 27, 33
Otter, 118, °120, 141
Otus asio naevius, see Screech Owl
Oven-bird, 70, 71, °105
Owl, Barred, 71
  Horned, °90
  Screech, 71
oxen, 47, 150

P

Pandion haliaëtus, see Osprey
Partridge, Hungarian, 145
Parus a. atricapillus, see Black-capped Chickadee
Passer domesticus, see English Sparrow
Passerculus sandwichensis oblitus, see Churchill Savannah Sparrow
Passerella i. iliaca, see Fox Sparrow
Passerina cyanea, see Indigo Bunting
Pediaecetes phasianellus campestris, see Sharp-tailed Grouse
Peeper, Spring, 54, °61-62, 137, 150, 152, 154, Fig. 32
Peet, M. M., iii, iv, 77, 81, 98
Perdix p. perdix, see Hungarian Partridge

INDEX

Peromyscus leucopus noveboracensis, see White-footed Mouse
  maniculatus bairdii, see Prairie Deermouse
  maniculatus gracilis, see Woodland Deermouse
Petrochelidon pyrrhonota, see Cliff Swallow
Pettingill, O. S., Jr., iv, 9, 86, 93, 102, 106, 111
Pewee, Eastern Wood, 70, 72, °94
Phalacrocorax auritus, see Double-crested Cormorant
Phasianus colchicus, see Ring-necked Pheasant
Pheasant, Ring-necked, °84, 145
Pheucticus ludovicianus, see Rose-breasted Grosbeak
Philohela minor, see American Woodcock
Phoebe, Eastern, °94, 146
Pigeon, Passenger, 76, 145
Pintail, °78
Pipilo e. erythrophthalmus, see Red-eyed Towhee
Piranga olivacea, see Scarlet Tanager
Pismire Island, 5, 30, 31, 36, °43-44, 45, 59, 117, 127, 137, 138, 146, 147, 149, °162, Fig. 19
Pitymys pinetorum scalapsoides, see Pine Vole
Plank, J., 48, 136
Plectrophenax nivalis, see Snow Bunting
Plethodon c. cinereus, see Red-backed Salamander
Plover, Piping, 72, °84
  Upland, 71
Podilymbus p. podiceps, see Pied-billed Grebe
Pooecetes g. gramineus, see Eastern Vesper Sparrow
Pope, C. H., iv, xi, 2, 4, 5, 54, 151
Porcupine, 115, °131, 141
Porzana carolina, see Sora
poultry, 47
Procyon l. lotor, see Raccoon
Progne s. subis, see Purple Martin
Purdy, W. B., 8

Q

Quaife, M., iv, 1, 29
Quiscalus versicolor, see Bronzed Grackle

R

Rabbit, Domestic, °132-133, 145
Raccoon, 115-117, °119, 122, 141, 145
Rail, Virginia, 72, °84
Rallus l. limicola, see Virginia Rail
Rana catesbeiana, see Bullfrog
  clamitans, see Green Frog
  p. pipiens, see Leopard Frog
  sylvatica cantabrigensis, see Wood Frog

Rangifer c. caribou, see Woodland Caribou
Rat, Wharf, 116, 118, °131, 141, 146
Rattus norvegicus, see Wharf Rat
Redhead, °79
Redstart, American, 70, 71, °106
Red-wing, 51, 53, 71, 75, °107, 138
Regulus c. calendula, see Eastern Ruby-crowned Kinglet
  s. satrapa, see Eastern Golden-crowned Kinglet
Reis, M. C., 8
Reynolds, A. E., 58
Richmondena cardinalis, see Cardinal
Riegel, O. W., 1
Riparia r. riparia, see Bank Swallow
Robin, Eastern, 73, °100

S

St. Helena Island, °44
Salamander, Jefferson's, 54, 55, °58-59, 143, 150
  Red-backed, 54-56, °57-58, 141-144
Sandpiper, Eastern Solitary, °86
  Least, °87
  Semipalmated, 74, °87
  Spotted, °85-86
Sapsucker, Yellow-bellied, 72, °92
Sayornis phoebe, see Eastern Phoebe
Scalopus aquaticus, see Prairie Mole
Scaup, Lesser, °79
Sciurus carolinensis, see Gray Squirrel
  niger rufiventer, see Fox Squirrel
Seiurus a. aurocapillus, see Oven-bird
  n. noveboracensis, see Northern Water-Thrush
Setophaga ruticilla, see American Redstart
Shelford, V. E., 146
Shoe Island, 5-8, 30, 31, 35, 39, °44, 59, 117, 127, 146, 147, 149, °162, Fig. 14
Shrew, Short-tailed, °118
shrews, 116-118, 141
Sialia s. sialis, see Eastern Bluebird
Siskin, Northern Pine, °110
Sitta canadensis, see Red-breasted Nuthatch
  carolinensis cookei, see White-breasted Nuthatch
Skilligallee, 24, 38, See Ile aux Galets
Skunk, 42, 115-117, °120-121, 141, 145
Smith, O., iv
Snake, Garter, 38, °67-68, 141, Fig. 34
  Green, 55
  Milk, 55, 56, 65, 66, °68, 142, 143
  Red-bellied, 55, °67, 141-143
  Ribbon, 55, °67, 141, 143
  Ring-neck, 55, °64-65, 68, 141, 142, 144
  Water, 38, 55, 56, 63, 65, °66-67, 68, 141, 142, 151

Snake Island, 45, 88
Snipe, Wilson's, °85
Sora, 74, °84
South Fox Island, iii, iv, 2, 4, 5, 7, 10, °11-
    21, 23, 25, 28, 30, 40, 42, °45-48,
    49, 54, 69, 72, 73, 75, 88, 117, 118,
    125, 133, 137, 138, 143, 146, 147,
    149, 150, 153, °162-163, Figs. 4, 6,
    9, 20-22, 36-38
South Manitou Island, iv, 4, 5, 7, 10, 12,
    13, 23, 25, 28, 30, 37, 42, 45, °48-
    50, 66, 69, 72-75, 88, 117, 118, 124,
    127, 135, 142, 145-147, 149, 154,
    °163-164, Figs. 23-26, 33, 34
Sparrow, Churchill Savannah, 73, °111
    Clay-colored, 74, °112-113
    Eastern Chipping, 73, °112
    Eastern Field, °113
    Eastern Grasshopper, 73, °111
    Eastern Vesper, 73, °112
    English, 75, °106, 145, 146
    Fox, 74
    Mississippi Song, 71, °113-114
    Swamp, 74, °113
    White-crowned, °113
    White-throated, 73, °113
Sphyrapicus v. varius, see Yellow-bellied
    Sapsucker
Spinus p. pinus, see Northern Pine Siskin
    t. tristis, see Eastern Goldfinch
Spizella pallida, see Clay-colored Sparrow
    p. passerina, see Eastern Chipping Sparrow
    p. pusilla, see Eastern Field Sparrow
Squaw Island, 5, 9, 13, 24, 30, 31, 44, °50-
    51, 52, 55, 72-74, 117, 138, 146,
    147, 149, 150, 152, 154, °164-165,
    Fig. 27
Squirrel, Fox, 116, 117, °126-127, 145
    Gray, 116-118, °126, 145
    Ground, 115, 141
    Northern Flying, 116
    Red, 116, 117, °125-126, 141
    Southern Flying, 116
squirrels, flying, 141
    tree, 141
Staebler, A. E., v, xi, 4, 5, 69
Stanley, G. M., v, xi, 2, 4, 5, °11-22, 38,
    40-42, 45-47, 55
Starling, 44, 71, 75, °102, 145, 146
Stelgidopteryx ruficollis serripennis, see
    Rough-winged Swallow
Sterna h. hirundo, see Common Tern
Stony Reef, 85, 88
Storeria occipitomaculata, see Red-bellied
    Snake
Strang, J. J., 1, 3, 6, 24, 29, 34, 37, 76, 120,
    122, 124, 126, 127, 132, 133, 135,
    136, 145

Strix v. varia, see Barred Owl
Strong, R. M., 87
Stuart, L. C., iv, xi, 4
Sturnella m. magna, see Eastern Meadow-
    lark
    neglecta, see Western Meadow Lark
Sturnus v. vulgaris, see Starling
Sus scrofa, see Domestic Hog
Swallow, Bank, 72, °95
    Barn, 72, °96, 138, 146
    Cliff, 72, °96
    Rough-winged, °95
    Tree, 71, °95
Swift, Chimney, 72, °90, 146
Sylvilagus floridanus mearnsii, see Cottontail
Synaptomys c. cooperi, see Lemming Vole

T

Tamias striatus, see Eastern Chipmunk
Tamiasciurus hudsonicus loquax, see Red
    Squirrel
Tanager, Scarlet, 73, °109
Taxidea t. taxus, see Badger
Taylor, F. R., 7
Teal, Blue-winged, °78-79
temperatures, 31, 33
Temperence Island, °51, 52
Tern, Black, 71
    Caspian, 6, 8, 38, 88, °89, Fig. 15
    Common, 38, 50, 85, °88, 89, 137
    Wilson, see Common Tern
terns, 6-9, 44, 51, 59, 137, 148, 150, 151,
    154
Thamnophis s. sauritus, see Ribbon Snake
    s. sirtalis, see Garter Snake
Thrasher, Brown, 73, °99-100
Thrush, Gray-cheeked, 70, °100
    Hermit, 73, °100
    Olive-backed, 70, 71, 75, °100
    Willow, 71, 75, °101, Fig. 36
    Wood, 71, 75
thrushes, 153
Toad, American, 41, 59-60, 150-152, Fig. 4
Totanus flavipes, see Lesser Yellow-legs
    melanoleucus, see Greater Yellow-legs
Towhee, Red-eyed, 73, 75, °111, 138
Toxostoma r. rufum, see Brown Thrasher
Tringa s. solitaria, see Eastern Solitary Sand-
    piper
Triturus viridescens, see Newt
Troglodytes a. aëdon, see Eastern House
    Wren
    aëdon parkmanii, see Western House Wren
    troglodytes hiemalis, see Eastern Winter
    Wren

INDEX

Trout Island, 5, 30, 31, 34, °51-52, 53, 54, 57, 72, 73, 117, 146, 147, 149, 150, °152, °165, Figs. 7, 29-31
Turdus m. migratorius, see Eastern Robin
Turtle, Painted, 55, °64, 143, 144
    Snapping, °63-64
Tympanuchus cupido pinnatus, see Prairie Chicken
Tyrannus tyrannus, see Eastern Kingbird
    verticalis, see Arkansas Kingbird
Tyrrell, W. B., 7, 8, 44, 76, 77, 80, 101, 103, 105, 113

U

Urocyon c. cinereoargenteus, see Gray Fox
Ursus a. americanus, see Bear

V

Van Tyne, J., iv, v, xi, 4, 5, 7, 34, 69, 145, Fig. 3
Vermivora r. ruficapilla, see Nashville Warbler
Vireo olivaceus, see Red-eyed Vireo
    philadelphicus, see Philadelphia Vireo
Vireo, Philadelphia, 70, °103
    Red-eyed, °102
Vole, Meadow, 51, 116, 128, °130, 139, 141
    Lemming, 116
    Pine, 116
    Red-backed, 116, 117
voles, 141
Vulpes fulva, see Red Fox
Vulture, Turkey, 70, 74, °81

W

Walker, B., 6
Warbler, Bay-breasted, 74
    Black and White, 73, °103
    Blackburnian, 73, °104
    Black-poll, 70, °105
    Black-throated Blue, 73, °104
    Black-throated Green, °104
    Canada, 71, 74
    Cape May, 74
    Chestnut-sided, 73, °105
    Magnolia, 73, °103
    Mourning, 73, °105
    Myrtle, 73, °104
    Nashville, 73, °103
    Pine, 74
    Western Palm, °105

    Wilson's, 70, °106
    Yellow, 73, °103
Ward, H. B., 6
Warthin, A. S., Jr., 34, 88
Water-Thrush, Northern, 74
Waugoshance "bridge," 57
    Point, 13, 51, 56
    Island, 34, 51, °52, 77
Waxwing, Cedar, 71, °102
Weasel, °120, 141
weasels, 116, 117, °120, 141
weather records, 31
Weed, Thurlow, 1, 6, 43
Whip-poor-will, Eastern, 72, °90
Whiskey Island, 5, 9, 24, 30, 31, 50, °52, 54, 73, 74, 117, 119, 138, 147, 149, 150, °152, °166, Fig. 28
Wilson, E., 127
Wilson, F. N., 8
Wilsonia canadensis, see Canada Warbler
    p. pusilla, see Wilson's Warbler
Wobbleshanks, see Waugoshance Island
Wolf, 115, 145
Wolverine, 115
Wood, J. H., 7, 8, 78, 79, 81, 83, 85, 86, 92, 94, 98, 101, 104, 105, 110, 111
Wood, N. A., 1, 7, 8, 76-86, 92-94, 96, 98, 100, 101, 105, 108, 109, 112-114
Woodchuck, 115, 141
Woodcock, American, 72, °85
Woodpecker, Eastern Hairy, 72, °92, 93
    Northern Downy, 72, °93
    Pileated, °92
    Red-headed, 72, °92
Wren, Eastern House, 75, °98, 146
    Eastern Winter, 73, °99
    Short-billed Marsh, 73, 74, °99
    Western House, 75, °98-99, 143

Y

Yellow-legs, Greater, °86
    Lesser, 74, °86
Yellow-throat, 73, °106

Z

Zapus hudsonius, see Meadow Jumping Mouse
Zenaidura macroura, see Mourning Dove
Zonotrichia albicollis, see White-throated Sparrow
    leucophrys, see White-crowned Sparrow

ENNIS AND NANCY HAM LIBRARY
ROCHESTER COLLEGE
800 WEST AVON ROAD
ROCHESTER HILLS, MI 48307